By David Morgan, the creator of the cult series of 2019 books.

He was inspired to write Detectivity after suffering concussion from a falling tree leaf, believed to be oak.

Other books by David Morgan

The 2019 Series

2019: The Beginning
The murder of a Countess starts an incredible series of events from Hong Kong and Paraguay to rural England. Why does billionaire Jessica Crowne want old documents? Who is the unseen Jerome Jones? What is the Octagon? Why do some people never age? Answers start on page one.   ISBN 978-0-9559767-3-5

2019: The Second Coming
Magick. Is the world changing? A mysterious man with two glamorous assistants launches an organisation promising peace and prosperity. Why do they seek an ancient golden cat? The Omasor Agency investigates, with help from Brick and Blonde, celebrity adventurers. ISBN 978-1846858932

2019: Athens 1 Atlantis 0
Atlantis fought Athens, 11,000 years ago for global domination. Their descendants intend to control the planet again using the Treasures of Poseidon and helped by the Temple Virgins, who are different to other women in interesting ways. Corruption, lust, kidnap, murder follows. Also some bad things. The Omasor Agency gets involved with help from Brick and Blonde, celebrity adventurers. ISBN 978-0-9559767-0-4

2019: Godsplay
Selena and Chris travel to the universe of the gods to save Jerome Jones. A journey through many strange worlds populated by humans and the gods are amongst them, disguised as fellow inhabitants. Is it life or death? Or just a game? Fast, fun action with twists and turns everywhere. ISBN 978-0-9559767-1-1

Also

Amazon Bear Joiner
John Smith is young, rich and bored. What to do with his life? Inspired by his favourite book 'The Exploits of Cadaver Wincepole Gentleman Detective', he sets up as an investigator, employing a sexy young assistant, Eliza. Their first case is to investigate the loss of his parents, killed while exploring in the Amazon. So begins an extraordinary adventure, something far greater than routine murders. With help from two unusual allies, they start to uncover an unearthly mystery. Deception, aliens, bears, monks, trees and a secret sect are all in it somewhere. ISBN 978-0-9559767-2-8

Detectivity

DAVID MORGAN

©David Morgan 2009

All rights reserved. No part of this book may be reproduced, transmitted, stored in any form by any means including but not restricted to photocopying, recording and transcription.

This is a fictional work. Characters, places, names and events are used fictitiously or are the product of the author's imagination and any resemblance to actual persons, alive or deceased, names of companies, organisations, locations or events are completely coincidental.

The moral right of the author has been asserted.

Published by

Living Designs Publishing

Campion House, Campion Terrace, Leamington Spa, CV32 4SU

www.livingdesignspublishing.co.uk

Living Designs Publishing 2009

ISBN-13: 978-0-9559767-4-2

This book is for all men like me who need to deduce the location of missing socks. Every morning.

1

Mapleton is not the most vibrant town in England. It lies to the west of the Midlands area, a distance from motorways and through traffic. 98,721 inhabitants with a high proportion of retired people and many of the younger ones work at Pokes chocolate factory just outside town. Not all the citizens were choc related. For example, the street in the southern side that comprised a row of pleasant houses, each with extensive front and back gardens, four bedrooms and a delightful conservatory at the rear.

8.15 p.m. and spring darkness had fallen. The front window of the fourth house in the street displayed the flicker of a screen. Two people in the room. They sat on different sofas, both angled to face the large screen TV. The man seemed entranced by the film, his eyes never leaving the screen. He was tall, six foot two inches with a lean body with still black hair brushed carefully back to feature a rather thin, hawkish face. The woman was reading a book called 'How The Picts Lived' that summarised the latest research into the traditional Pict lifestyle.

Philip Caldrock was now 61 and Heather, his wife had just turned 56. Two children, girl and boy who had both married Americans and now lived in California and New York respectively. Philip didn't sleep with his wife. Her routine of reading in bed until the early hours had resulted in an amicable agreement for separate rooms. It was always amicable. They had never argued in all their 36 years of married life.

Their partnership had now reached a point where meaningful conversation was rare. Boredom perhaps but never to be admitted.

"Tremendous," Philip chortled.

Heather looked up from her book.

"Sorry, dear?"

"This film. Tremendous," he responded without moving his eyes from the screen.

"Oh, good."

They were very secure financially. House paid for. Significant savings and Phillips private retirement pension. A multitude of long-term bonds and investments were still maturing, providing all the finance they needed.

Three or four holidays each year, always to new destinations but now all seemed the same. Sightseeing, small talk with fellow tourists, restaurant dinners. New places but so similar. Philip routinely played golf at the club twice each week. Newspaper devoured every morning followed by a stint in the garden. He had been a college lecturer, never out of academia since leaving university. That was where they had met. Both left with degrees, Philip with an acceptable pass in business and commerce, Heather with an exceptional first-class honours degree in Ancient History.

He had gravitated into teaching and continued for his whole working life. She had become pregnant before having to decide about a job. A mother and housewife for many years. She could have started a career some years later. Could have but didn't. Whilst bringing up the children, she had developed a voracious appetite for learning, devouring textbooks with joyous comprehension. Heather had attended many courses but usually found her rate of learning far exceeded the steady pace of the tutor and frequently abandoned them after a few months.

A job just held no attraction for her. She visualised herself limited to just one subject, the same one, day after day. Couldn't even consider it. Instead, she had initiated a series of interest groups, a new one each time she began a fresh subject. People subscribed. Newsletters, correspondence and a multitude of contacts worldwide. She subsequently we launched the groups on the internet and the membership increased dramatically. It had become a full-time job for her to handle all the e-mails and keep the sites updated but the income from subscriptions was substantial. Eventually, three years ago, she decided that the work had become a chore and sold off all the websites.

She had then returned to reading and self teaching and it coincided with Philip's retirement. For the last 36 months they had been together. Too much together.

"It's so long since I've seen that!" exclaimed Philip.

The credits were rolling in enhanced greyscale.

"An old film," Heather murmured without raising her head.

"Yes, made 70 years ago but absolutely brilliant."

Now she looked. Enthusiasm in his voice that she hadn't heard for at least two years. It merited further attention.

"Do I know the film?" she asked.

"I doubt it. More of a man's movie. 'Son of Wincepole'. An American production."

"Wincepole? I read those books some time ago. Cadaver Wincepole, premier archetypal English private detective."

"Yes, good old Cadaver. What was his associate's name? You know, that man who was always with him. Doogie? Bongo?"

"It was Pongo. Pongo Wittler," advised Heather.

"Yes, the chap who was at public school with him. The two of them were a bastion of England ramparts."

Heather groaned inwardly. Philip sometimes had an irritating way of expressing himself.

"From the title, I'm speculating that your film starred Cadaver's offspring?"

"Absolutely. His son, Buggsy Wincepole. The Americans couldn't get the license to remake the original so they invented a son who was almost identical to his father. Instead of London, the lad was based in Los Angeles. The same sort of consulting rooms and a very similar casebook. Murder at country houses, bank robberies and an arch enemy, Doctor Morgyll Grimace."

"And another Pongo Whittler?"

"It was made by Americans, my dear. They used some blonde girl who spent most of her time in a negligee. She was supposed to be a medical doctor but had trouble speaking words with more than five letters. Doctor Tilly Witson, can you believe?"

"The studios rotated contract actors at that time. Probably slept with the director. One day, I need to study the history of the cinema. I'll make it number six on the list."

"I'm reasonably up on the subject. You can always ask me for guidance," Philip announced complacently.

Heather smiled and nodded. He always said that. Professing expertise on every project she studied. In all their years together he had never admitted her knowledge of anything was superior to his own. Male ego. She understood it well, having spent some time learning interpersonal psychology. Understood and accepted. Their relationship had never been passionate or exciting but she was grateful for his security and consistency.

"Do you know, I've always thought of myself as a bit of a Wincepole," he remarked.

"You certainly look a little like him but I think you're more intelligent."

No obvious reaction but she knew the compliment had lodged with him.

"I really must read the stories again. I'll get an omnibus tomorrow. Now I'm ready for bed."

"Me too," Heather responded.

She rose and collected a number of books, just as every night.

He joined her on the stairs and kissed her cheek.

"Sleep well, dear."

She returned the kiss.

"And you, Philip."

En suite bathroom in both bedrooms. They'd meet again at breakfast.

30 minutes later, Heather was comfortably propped up on a stack of pillows, reading diligently. She paused as her mind drifted.

"I wonder," she murmured and then shook her head, returning to the book.

2 THE MYSTERY OF THE MANIFESTING TREE

Heather descended the stairs at 8.12 the next morning, her usual timeslot. Later that day, she planned to visit Mapleton University with a list of Pict questions for the professor there.

Breakfast was always toast or croissants with tea in the air-conditioned conservatory, a meal they both enjoyed. Philip invariably came down at exactly 8.30 and she took pride in ensuring that warm croissants were waiting for him.

Not this morning. He was already at the table writing on a large pad.

"Philip, are you well?" she asked.

He looked up, eyes far away.

"I feel absolutely excellent," he beamed.

Enthusiasm? She barely recognised it. Hadn't seen that for so many years.

"What's happened?"

He put down his pen.

"I have decided to begin a new career and I would like you to join me."

She recalled her passing thought in bed the previous night. No, surely not.

"Have you eaten yet?" She asked.

"Ah, no."

"Then I will prepare breakfast and you can tell me after we eat."

He nodded and continued writing.

Heather prevented him from talking until the repast had been consumed and they were sipping hot tea.

"Now I'm ready," she announced.

He paused, searching for way to begin and eventually settled on the direct route.

"I have decided to become an investigator."

She looked at him with a smile. Her bedtime musing must have been a premonition.

"Like Wincepole?"

"Exactly. I feel I am uniquely qualified for it. As you mentioned, I do have a greater intellect and am fortunate to possess considerable knowledge of a wide diversity of subjects."

"And you want me to help?"

"One does require an associate in this profession. Someone that can be trusted implicitly. Not of course like the vacuous blonde in the film last night. I require someone similar to the original Pongo Wittler."

"I'm afraid that I'm a woman."

He waved a hand.

"That's of no consequence. It's the absolute loyalty that I need. One who will obey without argument."

Heather smiled inwardly. The ego again.

"Have you considered the practicalities?"

"Indeed yes. As you see, I have made copious notes. I will naturally need consulting rooms but meanwhile will purchase another telephone connection, a hotline, if you will. Then I can work from here."

"I don't know of any other investigators in Mapleton but perhaps there isn't a great demand."

"My dear, I do understand. You are concerned that I will establish myself and subsequently be unable to procure any clients. I have planned an ingenious strategy to launch myself to the public. A way that is almost guaranteed to establish a reputation."

"Please tell me."

He took a deep breath.

"I will consult the local newspaper for news of unexplained events. Then I will visit the location to announce that I will solve the mystery without a fee. Thus, I will not only establish a reputation but also acquire publicity. Of course, that will purely represent a starting point as I anticipate that I will subsequently cover the whole country."

"I presume that, like Wincepole, you won't get involved with routine criminal cases?"

"Of course not. Simple crimes will be excluded from my prospectus. As will divorces and other such mundane matters."

"I understand there are specific approvals and legal aspects in establishing an investigation bureau."

"So I would assume. I'm playing golf with three senior police officers this week and will discuss it with them. However, I see no reason why I cannot offer free assistance to a fellow citizen immediately. I have already identified our first assignment."

He handed her a clipping from the local weekly newspaper. The headline was 'Mysterious Tree Appearance'. Alongside this was a woman standing next to a bushy tree.

Mrs Ada Pine returned from a weekend holiday to find a tree had been planted in her front garden. 'I just can't explain it. I've never seen anything like this on TV,' said Mrs Pine, 57. She lives alone in the house and is separated from her husband. Police and council officials declared themselves completely baffled.

Heather returned the clipping.

"It's certainly strange."

"A perfect beginning. I propose to visit immediately after breakfast."

"I have an appointment at the University this afternoon while you're playing golf. So the morning is free and I'll come with you."

"Well, certainly. I may wish to hear your observations."

72 minutes later they parked near the house, just behind a police car. Road works in the centre of the street. A square of temporary wooden screens with the sound of drilling coming from within. They approached the Pine residence to see a short, balding man just leaving.

"Inspector Foxhole isn't it?" asked Philip.

"Yes. Don't I know you from the golf club?"

"Certainly. I played a round with you last year. I'm Philip Caldrock and this is my wife Heather."

The man nodded a greeting.

"I suppose you've come to look at the tree. Strange business."

"I am here to cast light on this conundrum."

Foxhole gave a quick smile.

"Cast light? You need permission to put up lamps, you know and it's an elm, not a conundrum."

"I mean I plan to solve the mystery."

"Amateur detective then? Well I admit it's got us completely flummoxed. Best of luck."

Foxhole marched off to his car and they continued to the door where Ada was waiting.

13

"Are you from the FBI?" she asked, a question resulting from a surfeit of TV watching.

"I am Philip Caldrock, private investigator and I am here to solve your little mystery."

Her eyes lit up.

"A private eye? One of those tough guys eh?"

"Rather more cerebral, I believe."

"What's a cerebral?"

Philip sighed.

"Is this the new arrival?" he asked pointing at a thick bushy elm in the front garden.

"Yes, that's it. Came from nowhere while I was away for the weekend. I went on Saturday morning and when came back Sunday night, well, I ask you."

"Yes?"

"What?"

"You wanted to ask me something."

"No."

Heather jumped in quickly.

"A mound of soil?" she asked.

"I beg your pardon?"

"The obvious solution is that someone planted the tree while you were away. That would have involved digging out a hole for the roots. Did you have a pile of soil?"

"Oh, I see."

"Yes?"

"How would you know?"

"I meant well?"

"Did you? Let me tell you that those who mean well are often well, mean."

"Was there a pile of soil?" asked Heather patiently.

"No but that's easily explained. When Thor hurls the tree, it embeds itself directly in the ground without any digging."

"Thor as in Norse myth?"

"No, the one on that satellite channel."

"I see."

"I wish he hadn't thrown it just there. I'll show you."

She guided them inside to the front facing lounge where the window displayed only foliage.

"I used to have a perfect view across the road. That building opposite is the rear of the Balloy Bank. I often used to sit here, looking out of the window."

"I notice you have road works outside."

"Yes, they started the day after the tree arrived and seem to be working all the time, day and night."

"And you are unable to observe the workmen now that the tree is here?"

"That's exactly right. I'd like to know what they're doing. Sounds as if they're digging a tunnel."

"Can anyone else see this excavation?"

"No, this is the only house in the street. The other buildings you can see are just the backs of warehouses and similar."

"And the rear of the bank is directly opposite?"

"Yes. My friend Margery works there. She tells me that they've got a diamond shipment arriving tomorrow. It's going to be kept for a week in a vault right at the back of the bank."

"We will visit there next," announced Philip.

"But what's that got to do with the tree?" asked Ada.

"We investigators must apprise ourselves of all the facts, however insignificant they may seem."

"Oh, I see. I'm holding an open day at lunchtime tomorrow. Invited everyone to visit and look at the new tree. You're welcome to come."

15 minutes later, waiting for the manager in the bank.

"Well, if it isn't Heather!" exclaimed a suited, dark haired woman who emerged from a side office

"Hello Margery, this is Philip, my husband."

Heather knew her from a college course on finance, a couple of years previously.

"We've just seen Ada Pine and her new tree. She mentioned you were a friend."

"Well sort of. She's one of the richest but also meanest person in town. Never used a bank in her life. Says she doesn't trust us! Why, we're as solid as a rock!"

Margery banged the wall to emphasise. A security sign fell to the floor and a nearby window shattered.

15

"She believes that Thor hurled it into her front garden."

"That's stupid. He's just a character on TV."

"Also myth."

"Ms is the word you're looking for. Even my financée has to call me that."

"Is he rich?" asked Heather to confirm the financée word.

"Yes, very but I haven't actually got him to propose yet. I just need to nail him down for the marriage and I'll be laughing for the rest of my life. I meet him every day at the back of the bank so we can be seen. The only problem is that grey haired man who's always hanging around there."

"I understand," offered Philip primly.

"No, not that. I just don't want to be seen in public, begging on my knees."

Heather jumped in quickly.

"We would like to see the vault where the diamonds are to be stored," she remarked.

"Of course. Follow me."

She led them to the back of the bank. A thick steel door in a thick steel wall.

"Here it is. Impossible to enter without the code," she announced with pride.

Looking at a card taped to the wall, she read off a series of numbers and punched them into a keypad. The door swung open to reveal a compact chamber with metal shelving on each side.

"You see the walls and ceiling are nine inch thick solid steel. It would need a nuclear missile to get through," she announced.

"And the floor?" asked Philip.

"Oh, we don't bother too much about that. Just covered it with a thin plastic lining. There's good solid earth underneath. The diamond shipment is due at exactly midday tomorrow and it will be absolutely secure here."

"It seems very obvious," said Heather as they returned to the car.

"Really?"

"A criminal gang are burrowing a tunnel to the bank vault. They just needed to prevent Ada from witnessing them. I'd assume the robbery is planned for tomorrow afternoon or evening, soon after the diamonds arrive."

Philip appeared deep in thought as she spoke but now he smiled.

"I have a theory," he announced.

"I'm ready to listen."

"It is based on Ada's view of the street being blocked by the new tree."

"Right."

"Do you recall what Margery said?"

"Yes, a thin plastic floor."

He held up a finger.

"No. About her fiancée."

"Yes and I wasn't impressed. Marriage isn't just a way for a woman to get money."

"Did you mean to say the word 'just'?"

Heather performed an innocent smile and didn't respond.

"You recall she said they had regular assignations at the rear of the bank?" he continued with increasing certainty.

"To beg him to marry her."

"I can just see it now. The amorous pair planting the tree while Ada was away, ensuring that it masked the view of their meeting place."

"That seems rather unlikely."

"But if it's not impossible, then it may be the real solution."

"That's silly. Almost anything is possible. The tree could have been planted by anyone, including royalty, arboreal fanatics or just a bunch of crazy people."

"Nevertheless, my idea fits the facts perfectly. Tomorrow, I'll be tailing this woman. Then I can be sure."

"I'm convinced this is part of a bank robbery. Unless…"

"You've just recalled one of those women's romance novels where the ordinary bank assistant is seduced by a roving adventurer."

"Yes, Philip. That could be it."

The next morning dawned warm and dry. Over breakfast, Heather was still thinking.

"I just can't pin it down," she remarked.

"Don't worry. I'm leaving shortly to follow Margery."

"I might go back to look at the tree."

Heather did that. At 10 a.m., she was driving towards Ada's home. Parking the car, she walked past the road works. The hole was surrounded by tall wooden panels with a door in the side facing the bank. As she passed it, an unshaven man emerged. About sixty with greying hair.

"We're doing the water pipe," he said earnestly.

"Yes, good."

"Just routine."

"Yes."

"Right, I'm off for a snack."

"Good."

He pulled a thick grey balaclava over his head. It covered his face completely except for the eyes.

"Bit cold," he mumbled, walking away with shoulders hunched.

Heather attempted to memorise his face, ready for subsequent identification among police bank robber files. Then she continued to Ada's home.

Lots of signs with 'Open Day' written large. A crowd of people with drinks and eating things on little sticks.

Ada bustled up.

"I'm not paying for this, you know. The local newspaper sponsored the party," she announced with satisfaction.

"Can we have a little private chat?"

"Will it cost me anything?"

"No, just to talk about Margery and marriage."

"Then come on inside."

30 minutes later, Heather walked round the front of the bank to find a man with grey wig, beard and sunglasses in a car parked opposite.

"Good news, dear," he said as she climbed in the car.

"Yes Philip?"

"I followed Margery at lunchtime. She went to the back of the bank and met a man."

"On her knees?"

"Only when she was with him. I walked past them and pretended to tie my shoelace. Quite embarrassing really. She jus kept saying 'please, please, please' all the time but he didn't seem too interested."

"A young man?"

"I couldn't really tell. He was wearing a grey balaclava. Anyway, I think I have enough evidence now to make an announcement to the media. Look, there's Inspector Foxhole."

They intercepted the small man as he was walking round the side of the bank.

"Hello, Caldrock. I think I've finally solved the case," he declared with satisfaction.

"You have?"

"Very simple. Thieves have dug a tunnel from the road works to just beneath the bank vault. As soon as the diamonds are stored, they'll break through the floor and grab the loot. Back down the tunnel, into a car and off to South America."

"I think you may have been misled."

"Miss Lead? No, I've always been a man, more or less."

"I mean that there is another solution."

Heather jumped in before he could continue.

"Yes, Philip has told me and I'm sure he's right."

Both men turned to her.

"Perhaps I should tell everyone," declared Philip, noticing that a group of reporters had gathered around them.

"You some police expert?" asked one.

"I am Philip Caldrock. That's spelt with an 'a' by the way."

"Philap?"

"No, Caldrock."

Heather to the rescue again.

"Yes, Mr Caldrock was about to tell you that the one digging the hole is Ada Pine's ex husband."

"No wonder she separated from a bank robber," observed Foxhole.

"Am I certain of this?" enquired Philip.

"I saw him coming out of the road works and later, Ada showed me his photo."

Now her husband's face showed all the indications of a rapid deductive process occurring somewhere inside his cranium.

"Ah, yes. I recall that Margery mentioned a grey haired man who often lingered around the back of the bank. Now I see it!"

"Yes, go on Caldrock," enthused Foxhole.

"Ada Pine knew he was watching her and arranged for the tree to be planted to block his view. She is the perpetrator!"

"That's brilliant!" exclaimed Foxhole and the reporters murmured agreement, some already turning away to phone in the story.

Heather quickly raised her voice.

"That was Mr Caldrock's first idea but then he considered the road works. His investigations indicated that Mrs Pine was a person who never used a bank, despite her wealth. She therefore had the problem of storing her cash and valuables. What better place than buried in her garden?"

"That's where I hide stuff from the wife," declared a reporter incautiously.

"Mrs Pine admitted to me that she had done this and my husband immediately solved the case. When the Pines separated, Mrs Pine was awarded the vast majority of their money. Her husband resented this and determined to recover what he regarded to be his fair share."

"I covered that divorce. He wasn't a happy boy," remarked one of the crowd.

"He would wait until she was away for a weekend and then dig a hole where she normally buried her valuables. Unfortunately for him, she had changed the location. He had used a contractor to carry away the earth and was therefore left with a large hole. You should continue, Philip."

"Yes, right."

"And tell everyone how he filled the hole and then needed another way to find Ada's money."

"Oh, I see. Yes, well what could he do? On inspiration, he called another contractor and they came and planted the tree, perhaps early on Sunday morning. Both contractors were no doubt paid well for confidentiality. So Ada arrived back to find the tree but her ex husband hadn't given up. He decided to reach the garden by tunnelling through from the road. Then he could take all the time he needed by digging underground until he found the money. I think that about sums it up."

Loud applause from the gathered scribes and cameras clicking. Heather departed for her car as they surrounded Philip and it was some time before he joined her.

"Well, my dear. I think we can consider our first case to be a significant success."

"I rather enjoyed it, Philip. We will call it 'The Mystery of the Manifesting Tree'. I'm looking forward to the next one."

She kissed his cheek lightly and then they returned to their separate cars to drive home.

3 THE MAGPIE DID IT

The local weekly newspaper was published two days later with Philip on the front page. A photo of him next to the manifesting tree, chin raised and eyes apparently focused on somewhere distant. A regal portrait. The headline was 'Investigator Solves Tree Mystery' and the subheading read 'Residents praise amazing deductions'. Below that followed a story full of plaudits, mostly from Phillips own quotes.

Later that morning, the telephone rang and Heather answered.

"Is Mr Caldrock, the investigator available?"

A woman's voice.

"Not at the moment. I'm Heather, his assistant."

"You've got to help me! We didn't steal them!"

"You have been unjustly accused of theft?"

A sob before the woman responded.

"I'm sure the police are going to arrest us. We desperately need Mr Caldrock's help."

"Then I'll ask him to visit this morning."

The woman mumbled gratitude and Heather wrote down the details. She replaced the receiver just as Philip returned from a walk. Not his usual procedure but today he had the newspaper under his arm, carefully folded to display his photo.

"I'm afraid that my fame is spreading rapidly. Many people stopped me to express their congratulations and I perceived innumerable others looking with smiles as I passed."

"Perhaps you should discontinue the walks?"

"No, no. I started today to increase my muscular power and general fitness. I suppose I must suffer the adulation of celebrity status."

"A noble and trojan policy, Philip. I believe we have a new case."

"Ah, just as I anticipated. What are the facts? Spare no detail."

"Mr and Mrs Robar who live just 15 minutes from here. She's petrified of being accused of theft. Rather incoherent on the phone. We need to visit to discover the details."

Philip turned his head to gaze out of the window.

"If any citizen, however insignificant, pleads for my assistance, then I will go forth and investigate in the interests of justice and truth."

"I'll get the car."

The Robar's house was a large old property but with many signs of renovation in progress and a couple of men in overalls sitting outside, drinking tea. Two Robars in the doorway and the female one rushed forward, a thin, nervy woman of about 50.

"Oh you're here Mr Caldrock. I'm so, so grateful."

Philip continued to the door with the woman pattering beside him as she guided them inside. Her husband was heavily built with a round, florid face.

"Yer very welcome, Mr Caldrock. Come into the lounge," he invited.

Heather accompanied the trio into a freshly decorated large room with three sofas and several armchairs.

"First I have to know the facts. You must apprise me in a calm and precise manner," Philip announced, taking the most comfortable armchair.

Mrs Robar screamed and ran from the room.

"I'll tell you the story, Mr Caldrock. The wife's a bit upset by it all," declared Mr Robar, red cheeks deepening as he spoke.

"Rather strange that two people should require all this furniture," Phillips remarked detectively, taking the most comfortable armchair.

"It's not for us. We're opening as a guest house next week. Two rooms already booked."

"I see. Then pray continue."

"We're having the whole place renovated and it's a big job. The house had been empty for a while and we had bats in the attic, rodents and spiders everywhere and even a fox hiding in an outhouse. There are eight guest rooms altogether and the builders are finishing one room at a time. Two now completed with all the furniture in place and we even made the beds. Then we locked the doors so they couldn't get messed up by stray sheep or anything."

"You can't be too careful these days."

"These two rooms, numbers two and six, were finished a couple of days ago and we've already got bookings for them. Well, my wife is a bit of a fusser and she visited them to make sure all was well early this morning."

"The doors were locked, you say?"

"Yes. Not been opened for 2 days. Number two was fine but when she went into number six…"

Mrs Robar had just returned to the lounge and now burst into tears.

"It was horrible," she wailed.

"You found a body?" enquired Heather sociably.

The thin woman stared at her for a moment before running out again, renewing the screams. Her husband didn't seem too concerned, apparently used to the outbursts.

"No, Mrs Caldrock. Not a body but a necklace on the floor, right in front of her. Gold and diamonds. Worth a fortune."

"I presume that it didn't belong to you," said Philip confidently.

The man gasped.

"That's right. How could you know that? You're certainly a proper detective."

Philip looked inordinately smug, waving a hand airily in response.

"The necklace was such an expensive piece of jewellery and we were both convinced it must have been stolen. Almost certain that the police would be here soon to lock us up."

"Have you called them?"

Mrs Robar had just returned again.

"No, I telephoned you first. They won't know anything yet," she mumbled.

Inspector Foxhole burst into the room.

"Right, where's the loot?" he shouted.

Half the Robars fainted and the male part turned bright crimson.

"Who told you?" he blubbered as Heather rushed to tend to his wife.

"Anonymous tip off. He said you'd got the stuff stolen from Moat Manor. Hello Caldrock, you here already?"

"Just arrived, Inspector. What is this loot?"

"Four items were stolen from the Manor. A gold and diamond necklace with matching earrings and bracelet."

"These people found the necklace in one of the rooms. I will summarise their account and you will appreciate they are not the criminals."

"Ok, then. So who stole the jewels?" asked Foxhole as Philip completed his summary.

"First, I have to solve a locked room mystery. Do you have the necklace, Mr Robar?

"I kept it in a safe place. It's in my coat pocket in the hallway."

Five minutes later, the three men gathered in room six. Spacious, with one part open window directly opposite the door. A table in the centre and a bed on the right. The décor was unusual. On the walls were pictures of meals. Plates full of roast beef and vegetables, curries, stews and pies. Shelving to the left containing a number of realistic plastic food replicas. A lettuce, tomatoes, oranges and more. On the table was an imitation loaf of bread, onions and apples.

"You're obviously a food lover, remarked Foxhole, looking at Mr Robar.

"It's the missus. She adores that sort of thing, spends all her time in the kitchen. You know, she's got no sense of smell but can pick a ripe banana just by looking."

"And coconuts!" cried Mrs Robar who had just arrived with support from Heather.

"I'm partial to a bit of coconut. Best part is the skin, nice and hairy. I must ask the wife to get some in," remarked Foxhole.

Now the female Robar was in her element.

"Yes, yes! You can sauté the skin in coffee with a soupcon of white wine. Roast it gently for four hours and serve with radish sauce."

The Inspector had feverishly noted down the recipe but now Philip shattered the gastronomic affair.

"Where did you find the necklace?" he asked.

"It was there!" cried Mrs Robar, pointing at the floor between table and door.

Foxhole produced the necklace and laid it down carefully in the place indicated.

"Can't see how it could have got there. No! Hold on. The window's open. Someone could have tied it to a paper plane and thrown it from that tree outside!"

"Then where is the plane?" asked Philip.

Mrs Robar had been studying the room with a puzzled expression.

"Funny, I'm sure there's something missing but I can't think what."

Heather looked out of the window. A tall Birchy Elm outside, branches full of birds. Right on cue, one of them flew across to land on the windowsill outside.

"We have a visitor," she remarked.

"That's a magpie. Starlings, blackbirds and even owls there," said the nervy woman, looking up.

"The window was opened today?"

"Oh no. We left it open when the door was first locked. Keeps the room aired, you know."

"Open, you say?" asked Philip.

"Yes sir but the gap isn't big enough for a human to get through. Only something a lot smaller could do that."

Mr Robar chuckled.

"We've been here all the time and sleep in a room directly below. No one could have put a ladder against the wall, however big they were."

"Did you hear any noises coming from this room after the door was locked?" asked Heather.

"Not really. There were a few scuffling sounds but they stopped after the first day."

Foxhole sighed, reluctantly returning from an imaginary coconut feast.

"We're not getting anywhere here. How many workmen are on the premises?"

"Just two. It's a small company, just round the corner. The boss and his son have been here every day," replied Mr Robar.

Now Philip adopted a contemplative posture, gazing at the ceiling.

"A locked room. The inexplicable appearance of expensive jewellery. A lesson for all of you here. The most obvious explanation, however trivial, may indeed be the truth," he announced dramatically

Heather didn't reply immediately, her gaze still drawn to the window.

"Yes, Philip. Does your answer happen to involve trees or birds?"

"Birds? Why on earth would they want a gold necklace?"

They returned to the lounge to find Inspector Foxhole just ending a telephone call.

"It's coming together. The new tenant of room six is a known criminal fence and the necklace was obviously left there for him. We've had this man under observation for a time. Now I reckon someone got in the tree and simply threw it in through the window. Just need to find a thief with a strong arm," he announced.

Philip shook his head.

"Very unlikely they would have succeeded first time and then they would have had to climb down from the tree and start again. No, there is one other far simpler explanation."

"What's that? No, I've got it. The necklace was hidden under a corner of the ceiling paper before the door was locked but the glue didn't hold and it fell down to the floor."

"The ceiling is painted."

"No, forget that. These builders doing the renovation. They made the light fitting in the ceiling so it could be loosened from the room above. Then they simply dropped the necklace through the gap and fastened the fitting again."

"There was no ceiling light, just on the walls," observed Heather.

"A secret panel in the door then. Press a hidden catch and it springs open. Throw the jewels in and close it again."

"I checked the door and it's quite normal but you're in the right area," remarked Philip enigmatically.

"Doesn't anyone here know about the habits of birds?" asked Heather.

A pause while the others looked at her quizzically.

"Yes, they're very nice that we have mystery to solve. Ah, this must be the builders," said Foxhole finally.

Two burly men had entered, one a younger version of the other.

"I'm Bill Fornaught and this is my son Rob," announced the elder.

Mrs Robar rushed to the younger one.

"Hello again Rob. Sorry I haven't got anything ready for you today."

"Doesn't matter," mumbled the young man.

"He's always in the kitchen for a little snack," she announced in explanation to the others.

Philip stepped forward.

"Now everyone is here, I will reveal the solution. Please follow me back to the mystery room."

"Can you give me a few seconds there before you come?" asked Heather quietly.

Nearly 10 minutes later before they joined her in room six and she took position near the door, alongside Phillip. He waved a dismissive hand towards a magpie that had flown over to stand on top of the open window. It gave a bright eyed glare and fluttered back to the tree.

"The impossible can be explained by a person with the required intellect and deductive capability. To those select few, a locked room mystery is a mere trifle. Ladies and gentlemen, if I may speak immodestly, I am such a person."

He paused and looked round the bemused faces before continuing.

"What do we have here? A room with a locked door and window that no person could enter. I think we can dismiss the possibility of invisible aliens."

Pause for laughter but none came.

"But a necklace appeared in the room, about on the spot where I stand. A gold and diamond necklace that was stolen recently."

"Yes, just by your feet!" cried Mrs Robar, apparently impressed.

"The chronology is very simple. The thief stole four items of jewellery. I assume that he was able to quickly sell off three of them but not the necklace. A conundrum. He couldn't hand it to his usual contact who was being watched by the police and it was much too risky to keep on his person or at his residence. What to do? Nowhere to stash it, to use the expression of the criminal fraternity. Then he found out that his fence had rented this room and all he had to do was leave the necklace here for him."

"But that's impossible. Only my wife and I had a key," exclaimed Mr Robar.

"And you had no intention of opening the door until today."

"You're saying that we did it then?" Robar blustered, and his wife approached tears again.

"Not at all," Philip laughed.

Now Bill Fornaught stepped forward aggressively.

"Listen mate, I'm not a thief. We didn't have the key to this room either."

"The key? That is how the average mind works, presuming a locked room must need a key. I will show you how it was done. Hand me the necklace, Inspector."

The small man reached into his pocket and handed over the glittering jewellery. Philip held it up.

"How could it appear in this room? The answer is so obvious. Ladies and gentlemen, regard the door!"

He stood back as all gazed with blank expressions. Then he crouched down, placing the necklace on the floor and began to slide it forwards.

"Under the door! We'd never thought of that," exclaimed Mrs Robar.

A slight problem arose. The chain passed under the door but the first diamond wouldn't. Philip pushed it, hard. Several times. The builders began to laugh while the Robar couple looked at each other and then back to Philip.

"Call yourself a detective?" taunted the elder Fornaught.

Heather move forward swiftly to stand by her husband who had now risen to his feet, staring venomously at the necklace.

"It's very satisfying to see the relief on your faces. Just as you predicted, Philip."

He looked at her and nodded dumbly as she continued.

"Now our little distraction is over, we will disclose the true solution. May your assistant reveal it, Philip?"

Apparently regaining some composure, he waved a hand of assent and she turned to face the audience.

"In addition to the necklace, three other pieces of jewellery were stolen and not yet recovered. Mr Caldrock was immediately aware of the implications of this. Why were all the jewels not here? The answer is that they are. I think the jewellery has been in this room since soon after the robbery."

"That can't be right. There was definitely no necklace when we locked the door," said Mr Robar.

"And I don't see the other jewellery," added Foxhole, looking round.

Now two Magpies landed on the top of the open window and regarded the scene as Heather continued.

"Phillip saw the likely solution quite quickly but it was incomplete. Then he noticed the birds in the tree."

"Yes, the birds," added her husband with a knowing smile to cover his perplexity.

Foxhole clapped his hands together.

"That's right! Magpies. They love shiny things. So the little rascals carried the jewellery in through the open window. Difficult to arrest a bird though," he announced with disappointment.

"Philip considered the magpie possibility but soon dismissed it. If they brought the necklace, why not the other jewellery? It was also an incredible coincidence if they had decided to drop the necklace in the very room to be occupied by receiver of stolen goods."

"Maybe they were trained to do it," mumbled Foxhole but was ignored.

"The magpie is not the bird in question. It is the owl. I think it's time you showed something to our audience, Philip."

"Yes indeed," he agreed vehemently but didn't move.

Heather quietly whispered in his ear.

"The bread. Turn over and open it."

"What?" he murmured but moved with uncertainty to the table and picked up the plastic loaf. Turning it over revealed a circular section in the centre and he levered it open. Then tipped the contents on the table. Gold and diamond earrings and bracelet.

Gasps of astonishment filled the room and even the magpie chirped. Philip stood back with a casual look of satisfaction as Foxhole rushed forward.

"My word, you've certainly excelled yourself here!" he exclaimed.

"And now the culprit should be obvious," Heather continued.

"Rob Fornaught?" enquired Philip tentatively, mind now grinding into activity.

Heather nodded.

"That was your conclusion. He was the one who was always in the kitchen with Mrs Robar and had every opportunity to conceal the jewellery in the imitation food before it was displayed in this room."

"That sounds conclusive. You're under arrest, Rob Fornaught," announced Foxhole.

The young man seemed resigned to his fate.

"Only trying to make a bit extra," he mumbled.

"Mr Caldrock, you're a genius but what about the necklace? Why wasn't it inside the bread?" asked Mr Robar.

Philip bluffed bravely.

"Yes indeed, you may well ask. That was my biggest problem. Perhaps you should complete my conclusions, Heather."

She smiled.

"Yes, the necklace. Rob couldn't fit it in the bread and the other imitation foods have no compartments inside. Then he had an inspiration. Knowing Mrs Robar has no sense of smell, he embedded the necklace in a chunk of real cheese and substituted it for the artificial piece she had ready."

"Yes, cheese. I knew something was missing here," cried Mrs Robar.

"So where is it?" asked Foxhole.

"It was eaten by a mouse or more likely, mice. The cheese was on the table and during the feast, the necklace became exposed and was nudged to the floor. That was Mr Caldrock's solution but there was a problem. He knew that the house was originally infested with rodents but where were they now?"

"An owl grabbed them!" cried Philip with some certainty.

A silence for several seconds before applause rang out, even Rob joining in.

It was some time later before Philip and Heather left the house.

"That went well," she remarked.

"Well indeed. Did we ensure publicity?"

"I phoned the newspapers."

A gaggle of reporters and photographers outside the front door. Heather skirted past them and waited nearly an hour in the car before Philip arrived.

"Home, I think," he said, taking the passenger seat.

"Yes, Philip."

"Heather?"

"Yes dear?"

"I do appreciate your assistance, you know. Couldn't do this job without your support."

"When you love someone, you don't have a choice."

He touched her arm briefly and she drove away.

4 THE IMPOSSIBLE CIPHER

Now the regional newspapers ran the story. 'Master Sleuth Solves Another Mystery'. Heather turned down several requests for interviews. Not ready for that yet. She was surprised to see fan mail arriving and even proposals of marriage from female admirers. They were filtered into the garbage bin.

Two days later, she was reading a newspaper in the lounge when a police car screeched to a halt outside the house. Heather opened the door to receive a flustered Inspector Foxhole.

"I need to talk to Mr Caldrock, urgently," he demanded.

"Please come in and I'll fetch him," she responded, leaving the Inspector in the lounge.

She walked to a back room that had been converted into Philip's office. He was seated at the desk, hand on chin and apparently in deep thought. Heather shook his shoulder.

"Wake up, Philip. The police are here."

He grunted as his chin slipped off the supporting hand.

"What?"

"You were asleep. Inspector Foxhole is waiting to see you."

"Ah, yes. Mustn't delay the crime fighters."

He marched into the lounge to receive a grateful handshake from the small man.

"We have a problem and have reached a dead end. I thought you might be able to help us?"

"Of course, old chap. Please tell me all."

Philip took the primary armchair with Heather next to the Inspector on the sofa.

"I'd like you to look at this, Caldrock. Can you make anything of it?"

He passed a crumpled sheet of paper with words written on one side

'29TH elephant GANG termite ROBBING adder SAFE blackbird ESSWORTHY insect BANK thrush MIDNIGHT kestrel'

"Hmm, interesting. What is it?" asked Philip, passing the paper to Heather.

"That we do know. It's from one of our undercover men, Michael Smith. He's infiltrated a gang but can only send us messages by writing them on pieces of paper and throwing them out of a window. The words make no sense and I have an instinct that it could be some sort of cipher."

"Very perspicacious of you, Inspector."

"I passed it to our code experts and they studied it for hours. Tried all the best-known encryptions but can't decipher it."

"I see. The message seems to include a number of animals."

"That's what stumps me. I can make sense of some of the words like robbing and bank and as you know, coincidentally, the Essworthy Bank is the largest one in town. I've been told that they've got a big gold bullion shipment arriving today to store in their safe. But what on earth does this blackbird, elephant and thrush mean?"

"Indeed, yes. My appraisal indicates that no less than three birds are included among the menagerie and there's something else."

"What?" asked Foxhole, leaning forward.

Philip held up a finger.

"Only one of the creatures has four legs. The elephant."

"My word, I hadn't seen that. I knew I was doing the right thing in coming here. I do think I've worked out one word, the first. I believe that '29TH' indicates a date. Let's see, what is it today?"

Philip looked blank and Heather interjected.

"It's the 28th, Inspector."

"Then it could mean something is happening tomorrow. Curse this garbled text. My mind's a complete jumble of animals and birds. I feel like crossing them all out of the message and just concentrate on what's left. The fact that a lot of the words are in capital letters just makes it more confusing."

"May I ask if this gang your man has infiltrated have been active recently?"

"We reckon they're responsible for a series of robberies. You know that row of small warehouses on the edge of town?"

"I do."

"Six of 'em in line. The gold jewellery company has the first, followed by a precious stones store, furs in the third. Small but expensive consumer electronics in the fourth and designer watches in the fifth. A plastic bag supplier in the last."

"Security?"

"Well, it's pretty safe. There aren't any houses in the area so no residents there. The owners just lock the doors when they leave. They even have a watchman, although he only works in the day. It all seemed safe and sound but in the last week, five of the warehouses were ransacked during the night. Cleared out."

"All except the plastic bag place?"

Foxhole's eyes bulged.

"That's amazing. How could you know?"

Philip simply smiled complacently.

"You sound confident," Heather observed, after Foxhole had departed.

"I am indeed," he responded.

"Can I ask if your solution involves animals, or lack of them?"

He laughed.

"It may or may not. All will be revealed tomorrow. Do you recall one of Wincepole's major skills?"

"Punching people?"

"No, disguises. He was a master of impersonation. I am planning to use the same stratagem tomorrow. A friend of mine runs the local Dramatic Society and they have a substantial inventory of guises."

"And yours?"

"I recall Wincepole pretending to be a street seller, offering boxes of matches and ladies stockings. Rather think I could do the same."

"I believe that's a bit out of date, Philip."

"Yes, you could just be right. Very well, I will be a scruffy beggar."

He left at nine the next morning to allow time to prepare his disguise. Heather continued her studies until mid morning and then drove to the Essworthy Bank. No sign of any beggars, including disguised as ones. She waited with increasing concern and then began to think about the message again.

"Oh lord, I hope he hasn't gone to the zoo," she muttered.

Then her phone rang.

"Hello Phillip. I'm waiting outside the bank."

"The bank? Why on earth are you there? Anyway, if you come now, you'll just be in time. Elgate Road, just a couple of minutes away."

"Are you sure about this?" she asked but he had already ended the call.

Three minutes later, she pulled up in Elgate Road. Three police cars halfway down with officers milling around. A number of handcuffed people were being led to the cars. Then a scruffy tramp emerged from one of the houses. A mass of shaggy dark hair and a short beard that was coming off at the side. A shabby grey raincoat completed the disguise.

"Philip!" she called as she approached him.

"Ah, you recognised me. I suppose a wife would see through it."

"You're still wearing the golf club tie and those designer leather shoes."

He looked down.

"Ah, right."

"And half your beard is coming off."

"Yes, well. I think I will dispose with the coverings now."

He pulled off the hair piece, beard and raincoat, handing them to passing police officer who looked rather puzzled at the gift. Inspector Foxhole emerged from the house and immediately scurried to join them.

"Congratulations Caldrock. Brilliant work," he announced joyfully.

Philip glanced at him briefly, before moving his gaze to some distant point.

"Brilliant? Perhaps. One strives for perfection although always aware that even the greatest can err."

"Yes?"

"What?"

"You said 'can errr'. I was waiting for the last word."

"Not errr, Inspector. Err."

"Ur was a city in ancient Mesopotamia," added Heather, helpfully.

"Oh, right," the Inspector nodded.

The van drove away and most of the police departed, leaving just a couple of men guarding the door of the house. Then came the reporters. Swarms of them.

"I thought it only right to inform the press," he remarked to Heather as he posed for photographs, looking suitably complacent.

An hour before he joined her in the car.

"When you weren't at the bank, I feared you had gone to the zoo," she remarked.

"Really? How strange is your thought process."

"The message was pretty clear. '29th gang robbing safe Essworthy bank midnight'. I thought you'd be there."

"How on earth could you get those words from the message?" he asked.

"It doesn't matter."

"Surely it was obvious to you. '29 Elgate Road. Sables in bath. Mike'. The first two letters of each word. The agent had even given his name to prove authenticity. Not just the furs but also jewellery, watches, precious stones and video players. The police have rounded up the whole gang."

"Oh my lord," Heather exclaimed.

"Yes?"

"Philip, you really are brilliant."

"Yes?"

"And now I'll take you back home for tea."

"Yes, tea. Interesting."

5 THE GRUNTINGDON INHERITANCE

Heather was busy. National newspapers now. Inside pages but still a photograph. Clippings collection growing. Requests for radio interviews refused. Proposals of marriage increasing. Extra waste bin acquired.

Pleas for Philip's services were numerous. She dutifully sifted through them to prepare a shortlist of six that excluded missing cats, lost pencils and divorce case photography. One appealed to her and she carefully placed it last in the pile.

Philip entered the office, clutching a newspaper and smiling broadly.

"It seems my humble efforts have been recognised," he announced.

"You have several offers," she replied, indicating the papers on his desk.

"It is unfortunate that I am just a singular beacon amidst a raging sea of mysteries. Where shall my light be cast?"

She saw him flip through the pile and stop as planned at the last.

"Where is Gruntingdon Manor?" he asked.

"About an hour from here."

"Lord Gruntingdon appeals for my help. Whilst the poorest citizen means just as much to me as the noblest, there is something that interests me in this matter. Contact the Lord and tell him we will visit this morning."

"Yes Philip. May I ask a question?"

"Of course."

"Do you still love me?"

"An unexpected enquiry. Perhaps I should consider whether insecurity lies behind it."

"Don't consider. Just answer."

"Very well."

He paused, eyes moving to the window. Then he turned back to look directly at her.

"I loved you the first time we met and I still love you now."

She kissed him softly on the lips.

"If I promise not to read, can we sleep together again?"

"It would be an honour."

Another kiss.

"And I love you, Philip," she whispered.

He smiled.

"Of course, I can provide no guarantees for the future. My researches have revealed a large number of personal letters from ladies of various ages in the waste bin."

Heather smacked his arm.

Gruntingdon Manor was all that could be expected and more. A massive, grand mansion in acres of grounds, nestling in unspoiled English countryside. Heather pulled into the large gravel frontage where three rows of cars were already parked. As they approached the pillared entrance, a dark suited man emerged.

"Good morning. I am Bunty, manservant second-class. Mr and Mrs Caldrock?"

"We are," Heather declared as Philip paused to survey the building.

"Lord Gruntingdon awaits you in the Oriental lounge."

Grand entrance hall, exquisite lounge with oriental as the theme. Delicate wall hangings, sculptures and ornate furniture. A small grey-haired man stood near the fireplace.

"Lord Gruntingdon, I presume," said Philip, extending a hand.

"Philip Caldrock and your lady assistant. A pleasure to meet you both. Please make yourself comfortable on the sofa and Bunty will bring tea."

He lowered himself into an armchair as they took the sofa and Heather studied him. Grey hair brushed directly back from a weathered face. Sharp, quick eyes and a firm chin.

"I read of your exploits in the newspaper and was impressed. Very impressed. I hope you can succeed where others have disappointed," said the Lord.

Philip bent forward.

"I do not disappoint, I invariably succeed. However, I must counsel you that the truth may not always be desirable."

"You sound confident, Caldrock."

"Please tell me the details, omitting nothing of relevance."

"Indeed. Well, every year at this time, I invite a number of houseguests to stay for a month. It is a tradition, you understand. Six of them are family members but there are always five places reserved for the personal choice of the Lord, currently myself."

"I see," mused Philip.

"Everyone arrived nine days ago and all was well for the first two days. Then on the third day, my sister had an accident."

"Accident you say?"

"She was in the library when the book apparently fell on her head. Killed instantly."

"Apparently?"

"She was alone at the time and there were no witnesses to the occurrence."

"What was the book?"

"What? The Etruscan Concubine Directory."

Heather gasped.

"I know that book. It's huge. 3,123 pages."

The Lord nodded sagely.

"Indeed, yes. If only it had been the Babylonian equivalent."

"Pray continue," requested Philip.

"The next day, Larky Scrummer, my nephew also perished. Hit on the head by a croquet ball on one of the rear lawns. Tragic accident."

"A croquet ball?" exclaimed Heather.

"Yes, indeed. He was by himself so we can only surmise the details. However, it seems pretty obvious. There is a tree at the edge of the croquet lawn. He must have over hit his shot, the ball striking the curved edge of the trunk where the roots begin. It then flew into the air in an arc, landing directly on Larky's head."

"That seems conclusive," agreed Philip.

"At that point, my wife prevailed upon me to call for professional assistance. The police were not interested so I asked for help from a local amateur detective. She has been staying here since then but has not reached any conclusions."

"An amateur?" Philip declared dismissively.

"Yes. Dotty Parsnip. She has built a bit of a reputation. Do you know her?"

"It stirs a faint chord although I do not associate with amateurs."

"Despite her presence, there was another accident two days ago. My daughter Pompom. Riding her horse and bashed her head on the top of the stable door, we believe."

"I deduce that she was alone at the time."

The Lord looked impressed.

"Yes, very clever of you Mr Caldrock. We found her in riding gear, lying in the stables. Stone dead of course with her skull cracked open."

"And the horse?"

"Back in its stall in the stable. Pretty clear what happened. She saddled and mounted the horse but didn't remember to put on her riding helmet. Then she decided to charge out of the stables, forgetting to duck and striking her head."

"Then how did the horse get back?" asked Heather.

"Obvious again. It walked back into the stable, wriggled out of the saddle and untied the reins with its teeth. Then it trotted back into its stall."

"I see," said Philip.

"Now, what made me send you a message was this letter I received. Can't make head or tail of it."

He held out a sheet of paper with just a few words typed on it. Philip scanned briefly and passed it to Heather.

'Three down and two to go. Then it's your turn. When you've gone, the Manor will belong to me.'

"You say it means nothing to you?" asked Philip.

"Nothing at all. Three and two makes five. I thought it could be related to bowling. Three skittles down and two standing, if you read me. But you can't get five skittles in a proper formation. Six could be arranged 3-2-1 or ten as 4-3-2-1 but not five. My turn could imply that I have the remaining two skittles to knock over."

"And the last part?"

"When I'm gone probably refers to my holidays. I have a villa in the Caribbean where I stay every winter for two months. I just have a feeling about the word belong. It could mean possess but that makes no sense. I think it's a clever way of saying be long. That is, the writer is declaring that the size of this building will appear very large to them."

"I would imagine that a young child would say that. All buildings look larger when we are infants."

"Brilliant! I think you're onto something there," exclaimed the Lord.

"Do you have any young children here?"

"No."

"Who is currently in residence?"

"Just two of the family left. My wife, Bimba and our other daughter, Bubbles. Coincidentally, they are also the last in line to inherit the estate. Apart from young Billy Blackship, of course but I'm sure he's dead."

"Dead?"

"Yes, the young scoundrel. Always causing trouble by doing the servants' duties for them. Even made his own tea. He was sixth in line to inherit and would be third now. Still, he died in Ecuador two months ago."

"How?"

"It seems that he was exploring some ancient cave system by himself. They found his watch next to a deep hole. What made it conclusive was the note he'd written and pushed inside the watch strap. It said 'I've fallen down the hole. Don't bother looking. Billy'. That was it."

"A tragedy," Philip remarked consolingly.

"Not really. Little rascal was always full of ideas like planting more trees and stopping our deer and rabbit hunts."

"Does that conclude your account?"

"It does. Now what do you think, Mr Caldrock?"

Philip sipped tea as he paused.

"I think that certain forces are at work here. I will even theorise that other so called accidents are a possibility. Now tell me about your guests."

"Apart from myself, wife and daughter, I chose four others. They are Sensua Trim, the exotic dancer, Wilma Tryst, the nude model, Booby Hanced, the film star and Gluckweed Nightsock, the novelist. Then, of course Dotty Parsnip has joined us."

"When can I meet them?"

"Well, everyone regularly goes off by themselves, completely alone for long periods. They could be anywhere now. Your best chance is at dinner, tonight. You're staying, of course."

"Thank you. That is all I need."

Up in their room, Heather was contemplative.

"Any ideas, Philip?"

"I have various theories but it is much too early to speculate. We have eight people to investigate and I will need you to actively participate."

"I think I should take the three female guests. The model, dancer and actress."

"No. I will cover Wilma the model, the Lord, his wife and daughter. You have the remainder."

"Be careful, Philip especially with that model."

"Indeed I will."

Dinner at a long table. Six seats each side and one at each end. The Lord in the top position with model and dancer next to him then actress opposite Philip alongside them. Two clear places before the others. Lady Gruntingdon at the end, her daughter and the novelist with Heather facing Dotty next to them.

Dotty began during the soup course. A small, bright eyed woman with light grey hair, tightly fixed by a yellow elastic band at the back of her head. Thin lips and a knowing expression.

"Soup reminds me of poor old Tom," she remarked incitingly.

Lady Florence took the bait. A scrabble haired, lean blonde. Mid-fifties. Expensive dress and jewellery.

"Who is Tom?" she asked.

"He used to live in a little cottage in my village. People just thought of him as a lovable old rogue but I saw something else. When you get to my age, you see things my dears."

Lady Florence was intrigued

"What did you see?"

Dotty paused, waiting the moment.

"Death!"

Heather heard spoons clatter in dishes but continued her meal.

"That is so scary," cried Bubbles, the Lord's daughter. A flat chested, large eyed girl of 20. She wore a low-cut, strapless dress that kept slipping dangerously.

A chuckle from the man next to Heather. Gluckweed Nightsock, novelist. A massive, obese man with brown wavy hair that stretched down his back. Only 29 years old but he looked about 47.

"Ah death. The errant demon that visits us in the darkness, his long finger poking into us like shafts of, errr, flesh and bone," he remarked.

Bubbles stared at him, open mouthed but Dotty wasn't distracted.

"Yes, death! I could see death in the man. At my age, a woman gains the ability to discern such things. Like death!"

Lady Florence nodded vacantly.

"That's really fascinating, Dotty. What happened to this Tom?"

"Old Tom? What happened? I'll tell you. He died!"

Clattering of spoons again.

"Murdered?"

"Ah, my dears. In my profession murder and death! often walk hand-in-hand, like lovers on a seashore."

By now the soup had been removed and the main course arrived. Dotty waited until beef was approaching mouths before continuing.

"Death! Yes, old Tom died. Natural causes, said the doctor. But some of us knew about young Bessie going to visit him at night. A big girl and her head easily turned by a man."

Bubbles stared, fork held in front of her. The dress had shifted frighteningly lower now.

"You think Bessie murdered him?" she gasped.

"Ah, my dear. Just suppose she made strawberry jam, as I do. And let us say she added another ingredient before presenting it to old Tom on one of her visits. I happen to know he was partial to a bit of jam before retiring each night."

"Oh gross! Poisoned?"

"That's not for me to say."

Heather finally spoke.

"Why not? You're supposed to be a detective."

Not well received by Dotty. A silence as her lips compressed. Then she responded.

"When you get to my age, you know a lot of things, young lady."

Heather was unimpressed.

"How old was old Tom?"

"Well, he'd have been 109 next birthday if it hadn't been for death!"

"So he was 108 and being visited at night by a young woman. I'm sure he died happy. And how on earth did soup remind you of him, old lady?"

Dotty's face flushed.

"At my age you understand these things," she responded tartly.

"I know a few people your age. One of my neighbours, for example. Everyone calls her a silly old bat."

Silence again before Lady Gruntingdon stepped in.

"Talking about that, I'm so looking forward to our holiday this year. Caribbean, you know. Love to get the sun on me."

Nightsock looked up.

"Do you? Whose son?" he asked innocently and then backtracked quickly as brain connected.

"I mean huge sun in that area. It seems so much bigger than in England."

"There is much evil under the sun. Including death!" pronounced Dotty in a desperate attempt to reclaim attention.

"Did I mention why we have empty chairs at the table?" asked Lady Florence.

Nightsock shook his head.

"Well, my husband's sister, our nephew and our daughter have all been killed in accidents in the last week."

"Oh right. Sorry about that," he said.

"No need, I don't miss them. Actually I didn't like any of the three. I'd probably have hit all of them on the head with something sooner or later."

Bubbles nodded enthusiastically.

"Pompom was a horrible sister. I always wanted to bash her skull in."

Dotty was now becoming irritated by the loss of limelight.

"I had been investigating these accidents that involve death!"

"Have you reached a conclusion?" enquired Nightsock.

"I am forming a theory but I'll need at least one more person to die to confirm it."

Lady Florence nodded understandingly.

"Then let's just hope that happens, Dotty."

"Hope is like a jagged rock high in the Himalayas, that awaits the thrusts of rain drops that combine and course like waves within the cracks and fissures on its hard, bitter surface," mused Nightsock mysteriously.

Bubbles squealed.

"That reminds me. Andy, my boyfriend. We're planning to run away in secret next weekend."

Her mother smiled vacuously.

"A nice boy, public school. Is he still selling drugs?"

"Oh yes mummy. It's very lucrative."

"So are you getting married?"

"Of course not. We're just going to have sex all the time until I'm pregnant. Then I'll get loads of money and a free house from the government. I'll make sure it has a big cupboard for Andy to hide away all the drugs."

"That sounds lovely, dear. Don't forget to phone sometime but not for a few months. Or a year or two."

"Yes, super. Andy's already got two other girls doing the same thing. I really think he's hit on a growing business."

"Lovely, darling. Now if everyone is finished, we'll go to the African Lounge for coffee."

Crackling fire with a massive semicircular sofa around it. Lord and Lady in the centre of the arc. Heather found herself between actress and model who had obviously started a conversation over dinner.

"So Wilma, you're still doing the modelling then?"

"Yes, Booby. I was voted model of the year last week."

"Really? By a group of friends?"

"No. A national magazine, sweetie. It's supposed to be a secret until the next issue, so I can't say which one."

"I think I can guess. It must be a constant ordeal for you to keep the figure in shape. I mean, at a certain age, we all go rather saggy."

"I wouldn't know. That's what happens is it? I see your nose is different again and you seem to have grown around the chest."

"It's essential for an actress to maintain her beauty. I'm acquainted with so many famous actors and they are saying that I look better than ever."

"I'm sure. Don't you find your knees get awfully sore?"

A frigid silence broken by the Lord. He rose to stand in front of the group.

"Now we must all do our party piece. Tradition you know. I'll start it with my rendition of Greensleeves. The piano please, Bubbles."

His daughter scampered to the piano and clunked keys with grim determination while sounds emanated from the Lord's mouth. Pure chance would have hit one note correctly but both pianist and singer failed miserably. Lady Florence next, who read one of her poems. The opening was unpromising.

"Where bats and bluebottles flutter their wings

The little robin sings

Flitter flutter, chirpy, chirp

Mother nature, you cannot ever be usurp."

A noble attempt at a difficult rhyme but it worsened significantly and was apparently interminable. Polite clapping broke out several times but then a new line began unexpectedly. Consequently, no applause when she finally finished.

"And so every little creation who was in the forest and wood

Comes out to say hello as I think they should."

Eventually, Lady Florence curtsied and relieved acclaim burst forth from the audience.

The dancer, Sensua performed erotically but found life difficult with only three men present and frosty stares from the women. Then Heather was called. She related Phillips first case, the manifesting tree. Appreciated by most but Dotty kept muttering 'obvious' throughout.

Nightsock read an excerpt from his novel but sadly overestimated the attention span of his listeners. After six minutes, his words were almost drowned by coughing, scratching, clearing throats and shuffling posteriors on the sofa.

Heather squirmed as Wilma was called. What hidden talents could be possessed by a nude model? Surprise.

"I'm going to perform a song taught to me by a Chinese man I knew for a bit. I don't know what the words mean but it sounds nice."

She began to sing. An obscure, almost obsolete ancient dialect. Unfortunately, Heather had studied the language and was the only listener who appreciated that it was a lurid, grossly obscene account of the man's relationship with Wilma. As she finished the last line, translatable as 'And it only cost me five dollars', genuine applause rang out.

Philip was next. He performed a card trick. Sadly, no cards were available and he attempted it using whisky glasses, which proved much harder to palm.

Now Dotty stood up and briefly went through her recipe for marmalade. Distinct lack of ovation.

Finally Booby, the actress stepped up. She posed, spread her arms wide and opened her mouth to sing. Then the chandelier fell on her head. Several people applauded, thinking it was part of performance and some minutes passed before anyone looked at her.

"Stand back, I'm a doctor," Wilma cried unexpectedly.

"Really? I didn't know," said Lady Florence.

"Yes, I qualified after five years study. Took up modelling to pay the fees. My speciality is head injuries."

"Well, most of Booby's is still there, more or less."

Nightsock picked up something from the fireplace.

"You'd better have this. It was toasting there," he said, dangling a lump of something from his hand.

Wilma nodded.

"Brain tissue. I may be able to glue it back on, if we're lucky."

She knelt by the body and pulled a few pieces of glass from it. Then she stood up.

"Dead as a dodo," she announced with formality.

Lord Gruntingdon walked to the door and held it open.

"Never mind, can't be helped. Come on everyone, we'll go to the Alpine Lounge. The servants will clear everything up."

Philip paused at the door.

"I would like to examine the chandelier fitting," he announced.

Everyone stopped and encircled him.

"Why?" asked Sensua.

"It is possible that some tampering occurred."

"You think so? That hadn't crossed my mind," said the Lord.

He led them all to the room above the lounge and summoned a servant to remove a panel in the floor.

"You can see it was held securely by string," said Lady Florence.

Philip bent down.

"Yes but what is this?"

He held up a short piece of string with a pink tape wrapped around it at the bottom.

"Goodness, that's acid tape. You wrap it round something and it gradually eats it away. We always keep some in the house. Use it to slice bread. A real time saver," remarked the Lord.

"How long would it take to eat through this string?" Philip asked.

"Pure guesswork but I'll have a wild stab at it. I'd say one hour 47 minutes 18 seconds, give or take two seconds."

"Then it must have been affixed 30 minutes before dinner began," Philip stated gravely.

"Anyway, it's no problem. The servants will have the chandelier up again in no time. We've got a big roll of string in the kitchens."

Dotty stood in the doorway. A final attempt.

"Death!" she cried, holding up a finger.

Everyone walked straight past and down to the Alpine Lounge. A pure white room with several pairs of skis mounted on the walls.

Lord Gruntingdon stood in front of them.

47

"Right, everybody. I'm off to bed and no doubt you'll all be going alone to different parts of the house as usual. See you all at breakfast, if we're still alive."

The room emptied quickly leaving just Heather and Philip.

"I think we're getting to the bottom of this," he said.

"So did I before Booby was killed. This man, Billy Blackship will inherit everything if the Lord, his wife and daughter die. But what's the connection with the actress?"

Philip looked upwards in postured muse configuration.

"Perhaps, just perhaps she was not the intended victim. Either the initiator incorrectly estimated the speed of the acid tape or the performances were not in the expected sequence."

"Everything is possible but Blackship is the only probable murderer I can come up with."

"All are suspect, except the servants. I had been considering the first so-called accident in the library. How could that book have fallen? One wonders if a place like this has secret passages."

"Only in films, Philip."

The panel opened in the wall and Lord Gruntingdon emerged.

"Couldn't help overhearing," he said.

"Nor me."

Lady Florence entered through another hidden panel near the fireplace. Five more doors opened in various places and the others joined the throng.

"I was looking round my room and suddenly found a secret door," said Sensua.

"Me too," announced Dotty, Nightsock and Wilma in unison.

"Well, I know all the passages. Used to explore them when I was a girl," remarked Bubbles.

"So you think one of us is a murderer?" asked the Lord

Philip nodded.

"Not necessarily. This Blackship could be still alive."

Wilma raised a hand.

"I saw a face in the window of my room."

Everyone turned to her.

"Who?" asked Heather.

"It was horrible. A sort of phantom that grinned at me. Like a ghostly TV image."

"Do you have a TV in your room?"

"Yes."

"Did the face look like someone on TV?"

"Now you say it, it did. That young newsreader."

"Okay. Did anything else happen?"

"The face disappeared and I saw something even stranger in the window."

"Yes?"

"An advert for washing up liquid."

"Right."

"Then I turned off the TV and went to bed. When I looked, the face and advert had gone."

Sensua stepped forward, seeming to resent the attention grabber.

"Something happened to me last night. I had a shower and was lying naked on the bed when a man entered."

"Really? Who was it?" enquired Heather.

"Obviously, I can't tell you that."

"Well, yes. I think we'll forget about it. The main thing is that we're all alive," the Lord interjected.

A pair of skis toppled from the wall and struck Nightsock on the head. His huge body fell with a reverberating thump.

Wilma rushed to the scene.

"I need to conduct rapid removal surgery," she announced, wedging a foot against his shoulder to pull the skis from the head.

They were deeply embedded and the Lord gripped her waist to add his weight to the effort. Finally they came free leaving two massive notches in Nightsock's scalp, nearly down to his ears.

"Just a bruise, I trust?" enquired the Lord vaguely.

"I think he's dead but I'll just do a medical test to make sure," responded Wilma.

She kicked the body violently in the ribs. Twice.

"Nope. He's what we doctors call a gonner."

"So you think those skis were cursed do you?" asked Dotty.

"No one said that," responded Heather but the old woman ignored her.

"Ghost skis have watched over this room for generations. Watched and waited for the right person. The right moment to strike. Strike for death!"

"Shut up you old windbag," Heather remarked.

"Ah, you may say that but deep down, you also believe. The Skis of the Gruntingdons. Hidden powers we do not comprehend."

"Are you a loony?" enquired Philip politely.

Dotty gave him a frosty look and walked to the door.

"Mark my words well," she said and then left.

Bubbles stepped over the corpse to reach her mother.

"Can I go now, mummy? I've just had a call from Andy. He says he's had to go to South America for a few weeks so I can't run away as planned. But he hasn't let me down. He sent another man to make a baby with me."

"That's good of him, dear."

"Well, he's waiting in my room now and I'm itching to get started."

"Yes, of course. You run along."

The girl scampered joyfully from the room.

Lord Gruntingdon strolled back to the hidden door.

"I'm off to have a nice relaxing bath. It's a bit hot, so I'll balance at an electric fan on the edge to keep cool," he announced before leaving.

"I need to practice my new dance routine where I throw knives in the air and catch them with my teeth," said Sensua as she departed.

Wilma looked at the corpse.

"I'd like to give it another kick but I'm not qualified. Now I've got to go as well. As a doctor, I always carry several bottles of poison around in my case and one of them broke, saturating the postage stamps next to it. I need to prepare lots of letters tonight."

Just Lady Florence left.

"I'm going straight to bed. Are you two coming as well?" she asked.

Philip shook his head.

"Better to let you sleep alone, I think."

"Oh very well."

They accompanied her up the stairs. At the top, they found a wild haired, unshaven man crouching down. He wore a scruffy grey overcoat.

"Are you a servant?" asked Lady Florence.

"Umm, yes. A servant. Yes."

"Strange, you look remarkably like Billy Blackship, our dead relation."

"Never heard of him."

"What is your name?"

"Billy. No it's John."

"Billy Nowitzjon? Are you from Bulgaria?"

"Yes and no."

"Good. Lovely. Come and run my bath and you must make sure I'm naked before I get in. Can't have my clothes getting wet, can we?"

"Yes, run the bath. Never done that before. How does it work?"

"Don't worry, Nowitzjon. I'll show you everything."

She led the man away, leaving Heather and Phillip to continue to their room.

"Everyone seems safe enough for now," he remarked, sitting on the bed.

"But we're no nearer a solution to this mystery."

"On the contrary. I begin to see light at the end of the tunnel."

"Well, I'm thoroughly confused."

The next morning, they reached the breakfast table to find only Dotty Parsnip.

"Been up since six making marmalade. Try some," she offered meaningfully.

"It's got glowing green bits in it," observed Heather.

"Oh yes. My little extra ingredient, minced uranium. I get it in the village shop. Gives a lovely flavour."

Wilma entered, yawning. She wore a short, flimsy nightdress that barely covered anything.

"Morning everyone."

"How did you get on with the poison?" asked Heather.

"All tidied up. I licked all the stamps and then licked everything else in the bag. It's all clean now."

"Wasn't that dangerous?"

"Not at all. I wore what we doctors call plastic gloves."

Lord Gruntingdon was next.

"Had a bit of a problem last night. Damned fan kept falling into the bath. Broken now with all that water in it."

He plopped a spoonful of Dotty's marmalade on his plate and wolfed it down.

"Where are the others?" asked Heather as he finished.

"We'll Bubbles won't be here. She smashed her head in by banging it against the headboard 19 times. Wilma came, of course."

The nightdressed one nodded.

"It's clear from my examination. The second impact killed her."

"But she then hit it another 17 times?" asked Heather.

"Yes, quite normal. What we in the profession call PDHB. Post death head beating."

"Lady Florence must have been upset."

The Lord was now consuming eggs and bacon and it was a few seconds before he responded.

"No. Not at all. Old thing managed to get killed herself. Another accident."

He filled his mouth again and Wilma took over.

"A sad misfortune. She must have been asleep when the brick fell on her head."

"Brick, you say?" enquired Philip.

"Yes, it was beside her on the floor. Must have fallen from the ceiling as she slept."

"How did she get on the floor?" asked Heather

"Very common in this situation. We doctors see many such cases. The impact of the brick on her skull caused a tremor to run through her body. This compressed the bedsprings and they rebounded to propel her body out of the bed and on to the floor. Perfectly normal. Sorry to use all that medical jargon but I can't be more exact."

"And Sensua. Where is she?"

Wilma grimaced.

"That nasty cow? Dead, I'm pleased to say. Killed by a bear."

"A bear? Grizzly?"

"Well, I hope she cried a bit. Not a real bear, of course. It was what we medics call a big teddy. Just to explain, that means a purely representational bear figure, created from synthetic materials and adapted to enhance aspects of humanity that are not normally found in the natural bovine configuration."

"You mean ursine," observed Heather.

"Yes I do. Anyway, this bear was a good 'un. Killed that rancid bitch."

"What are the details?" asked Philip.

"Well, Lord Gruntingdon had generously supplied her with this teddy to keep her company in bed. It was large, nearly one third the size of a human. Like many bear collectors, the Lord had replaced the stuffing in its legs with heavy lead weights."

"Why?"

Wilma laughed.

"You're obviously not a teddy expert. The added weight prevents the bear being stolen by young children. Too heavy for them to carry. A bonus is that it keeps the bear on the bed in gravity free environments, a space station for example."

"What difference would weight make if there is no gravity?"

"Ah, you wouldn't know of course. I used the expression gravity free in the same way as pepper free in food, where 3.99852 percent of pepper is permissible within the law."

"And how did Sensua die?"

"That revolting tart? Obvious again. The bear jumped from the bed directly on to her cranium while she was lying on the floor."

"Jumped, you say?" asked Philip.

"Indeed yes. The evil witch must have been lying on the floor, having mistaken it for the bed. Then she was jumped on."

"By a teddy bear?" enquired Heather.

"I have to reveal one of the little-known medical laws that are normally kept strictly within the confines of hospitals and healing colleges. When any artificial copy of a creature is created, it is imbued with the power to leap once and once only during its existence. This is known as the law of Genetic Subethical Leap Transference. In practice, it means that every soft toy has got one good jump in them."

"Does that apply to human representations? Inflatable ones, just for example?" asked the Lord.

"It does. You will need to be careful."

"Fascinating," murmured Philip.

"So only us left. Plus Billy Blackship," remarked Heather.

"He's dead," said the Lord.

"I saw him last night with Lady Florence."

"No, that was Billy Nowitzjon, the new servant from Bulgaria. A good fellow. Used to work for Lord Poncewort."

"What about the man who was seeing Bubbles?"

"Oh, he went quite early. Said goodbye to me. Bubbles was there, trying to drag him back to her room but he'd had enough."

"We are also departing," announced Philip, rising from his seat.

The Lord rose, face reddening.

"Really sir? A failure then?"

"Not at all. The case is closed."

"What? Then who is the killer?" asked Wilma.

"The killer, as you use the name, is…"

He paused

"… misfortune."

"Who is that?" asked the Lord

"Misfortune or Act of God for the uninitiated. This house has a severe dose of it. Every death was simply an ACVUA."

"ACVUA?"

"A Chapter of Very Unfortunate Accidents."

"Brilliant! My word, you're a genius. Your reputation is well founded Mr Caldrock."

"I did tell you when I arrived. I do not fail, unlike some others."

Dotty wasn't pleased.

"I'd nearly got there. Two more deaths than I'd have been sure. I believed they were accidents all along," she blustered weakly, only to receive scornful looks from the others.

Wilma moved close to Philip, eyes shining and nightdress strap slipping dangerously down her shoulder.

"What a man!" she exclaimed breathlessly.

"Off we go then," Heather announced, forcing herself between them and grabbing Phillip's arm.

"I'm willing to give you a check-up any time," Wilma called after him as they departed.

6 THE RECEPTIONIST COMETH

Two weeks later, Heather stood in a newly furnished office suite in a quiet street near the centre of Mapleton, the rental paid for by the massive cheque received from Lord Gruntingdon. She was in the reception chamber that contained a desk, computer and filing cabinets with a long leather sofa along one wall. Two doors. One leading to her room, the smallest. The other door led to the largest room, Philip's office. A large oak desk, paintings on the walls, two cabinets and four padded chairs.

She entered it to find him lounging behind the desk.

"Are you comfortable?" she asked.

"Yes dear. Any applicants yet?"

"They're due in five minutes. Try your screen."

"Oh yes. Forgot that."

Two screens on a desk extension to his right. He clicked on the second. A picture of the empty reception room outside.

"I think we should have sifted them first," Heather remarked.

"No, no. I well recall how Wincepole did it. He placed a job advertisement in a newspaper and asked everyone interested to attend at a specific time. I've copied his example."

"I think you should have been more explicit. She read the advert again. 'Person wanted by brilliant investigator. Interviews 10 a.m. Thursday'. The office address followed.

A movement on the screen. A young woman entered and stood uncertainly in the room. Then she noticed a mirror on the wall and walked over. After a few moments, she opened the top button of her blouse and moved to the sofa.

"Not suitable," Heather announced.

"Maybe we should keep an open mind."

"Not suitable," Heather repeated and walked out into the reception office.

The girl sprang to her feet.

"Hello. Am I in the right place for the interview?"

"You are."

"My name's Clarissa Hartwin. I've just received a first class honours degree at university, specialist subject was investigation and detective work. The faculty awarded me the best student prize for three years running and I was voted best person at university by the student body. I nearly made the British Olympic team in martial arts and I was university chess champion last year. I'm not really boasting about any of that, just stating the facts."

"I see. Well, I don't think we can offer you sufficient salary."

"Oh don't worry about that. My father is a billionaire. I'd be happy to work for nothing."

Heather hesitated, desperate for a reason.

"We're expecting more applicants and obviously can't decide now."

"I understand. I'll just wait here until you're ready. I'm not going to apply to any other jobs. All the multinationals have been after me but I said no. This is the one I really want. I'll work any hours, seven days a week. I hardly ever take holidays and I'm definitely not going to get pregnant."

"Right. Ah, here's another applicant."

A middle-aged man in a dirty raincoat. Unshaven with wild, staring eyes. He was covered in grime and a nasty smell filled the room as he entered.

"This the interview place?" he asked.

"Yes," replied Heather, reeling back from the stench.

"Need to be careful. They're after me."

"Who?"

"Them that have no name. Demons, I call 'em. Arrived in those little spaceships outside my house. Follow me everywhere. But they'll never take me!"

Heather flinched as he opened the raincoat. A garden scythe was tied inside it.

"I'll get 'em with this," he declared, pulling out the gleaming blade and swinging it over his head.

Heather squealed and stepped back but Clarissa rose to face the man.

"Now, now. What's all this then?" she asked, swinging her silver pendant in front of his eyes.

The man grunted with eyes fixed to the jewellery.

"Now you want to go to your doctor, don't you?" she continued.

He nodded dumbly.

"And tell him you're suffering from Impagrillicatus Aphyloxtilly. He'll give you some tablets that you will take every day. Do you understand all that?"

Another willing nod.

"Then off you go. Have a nice day," said Clarissa cheerfully.

The man departed and she returned to her seat.

"What did you do?" asked Heather.

Clarissa looked up.

"Oh, nothing really. Just something I picked up when I qualified as a psychiatrist."

"Really?"

"Well, yes. I took two years out before university. Went to some colleges and did a few qualifications."

"A few?"

"Oh one was to become a medical doctor. Did the psychiatry thing concurrently. Silly really but the tutors said they'd never seen anything like it. I finished 10 years training in 21 months."

"Holiday for the other three months?"

"Oh sort of. Just messed around writing."

"A book, I presume?"

"Just a few jottings. Didn't even give it a title but the publishers called it 'The Definitive Absolutely Complete History of England' or something like that. Bit boring really. A few universities are using it as a standard course book. You know, Oxford, Harvard, Cambridge and others but it's not really worth talking about."

Heather was nodding as a new applicant arrived. A young man with a shaven head in tattered jeans and scruffy jacket.

"All right, love?" he asked, looking at Heather.

"You're here for the job?"

"Forced to. Probation people sent me round. Got no choice."

"So you're not interested really."

"Na. I get enough handouts to buy my alcohol. You keep some here?"

"No."

"Any drugs then? I'm not fussy what sort."

"No."

He began to shout. 85 percent expletives. Then stepped foward.

"Give us money then," he yelled.

Clarissa was up again, gripping his shoulder.

"Come on now, behave young Bobby," she declared with authority.

His face contorted as he spun round to face her.

"Clarissa?" he said and then began to weep.

"Now Bobby. What's been going on?"

"I'm sorry. You were so good to me but I fell into the old ways again," he blubbed.

"Stop that crying and look at me," she said firmly.

The sobs subsided and he stood erect with eyes staring.

"I know. I've got it in me. You told me that. I promise it will never happen again."

"And you'll go back to that nuclear fission course?"

"Yes, Clarissa. I give you my word."

"Then you'd better get started. Nice to see you again, Bobby."

"Thank you. Thank you. And just to say again I'm very sorry."

He departed with a new spring in his step.

"I won't ask," remarked Heather.

"Oh, just a lad I helped a bit. Student life is a bit boring in the evenings so I joined the police as a night officer. Only a temporary part-time thing, not worth talking about."

A smart suited woman came in next. Tidy blonde hair, white blouse. About 38. She gave a correct smile.

"Good morning. My name is Stopper. I'm here regarding the position," she announced.

"I'm sorry. I think we may have already decided."

"I beg your pardon. That is totally incorrect. You are obliged by law to conduct fair and proper interviews with all applicants."

"Really?"

"Furthermore, I have every reason to believe that your blunt refusal relates to the fact that my grandfather stole apples."

"Apples?"

"Blustering like that will not help you. The accusation clearly stated that three apples were taken and he was totally innocent of the crime. I propose to initiate legal proceedings against your organisation immediately."

"Grimwell Stopper," Clarissa said loudly.

"What?"

The woman turned quickly and Clarissa rose to meet her.

"Grimwell Stopper. Petty larceny. Case 43877 at the Morchester Assizes, 51 years 203 days ago. He was found guilty."

"Well, Miss Smart Legs. I tell you he was innocent."

"I remember the case well from my studies. The Crown correctly charged him with purloining three items of fruit, hereinafter known as apples. One was dropped by the miscreant as he ran away and consequently only two remained when your grandmother received them."

"No, I don't believe you."

"After he had been fined, he made a full confession to the newspapers. The story was printed on page 4 as I recall."

Stopper put hands over her ears.

"I won't listen! I won't!"

"In addition, the procedure adopted on these premises today has been demonstrably fair and just. Your arrival was 4 minutes and 13 seconds after the time specified in the advertisement and thus your position is one of Delictum Solitus Fortunas, as recognised under British and European law. For non-Latin speakers this is known as 'Corpum Darnitus Meliforantis Saysum' although the strict translation is 'Bloody hard luck'."

Stopper sighed.

"I apologise. I was wrong about everything and I'm so grateful your honesty and openness. You've changed my life forever and I thank you from the bottom of my heart."

With that, she left the building and Clarissa returned to her seat.

"Thanks," murmured Heather.

"Not at all. Sometimes I can't seem to forget my legal training. You'd have handled it better, I'm sure. Sorry if I've been a bit of a pest, it's just that I really want this job."

"I've just noticed that the top button of your blouse is undone," Heather mentioned innocently.

"Yes, absolutely. I've only just remembered to do it."

"Remembered?"

"Of course, you won't know. The research hasn't been published yet. A woman should always leave the top button unfastened to ensure correct air circulation around the chest area."

"Oh, right. Come in and meet Mr Caldrock."

A surprised smile and the girl followed Heather to Philip's office. He was poring over a clutch of papers.

"Clarissa, I presume," he announced.

"That's amazing. I saw the video camera and microphone in the next room but never thought you'd be able to memorise a person's name."

"A mere trifle."

"May I say that your wife has been very courteous to me."

"You believe this lady is my wife?"

"She has a few grains of powder on the hem of her coat and you have the same on your shirt. I can't mistake that powder. It's from a stone used in the construction of house doorways and only six residences in the town were built like that. You are also both wearing wedding rings."

"Circumstantial conjecture."

"Finally, your names are printed on the doors of your offices."

"Yes, I see," Philip murmured, leaning back in his chair.

"Am I suitable for the job?"

"I think we can offer you a trial period. Do you have transport?"

"Yes, I've got two cars actually. And a helicopter but I don't have an aircraft yet," she responded, somewhat downcast.

"No plane?"

"My father offered me one but I didn't want to sponge off him. However, I've just received a large amount for a few academic awards and my book sales. I hope to have one soon. I'm already qualified to fly just about anything."

"Good, good."

Heather interjected.

"I'm afraid the job involves a lot of reception work, greeting people, answering telephones and other rather mundane duties. Plus typing."

Clarissa beamed.

"That's great. I love all that. I hope you don't want me to leave at lunchtimes. I'd rather bring a sandwich and carry on working. I'll be here seven days a week, if that's okay?"

"When can you start?" asked Philip.

"Now, if possible. I can't wait."

"Very well. Heather will show you everything. I'm expecting our first clients imminently."

7 THE SQUIRREL OF THE CRUMMS

3.14 p.m. Having tidied the office four times, Clarissa was correcting a textbook of brain surgery and drinking tea. The door burst open and a chubby faced figure staggered in.

"For god's sake. I've got to see Caldrock," he cried, mopping his brow with a handkerchief.

She dutifully spoke on the intercom and led him to Philip's office.

"He's not too bad, just slight twinge of Traumaticali Versum Bungalus. That translates as blind panic," she announced.

"His name?" enquired Philip.

She clasped a hand over her mouth.

"I forgot to ask. I'm so really sorry. Stupid of me."

"Sheltrick Crumm," the man gasped.

"Sit down Mr Crumm and compose yourself."

Philip pressed the buzzer and Heather joined them.

"Tea for three then?" offered Clarissa.

"Yes, thank you and also biscuits," Philip replied.

"You're brilliant, Mr Caldrock. The average biscuit contains trace elements of Vaselectomal, a proven remedy for panic."

She left the room after bestowing an admiring glance at Philip.

Heather pulled up a chair as Crumm mopped his brow and began his account.

"I'd better tell you what's happened from the beginning. My wife and I live on the outskirts of town, in a secluded house. Trees all around us and we love the privacy. It all started nine days ago when I was pruning my Bustrellis in the garden. Old Mrs Grapefull came past and asked me if I thought it was going to rain. I said no and she said occasional showers were forecast. Quite a shock to the system, I can tell you."

Heather looked at Philip hoping he would ask the 'are you a loony' question.

"Are you a loony?" he enquired.

The man rose to his feet, face reddening.

"Loony, sir? Loony, you say? This business is enough to threaten the sanity of any person."

"Please sit and continue with your account, Mr Crumm."

"Very well. The unexpected, not to mention disturbing news of imminent precipitation caused me to return to the house to fetch my umbrella. Another shock. It had been moved."

He sat back, awaiting their response.

"Moved from the place where you expected to find it?" asked Heather sympathetically.

"Indeed, madam. Yes indeed. I invariably leave it on the stand to the right of the hall table and now it was on the left."

"Perhaps your wife was tidying up?"

"Minerva? No, absolutely not. She knows my possessions must not be touched. I did question her on the matter and she broke down in tears but denied any umbrella interference."

"Is that it?" asked Philip, doodling on the pad in front of him.

Another red-faced rising.

"It, sir? It, you say? Not at all. Oh no!"

"Then please expedite your account."

Crumm sat again.

"So be it. Of course, it will be very clear to you detectives that the umbrella had been temporarily borrowed, shall we say, in order that it could be sniffed by the wild creature designated to attack me. Subsequently it was returned and incompetently left in the wrong place."

Philip leant forward over the desk.

"I will deduce. You will relate," he said firmly.

"Then to continue. At this point I must tell you of a family legend. A story of bloody horror that is passed down through generations of my family. You may have heard of 'The Great Red Beast of the Trees that Seeks the Crumms'?"

No response.

"Well, I'm sure most people in this town will know it. In 1733, my ancestor Bisquet Crumm lived in the house. You will note from the name that our origins are in France. A little village called Pillinquette in the Massif Central region. There are 26 Crumms still living there. It's an ideal base for touring the area. You can stay at the Hotel Rumpatelle, a pleasant and not too presumptive establishment. I have visited several times with my wife to sample the delights offered by the village. A quaint museum, antique shops, cafes, patisserie and a well-stocked brothel. So great is my affinity with the place that I am actively considering whether to purchase a residence there. A tranquil paradise in which to spend my retirement years."

Clarissa tottered in with a tray of tea. Still a little left in the cups and the biscuits were dry, being positioned on a plate above tea level.

"Sorry. Bit clumsy with trays," she said and thrust the biscuits under the visitor's nose.

"Take one now, Mr Crumm. It will calm you down."

"No thank you."

"Now come along. Open up."

"Shan't."

He placed a hand over his mouth. Clarissa looked sternly at him for a second. Then she grabbed the offending digits and twisted them back while forcing his jaw open with her other hand. Gripping a biscuit between her teeth, she pushed it into his mouth. Then she clamped the jaw shut and held it tightly.

"I want to see you swallow," she asserted.

The rebelliousness went from his eyes and he gulped dutifully.

"There's a good boy. Now you'll feel a lot better."

She turned to Philip.

"Sorry about the spilt tea. Shall I make another attempt?"

"No. You've done very well," he responded and she left the room.

Crumm smiled and relaxed in his chair.

"I do feel so much better. That woman is wonderful. Now where was I?"

"Before descending into mere gibberish, you had told us of some family curse," responded Philip amiably.

"Ah yes. 'The Great Red Beast of the Trees that Seeks the Crumms'. Well in 1733, my ancestor Bisquet Crumm lived in the house. You will note from the name that our origins are in France. A little village called…"

"What happened to him?" Heather interjected quickly.

"It was horrible. One night he was asleep on the back lawn. You'll be aware that many people did that in the eighteenth century as beds were most uncomfortable then. When he awoke, he found his mouth was stuffed full of nuts. Can you imagine his terror? At any time he could have swallowed!"

"He was allergic to nuts?" asked Heather.

"No but perhaps you can understand why I was so afraid of that biscuit being pushed into me. There is obviously something in the Crumm genes, some revulsion at force-feeding. Anyway, Bisquet subsequently told the story to a neighbour who reported seeing some red creature in a tree on the property. A tree immediately adjacent to the sleeping position of my ancestor!"

Philip sighed.

"The nuts were placed in his mouth by an animal that had mistaken the orifice for a hole in the ground. The perpetrator was a red squirrel."

"Squirrel?"

"A red squirrel."

"You know this creature then? What is its appearance?"

"Does the word squirrel mean anything to you?" asked Heather patiently.

"Not a thing. But I am no student of the residents of hell. No doubt you've found the name in some esoteric manuscript."

Philip swung round in the chair to turn his back but Heather was more sympathetic.

"I'll show you," she said and pulled a book from the shelves. She opened it at a full page, captioned picture.

"Oh that. You mean Skew-weel. What a strange colour. They're always grey. Is this some devilish mutation that you show me?"

"Red squirrels were indigenous in England but the grey came across in ships from Canada. They were more aggressive and carried a virus that was fatal to the red and they are nearly extinct in England now."

"I see."

"That solves your case Mr Crumm. Our fee is five thousand pounds," Heather continued.

"Solves it? Not at all. The creature seen by the neighbour was different altogether. Nearly the size of a very small man."

Phillips spun his chair round quickly.

"A small man?"

"Yes or a child. It was covered in red hair with long arms and a vicious fanged mouth."

"An ape or a monkey perhaps?" enquired Heather.

"What?"

Back to the book.

"Oh you mean an A-pee or Mon-uk-yea. No, no. They were very common in England in the eighteenth century. This creature had six huge tusk-like fangs that hung down, nearly as far as its jaw. Bright crimson eyes and pincer like hands. Its feet were like plates. Circular and flat."

Heather pushed the book to one side.

"Has this creature reappeared since?" enquired Philip.

"Yes, several times. In 1784, 1821, 1886, 1924 and 1969. And also last night!"

"Last night?"

"That is why I'm so distressed, Mr Caldrock. I will recount the events. We retired exactly at ten. Now I have to tell you that my wife has an unpleasant habit in bed."

"Really?"

"Full length and a disgusting shade of grey. She has recently indicated a desire to become a trainee nun and despite my protestations, insists on getting used to the clothing."

"That is her habit," observed Heather.

"No, she wakes up at the slightest noise. At 1.30 in the morning, she roused me. On enquiring the reason, she put a finger to her lips and whispered that she'd heard a noise outside our window. A first-floor window!"

"Go on," encouraged Philip.

"I pulled on my clothes as quickly as possible and then crept to the curtains. Lifting one edge, I peered out. There, directly outside the window was the creature! I could see its red eyes and the huge fangs. For a second, our eyes met. A sight to make a brave man scream, I can tell you. My wife joined me and also witnessed the next action of the beast. It gave a hoarse cry and climbed upwards until it was out of sight. It's coming for me, Mr Caldrock. I'm certain of it!"

"I have some questions, Mr Crumm," said Philip.

"Yes, of course."

"On any previous appearances, has this creature harmed anyone?"

"Harmed? Yes indeed. Every previous visitation has resulted in a leg of a Crumm being broken."

"The creature struck them?"

"No, they all fell from the tree while searching for it. That is the devious nature of the beast, Mr Caldrock. It displays fearsome cunning in its attacks."

"Another question. Do you know anyone who wishes to harm you? An enemy, someone you may have upset?"

Crumm nodded.

"Absolutely not. Everyone likes me. Except perhaps one person."

"Who?"

"Oh, I'm sure it's unimportant."

"I will be the judge of that."

"The man who lives at the back of us. His garden adjoins mine. Roger Mudd is his name. A small fellow about the size of a child. I invariably greet him cordially when I see him. 'Hello you swine', I call but he rarely replies. Just gives me a sour look. I encounter him quite often as he runs his business from home."

"Business? What sort of business?"

"I'm not certain. Some trivial merchandise. Fancy dress, costumes and the like, I believe. I often see him dressed up. A clown, lion, fairy, panda and suchlike."

"Has his family being in the house long?"

"Indeed, nearly as long as the Crumms. They first took over the place in the 18th century and even his ancestors were little swine."

"The dislike is mutual then."

"Oh yes. Our family believes that his property belongs to us. It goes back to 1731 when old Crachpot Crumm sold the land to the Mudds. He must have been stupid at the time. They moved in just before old Crachpot died. He was 104, you know. When Bisquet took over he went to them to explain the mistake and asked the Mudds to leave. But disgracefully, they refused and so Bisquet quite reasonably shot them all. All except one son, that is. To our family's utter disgust, he went to the authorities and Bisquet was forced to return the land. Until this day, the swine's successors remain a painful thorn in our side."

Philip sat back.

"Mr Crumm, I will take your case. We will visit you early tomorrow morning when the solution will be revealed."

"Oh really? Very well. Early tomorrow then."

He mumbled words of gratitude and departed.

Heather was on her feet immediately.

"We need to go immediately, not tomorrow," she said.

Philip grinned.

"You read my mind. I want our assistant with us."

They rushed to the reception room where Clarissa was mopping up a pool of coffee around her cup.

"You're coming with us. We need a gun that doesn't kill, just knocks out," he called.

"I've got one," she responded, opening a cupboard. It contains an array of weapons and she grabbed a pistol, stuffing it into her waistband.

Heather knew the answer. The land dispute provided the motive. Neighbours who hated each other. A man who stored costumes in his home. Clever but not clever enough. She estimated that Crumm must have arrived back 15 minute before they parked up the street, a short distance from his house. Clarissa leapt out, drawing the pistol and crouching.

"Not yet," called Philip as he turned to the house. He didn't try the door, just walked directly round the back and then continued down behind a row of bushes with Heather and Clarissa following closely

A raised voice. Sheltrick Crumm.

"Come on Mudd. Put on that costume and come out here," he was yelling.

No response.

"You're a coward, you swine. Come and show yourself."

Helen moved closer, behind another clump of bushes. Now she saw a dour woman running from the house to join Crumm. She was wearing a solid grey habit that brushed the floor. Must be his wife. She held a basket behind her back and in it was a shot gun.

"I want you in that costume. Now!" yelled Crumm.

"I'm coming," came a faint reply.

Heather moved forward again. Now next to the hedge that divided the property. She was still hidden from view behind a Fusilium Carmonthus Bush, an evergreen with a unique leaf pattern admired by naturalists for hundreds of years. The substantial yet delicate foliage provides excellent coverage and is ideal to conceal those less appealing sectors of any garden, particularly any gaudily coloured plastic gnomes that may be present.

From her new vantage point, Heather could see the neighbour's garden and in it was a low white building a few metres from the hedge. The Crumms were directly in front of her. Now the wife had started.

"Show yourself, you toad," she screamed.

"Yes, come on. Let's see you in that stupid animal disguise," added her spouse.

Heather saw movement on the other side of the hedge and gasped. A huge rabbit had emerged from the white building and was moving slowly forward.

"No! Not that costume, you swine. The red one."

"That's right. We want you in the red one," the pseudo-nun shrieked loudly.

"Oh, very well. But it will have to be quick," replied the rabbit as it disappeared into the building.

The woman pulled the shotgun from the basket and handed it to Crumm. Then she began to tremble with some unknown emotion.

"Are you ready? I'm coming!" yelled the neighbour.

Heather sprang forward.

"Stop! This little game is over, Mr Crumm. We listened to your little tale and I admit it was clever. Invent a mythical creature that exactly matched one of the costumes used by your neighbour. Pretend that it was about to attack you to provide justification for your actions. A shotgun fired in self defence but in fact it is premeditated murder. And your wife is assisting you."

The couple turned to her, open mouthed as she continued.

"Come on out, Philip and Clarissa."

Bad news. No one appeared.

More bad news. Mrs Crumm's habit had fallen open to reveal a short red dress underneath. Not trembling but unbuttoning. Even worse news. A red wolf emerged from the white building.

"You don't like Little Red Riding Hood, I take it," shouted the wolf.

"What?"

Crumm stepped forward.

"We do this all the time. My wife is the star, Mudd is the wolf and I come along with a shotgun just in time."

He opened the weapon. No cartridges.

"Oh."

"Was this some investigator's trick?"

"Exactly, Mr Crumm. That is precisely what it was," said Philip, marching towards them from the house.

"I told you we would arrive tomorrow to avoid unnecessary worry. As your wife is a light sleeper, your night would have been restless in the extreme," he continued.

"But why have you come?"

"To rescue something unique. Show them, Clarissa."

He turned as the girl emerged from the house, carrying a large sack. She opened it in front of them.

"My God, that's revolting," exclaimed Heather.

A hairy, multi fanged creature, apparently asleep.

"A sabre toothed baboon," Philip observed.

"It's incredible. Multiplus Vampiricus Bigabus Puspus, a native of the Massif Central region of France until it became extinct several hundred years ago," cried Clarissa.

"I believe it stowed away in your ancestor's hand luggage in 1731," added Philip.

"It can't be that old," exclaimed Mrs Crumm.

Clarissa smiled.

"Indeed yes. It normally lives for nearly 500 years and needs very little food. Just a couple of nuts every month are more than enough. Obviously, it is also partial to sucking a little blood from a young woman's neck but that's purely for pleasure."

"How did they become extinct?"

"Very sad. They have just one predator, the squirrel. A most unfortunate quirk of nature as it is the only creature that squirrels like to eat. The population was decimated by a rampaging squirrel gang in the 17th century. We're so lucky to have found this one. I'm really sorry about dropping it a few times, Mr Caldrock."

"You've done well," he responded and she carried the sack back towards the car, only dropping it twice more before disappearing from view.

"Remarkable. Quite remarkable. Where was the creature?" asked Mr Crumm.

"Have you ever been to your attic?" responded Philip with a smile.

"No, never. Nor have any of my family since we moved here. I see. Brilliant, Mr Caldrock. I must pay you handsomely for this."

"Me too," cried the neighbour.

"My assistant handles all such financial matters," Philip declared regally as he strolled back towards the car.

8 THE MISSING POSTAGE STAMP

"A woman approaches," declared Philip turning in his chair as he observed the screen that displayed the pavement outside their premises.

"A customer?" asked Heather, looking over his shoulder. She could see a rather elegant, blonde woman pacing uncertainly outside the entrance.

"Indubitably. A rich widow who plans to move to Spain shortly."

"I can see the approved Spanish resident's permit sticking out of her bag. Her clothes and jewellery indicate wealth. Widow? Was that a guess?"

"I do not guess. Many will observe but see mere fragments whilst a few of us barely glance and compose a picture like pieces from a scattered jigsaw that have fallen from the table of life within the games room of existence that lies inside the great residence of the universe, glittering with a myriad of aspects that dazzle the imagination."

"A guess then."

He held up the local newspaper, page five. 'Model in the Money'. A photo of the blonde woman outside, Melda Swivel. Heather scanned the story. Melda, 31 had inherited six million pounds after the death of her husband, 97. 'I was getting too old for modelling so I searched around for some rich old man who'd die soon. I made him redecorate the entire house and dig the garden every day. Finally, I finished him off by demanding he personally build a sun house using massive stone blocks that he had to lift in place. Now I've got the money and I'm off.'

The man's sister was also quoted. 'I'm so pleased for Melda. They were only married a short time and we never met but she deserves to get all his money. In fact, I'm sending her a cheque in gratitude and commiseration.'

"Ms Swivel seems a good sort," remarked Philip.

Heather pursed lips.

"She's decided to come in."

A minute later, Melda entered. She was accompanied by Clarissa, walking on her knees and dabbing a cloth on a large ink stain on the blonde's short skirt.

"I'm so sorry. I was creating an illuminated manuscript and the ink bottle just caught my hand. Luckily, with my training in textile chemistry, I've prepared a solution that will remove the mark. You simply mix water and salt with liquefied yak fur. Cleans almost everything."

She finished dabbing and Melda smiled regally.

"Thank you, lovey. Now bring me a nice mug of coffee."

Clarissa hustled out of the room.

"Please be seated, Ms Swivel and relate your problem to us," invited Philip.

"Thanks dear."

She sat in a fizz of nylon and her skirt rode up high to reveal pink underwear.

"Amazing," Heather exclaimed.

"Yes, my legs. Aerobics is what does it," responded Melda.

"No, your skirt. The stains gone."

"Oh, it didn't matter. I only wear things once and then buy something else. Saves on cleaning bills, lovey."

Philip shuffled in his chair.

"I am Philip Caldrock, investigator. You wish to consult me?"

"Yep. I couldn't make up my mind but decided I would."

"I accept only the cases that interest me."

Melda turned her steely gaze to him and formed a plastic smile.

"You look like you're worth a bit. Married?"

"That is my husband," Heather announced with malice aforethought.

"Okay, dear. Keep your knickers on. Just asking."

"What is the reason for your visit, Ms Swivel?" Philip interjected.

"It's a shame and all that. A real mystery. I'll start at the start. I got the old man dragging those big stone blocks in the garden to make my sun house. Fit as a flea, he was. Anyway, eventually I bribed the delivery men to drop a block on his head. I got this doctor friend of mine to sign it off as accidental death and then showed a couple of potential buyers round the house. I'd already set it up with the estate agency. After that, I started to work out all the money I'd got."

"It must have been very distressing for you," observed Heather.

"Well, yeah. I mean, adding up isn't my strong point. So I put the papers in an envelope to send to my accountant. That's when the mystery began."

"Yes?" asked Philip.

"The stamp had disappeared."

"What? A postage stamp?" exclaimed Heather.

"Yer on the mark, lovey. A postage stamp. There was one in the drawer of my desk. I saw it earlier that day but it had disappeared!"

"How many other people had access to your desk?"

"There's no one else staying in the house. I got rid of the servants in case they saw something when the old man died. Nobody ever went to my office room apart from Denis, of course."

"Denis?"

"My boyfriend. Came round regularly for, you know but not that day. He was already in Spain, buying our new home."

"The people who delivered the blocks?"

"They never went in the house. I paid them off and they drove away."

"Only one possibility then. The prospective buyers of the property."

"Never thought of that but they did look round my office. Two couples. The first was that TV sports commentator and his wife. They had a quick look but weren't interested."

"And the other couple?" asked Philip.

"Some foreign bloke, Victor Velpronov and his woman, Virginia Incent. They didn't seem to like the place much but he agreed to pay the full price. He's some sort of billionaire and I've made a note in my diary in case he becomes available. They're moving in next Monday."

Philip sat back, hands clasped in front of him.

"This man interests me. Can you describe him?"

"Sort of average height, dark hair and a great smile. I reckon he's about thirtyish. Nice tan as well. Real good-looking. Didn't like his girlfriend though. Long dark hair, perfect figure, beautiful face and intelligent. Just the sort that other women don't want to know."

"Was the drawer locked?"

Melda nodded.

"Yes and also sealed with clear sticky tape. I do that for extra security."

A pause and Heather was deep in thought for a few seconds.

"Did you happen to notice the woman's leg covering?" she asked unexpectedly.

"Yes, of course. She had this very short dress on and I followed her up the stairs. Old-fashioned suspender belt and stockings."

Another pause as Heather smiled and then Melda clapped a hand and her mouth.

"Oh my gawd. You're brilliant!"

Phillips face was a picture of incomprehension but he wasn't going to ask. Heather took pity on him.

"You wouldn't understand, Philip. It's a woman's secret. Traditional suspender belts have a clip that can be twisted into a key that will fit any keyhole. In addition, sticky tape is an essential complement to secure the stockings in position. Now you mustn't reveal this to any other man."

He nodded dubiously but Melda looked uncertain.

"Can he be trusted?" she asked.

"Yes, absolutely," Heather assured her.

Clarissa entered, biting her lip with concentration as she carried the loaded tray to the desk. She nearly made it but two mugs fell to the floor.

"It's okay, I expected that. I made extra as contingency cover," she said smugly.

Rescuing three mugs from the ocean in the tray, she placed them carefully on the desk.

"My researches have shown that if three mugs are situated in a triangle of the correct proportions, it creates a gravitational field that ensures the contents remain hot indefinitely."

Returning to the door, she picked up the fallen mugs and dropped the tray. Then she tripped over a chair leg. Another three minutes before tray, mugs and Clarissa left.

Philip took a sip and gasped as his tongue was burnt.

"Ms Swivel, your case intrigues me and I will take it."

"So what do I do then, dearie?"

"Push off to Spain and don't come back. Before you go, you will pay Heather in advance."

"Okay, that sounds fair," Melda responded, rising from her chair.

Heather returned to the office a few minutes later.

"She's gone. I can't believe you agreed to investigate the theft of a piffling postage stamp. Apart from getting some money from that obnoxious witch."

"It is the very triviality that draws me. One may see the tiniest hair moving on a great mountain and ignore it. However the hair could be on the tip of the nose of a shaggy brontosaurus, emerging from a cave."

"I didn't like that blonde creature."

"Come, come my dear. A sincere young woman with a few rough edges but a heart of gold."

"She can afford a gold one now. What is our plan?"

"We must endeavour to find out about this Victor Velpronov. Then we will visit on the day he moves in. Next Monday. Why was the stamp taken? Why did he purchase the house? These are the vital questions."

Research proved singularly productive. Victor had suddenly appeared in England, four weeks ago and undoubtedly possessed excessive riches. The source of his wealth was reputed to be the ownership of the only mine in the world producing Zazac, an essential element used in every computer in the world. His age was uncertain but most sources showed it as 33. Unmarried and consequently now the target of virtually every woman in England. Since arriving, he had attended a few parties and held meetings with government ministers. Nothing else and no mention of Virginia Incent.

2 pm Monday.

Heather pulled up in the street on the opposite side to the house. An imposing old structure, originally on the outskirts of town but a tide of new buildings had now encompassed it. Three floors with four windows on each. Just enough garden around to keep it aloof from its neighbours. Velpronov had paid a substantial amount for it.

"We'll look round first," Philip announced.

They began a tour round the building. Streets in front, along the rear and down one side. On the other side was a recently refurbished commercial property. A large store with 'Cheap Gold Jewellery Warehouse' in fluorescent yellow on a large sign outside.

"We will go there first," declared Philip.

They walked into a massive air conditioned room with rows of shelves and stacked up on each was a pile of glittering jewellery.

"Can I help you?" asked a grinning woman, wearing a pink sash with a store logo.

"Just browsing."

"That's fine, go ahead."

Heather led the way past the first row of shelves.

"Have you seen the prices?" she asked.

"Not inexpensive."

Heather checked again. A pile of gold and ruby necklaces, 50,000 pounds each were stacked up, every one in a shrink-wrapped package. 75,000 pounds rings in polythene bags. The centrepiece was a massive heap of small, fluorescent yellow boxes with transparent plastic fronts. A large, handwritten sign behind. '24 Karat gold bracelets with eight different precious stones. Special purchase, just 150,000 pounds each. Grab one now before they're gone."

Now a suited man approached.

"Good morning sir, madam. My assist you? I see you are looking at our lower-priced articles. Excellent value, though."

"Do you have security here?" asked Heather.

"Yes, of course. There's a camera over by the door. It shows the entire area perfectly. Sends a picture to a screen in my office."

"But you're here."

"No need to look at the screen while I'm here in person is their madam?" he responded with a faint sigh.

"But surely people just take things from the shelves?"

"Of course. That's the idea. We're using a supermarket approach. In time it will certainly replace those old fashion jewellery shops where everything is kept locked away behind a counter."

"You must have shoplifters?"

"A thorn in the big toe of every retailer. We just write it off. It's called shrinkage, you know."

"Attractive decor," Philip observed vacantly.

"Yes indeed but it's better when the sun shines. The roof slides open automatically to give that open-air experience so desired by our customers. There it goes now."

They looked up to see the roof split into sections that gradually receded, leaving most of the ceiling exposed. From her position, Heather could see the top floor of the adjacent house. A face just visible at the second window.

They departed after refusing the manager's offer of a 'buy one get one free' emerald necklace.

"The house overlooks that place. All they need is some form of lifting mechanism, like a crane," remarked Heather.

As she spoke, a vehicle pulled into the grounds of the house with a crane mounted on it.

"We will pay a visit to Mr Velpronov," said Philip and walked towards the outer gate of the house where surveillance cameras had been mounted.

"Can't come in here."

A large, shabby man blocked the way. He was quickly joined by another who wasn't quite as large but just as shabby.

"I wish to see Mr Victor Velpronov," announced Philip.

"He don't see anyone."

"He will see me. I am Philip Caldrock, investigator and this is my assistant."

"So what?"

"Contact the owner and tell him that I am here."

A bleep came from the man's pocket. He pulled out a communicator and listened for several seconds, nodding. Then he returned it to his jacket.

"Boss says go in while we kick each other for incompetence."

Philip headed towards the building as the two men began the kicking.

A number of people in blue boiler suits moving around near the house and the crane had been taken around the back. Sounds of machine tools from that area. As they reached the entrance, the door was opened by a woman and even Heather was stunned by her beauty. Long, gleaming deep brown hair, styled expertly to frame a face that could have modelled for any cosmetic. Large, dark eyes and full, natural lips that were now parted in a brilliant white smile.

"Mr and Mrs Caldrock, you are most welcome. I am Virginia Incent. Mr Velpronov is waiting for you in the library."

She stood back to allow them to enter and then clicked her way across an elegant hall to stand by an open door. Heather grudgingly noted that her figure was as perfect as her face and was clad in this season's Visitanti Superior peach dress, one of only three made each year.

They entered the room. Floor-to-ceiling oak bookshelves on every wall. A leather sofa and two armchairs around a coffee table.

An astonishingly handsome man sat in one of the chairs, fingers together but his dark eyes were fixed on the visitors. About 30 with dark, groomed hair and tanned complexion.

"A pleasure to meet you at last, Mr Caldrock. I am Victor Velpronov," he announced in a silky, rich voice.

He made no attempt to rise but maintained the incredibly magnetic smile. Heather returned his gaze, finding him attractive in an irresistible sort of way. Very attractive and totally irresistible.

Virginia moved to sit in the adjoining chair. Dragging her eyes away from the man, Heather felt Philip taking her arm and leading her to a sofa where they sat facing the couple.

"I anticipated your arrival. Let us say it was predicted in the stars," remarked Victor.

Philip smiled.

"I somewhat doubt that the current Capricorn ascendant is related to my visit. A man with your wealth and power can create his own night sky, using laser and hologram technology."

"But I'm sure that one with your perspicacity would quickly observe any misplacement of Sirius."

"Every dog has his place, even in the dome of the universe."

"However, the dog may savage a man or woman unless given a bone to suck."

"Those that suck the bone of avarice find their lips rapidly grow weary."

"The lips of a wise man are invariably restored to vigour by the tender taste of a woman."

"A woman's tastes may change on a whim whilst the tainted pearls of nefariousness remain in perpetuity."

"The weather is nice today," Heather remarked, looking at Virginia.

"Yes. I'm hoping to get out in the sun later," she responded.

Victor seemed unsettled by the interruption and rose to his feet.

"I believe that you wish to ask me something, Mr Caldrock."

Philip stood and moved close to him. A few centimetres taller.

"Just one question. Why did you steal the stamp?"

Heather heard Virginia gasp and saw her eyes widen.

"How did you know?" she exclaimed.

Victor also appeared disconcerted.

"Your reputation is well deserved, Mr Caldrock."

He took a notepad from his jacket and wrote quickly. Tearing off the sheet, he handed to Philip who placed it in his pocket without looking. The smile returned to Victor's face.

"You have your answer. Now we will see if the so called great detective can comprehend it."

"Comprehension is the spouse of deduction."

"But deduction constantly opposes his brother, addition."

"As wrongdoing can multiply, so may it also be divided."

"Still the numbers remain, bonded to the cosine."

"Like vicarious lemmings, they fall exactly from the decimal point."

"Only to rise once more from the aggregate below."

"For just a day in the sun before the steeds of righteousness come down to restrain them."

"The twin steeds of power and wealth can never be saddled by any mortal."

"But the fence of justice will always contain them, segregated from those on whom they prey."

"Fencing requires swords and the one with the largest sabre may break through any restraint."

Heather rose from her seat.

"We'd better be making our way," she announced.

"Every move is an action and nature decrees there will be a reaction," responded Virginia.

"Yes, right. Come on, Philip."

Victor held up a hand.

"One who comes on can not come off," he declared.

Heather shepherded Philip to the door.

"But deduction will always come off," he called in triumph as they walked away from the house.

No conversation until they reached the car.

"Let's not dwell on that repartee. Shall we look at the paper?" asked Heather.

"Wait until we reach our base when the full force of my intellect can be applied."

Back in the office and Philip made three photocopies of the sheet of paper. He gave one to Clarissa who was furiously removing lipstick from her nose and ears.

"A cipher! Thank you, thank you!" she cried abandoning cosmetic removal in favour of a pen and pad.

Heather joined Philip in his office, reading her copy. Just a few words.

'The answer is - double correct, pair potmaker'.

"Very clever," Philip murmured.

"You've solved it?"

"No. Victor Velpronov is very clever. An opponent worthy of my attention."

"There's no evidence that he's a criminal."

"He will certainly not leave evidence. The man is astute in the extreme and his words lead me to believe that he is setting down roots here."

"An evil mastermind?"

"That we cannot say at this time. What is this clue he gave so freely?"

"I tried the first two letters of each word as you did before. It gives Docopapo," remarked Heather.

"A place perhaps? Africa? South America?"

"I'll check."

It wasn't a place.

"Okay, what about the last two? That gives Lectirer," offered Heather.

"Promising. A misspelling of lecturer? An I for a U. That could indicate a university or college perhaps."

"It's not precise. There must be hundreds of lecturers in this area."

Clarissa burst in, carrying a whiteboard. She dropped it on her foot, cursed then picked it up and placed it on the desk.

"I've got something!" she cried, sparkle eyed.

"Go on," responded Philip.

"Well, I tried the quad shift Kopinski Cipher currently used by the US military. They have a 47 bank supercomputer to do the coding but it's not really difficult. Anyway, I decoded the message."

"What does it say?" asked Helen.

"Glibsnubbyringbatpkinto."

"Right."

"But I then translated those letters into ancient Mesopotamian characters, the east side version of course."

"And?"

"I placed the hieroglyphs in a Carter-Welstad mathematical formation. Look, I'll show you."

She drew rapidly on the whiteboard and then held it up proudly.

"What about that!" she declared.

"It's a penguin," observed Philip.

"Yes, exactly. I'd say it was the Canveski variety of the species, found in only one place on this planet."

"Where's that?"

"A transient iceberg that currently lies 92.8 kilometres off the east coast of Greenland."

"Is there anything on or near the iceberg?"

"Nothing at all apart from the penguins. It's only 100 metres across."

"Can you relate it in any way to a postage stamp?"

"Yes I can."

"How?"

"To use a geophysical expression, it's a lot bigger."

"Right. Good work Clarissa," said Philip.

"Would you like tea now?"

"No thank you. You may wish to continue with the removal of lipstick from your ear."

"Yes, certainly Mr Caldrock. Thank you," the girl effused and left the room.

Philip idly began to draw spectacles on the penguin.

"I must not fail this test," he remarked without passion.

"It doesn't help a lot until I get to a computer. Even then I'm doubtful," Heather smiled.

"Sorry?"

"The solution. I saw it when Clarissa was animal drawing. It's simple."

"Yes?"

"Alternative homonym substitution. Double and pair both mean two. Sounds like to. Correct means right, sounds like write. And potmaker is potter. To write to Potter. That's the answer to why he wanted the stamp."

"Ah yes, of course. I was already thinking on those lines."

"Yes, Philip. Shall we try the internet?"

Hundreds of Potters in the area and what seemed like millions in the world.

"As I suspected. Not much help," Philip remarked.

"Well, we do have a name. My feeling is that this Potter is some criminal with expertise in burglary. It can't be coincidence that the house is next to the wide open jewellery store."

"We need more information. I wonder if I can undermine Mr Velpronov by getting closer to that young lady, Virginia?"

"Only if I'm with you at all times."

"Of course, my dear. We began with two questions. Why the stamp was taken and the reason for purchasing the property. The Potter reference helps with the first. Now we need to dig deeper."

"We could wait outside the house and follow Virginia when she goes out," suggested Heather.

"Exactly my plan. However, we will need disguises."

The next morning Heather squirmed uncomfortably at a cafe table. Frumpy grey skirt and jacket with an itchy wig of long blonde hair. Philip sat opposite, his head a mass of curly grey, topped with a trilby hat. Virginia Incent was four tables away, sipping coffee and reading a magazine. She was alone.

"What now?" whispered Heather.

"Just watch and wait."

A muscular man marched in and joined Virginia at the table to begin an intense conversation. Heather pulled out her phone and took a series of silent pictures as she pretended to make a call.

"Who is it?" she whispered.

"I'd deduce that we will find out shortly," Philip responded.

The couple had left the table and approached them.

"Hello Phillip," greeted Virginia.

"A pleasure to meet you again" he said, somewhat unhappy that his disguise had proved ineffective.

"As you and your assistant had been following me all morning, I thought I should introduce you to someone."

"I'm sure your friends are good company."

"This one isn't. Burg Stonewall, until 12 months ago an officer in the British Demon force. He now works for Mr Velpronov."

"Ah yes, the most elite group in the Army. A pleasure to meet you, Mr Stonewall."

The chunky man regarded him steadily with cold grey eyes.

"Killed 392 men like you," he responded in a gravel voice.

"That's nice for you. Where are you holidaying this year?" asked Heather.

He turned his gaze to her.

"Also 198 women. Florida," he gravelled.

"Such a lovely place. Does the humidity bother you?"

"Wandered Sahara Desert three days. No water. Ran naked round North Pole."

"Army service demands great endurance."

"Not army. Last two holidays."

Virginia smiled.

"That's lovely. You've made friends already. Well, we must be going. Say goodbye, Burg."

As she moved away, he picked up a cup and crushed it in his hand. Bits of porcelain fell from his fingers. Then he deposited the remains on the table and wiped his hand on Philip's coat.

"Nice to meet you," he said and departed athletically.

A brief silence.

"Makes you proud to be British," remarked Philip.

"Meaning one of our ex-military," asked Heather.

"No, the cup was of foreign manufacture. He'd never have tried on one made in this country."

"Well, we know one thing. He's not our Mr Potter."

"I'd quite forgotten about that. Let's see if we can catch her."

They rushed outside to find Virginia entering a pure white Caballini with Burg at the wheel. She saw them and paused.

"You want to ask something, Mr Caldrock?"

"Just to enquire if Potter has arrived yet?"

A dazzling smile.

"Without the clue, you'd need to be first," she said, then was into the rear seat and the car pulled away immediately.

"I still don't like her," remarked Heather enviously.

"Really? I find her most intriguing. The inner innocence of a fair young maiden."

"Philip, she's about as maidenly as a lap dancer."

"Yes, exactly," he responded mysteriously.

Back in Philips office where Clarissa was mopping up another puddle of coffee from his desk.

"Just doing some trial runs. Only dropped 37.84 millimetres this time," she remarked.

"That's excellent. Well done," Philip congratulated.

"I've been thinking. Virginia's response was strange," remarked Heather.

"Not at all."

"It could be another code. 'Without the clue, you'd need to be first'."

"I believe I know the solution but would you like to reveal it, Clarissa?"

The girl was on her knees, rubbing a stain on the carpet with a pink coloured solution from a test-tube.

"Me? Oh, thank you. Thank you. It narrows the Potter search, probably uniquely. 'Without the clue' means look up the first three words of Velpronov's text. That was 'The answer is'. Need to be first means take the initial letters. T–A–I are Potters initials."

"But you came up with a penguin," remarked Heather.

"Oh, I saw the writing to Potter one immediately. It just seemed too simple."

Philip was already on the computer.

"Thomas Alistair Ignatius Potter. A scientist of no fixed abode. His expertise extends from nuclear fission to trout history."

Clarissa's eyes sparkled.

"That's my sort of man," she gasped.

"Only 29 years old. Tall and quite good looking in a scruffy professor sort of way."

"I hate good-looking men and he's much too young for me."

"But you're only 21," Heather observed.

"Yes and anyone who has studied DNA in relationship to the Pelgrant Numeric Sequence applied exponentially will know the perfect match for me. He's got to be exactly 33 years and 121 days old as at now. I'm surprised they don't teach the system to all schoolgirls."

"So every woman should marry an older man?" enquired Heather.

"Oh, no. It depends on the multilinear relationship of the DNA molecules. It helped to find a husband for my friend Polly. She's blissfully happy now they're together in the cave."

Heather nodded.

"Right. Well where is this scientist man?"

Philip was reading from the screen.

"It appears that he is currently on the move, selling his services to the highest bidder. He spent a month in one country designing an invisibility uniform for the Armed Forces. Then some other place for a couple of weeks where he built a moon rocket out of discarded soup cans. He was last seen discovering a new oil well in the main street of Las Vegas."

"A typical mad scientist," Heather remarked.

"Actually, he's rather cute," said Clarissa.

"So what would Victor want this man for?"

Philip shrugged.

"It could be anything. He's an expert in so many subjects. Maybe to manufacture a flying saucer. This man Velpronov is devious in the extreme."

"To be fair, he did answer your question. You only asked why he took the stamp."

"Perhaps we should visit again?"

"I don't think I could stand any more verbal jousting."

"I could phone Potter, if you like," offered Clarissa.

"You know him?"

"Not really. We met a couple of times at science conventions when we were both presenting papers. Exchanged telephone numbers but we didn't get in touch as I'd already confirmed he was the wrong age."

"Why didn't you tell us earlier that us you knew him?"

"You didn't ask me."

"Excellent work, Clarissa. Would you like to phone now while we're together?" enquired Philip.

"Certainly. I'll just get his number from my scientist's contact book."

She hastened the room, tripping over the chair again on the way. Within 20 seconds she was back, struggling under the weight of a mighty volume.

"I had the binding specially made for me," she gasped and then dropped it.

Heather moved to help and they placed the massive article on the desk. A loose leaf book of terrifying dimensions. Clarissa began to heave over stacks of pages to reach the 'P' section. She had written a mass of names and numbers on every sheet, some with brief notes alongside.

"Yes, here it is," she cried.

"Use this loudspeaker phone," suggested Philip, pushing the handset towards her.

Clarissa began to push the numbers, cursed and then started again. After the ninth attempt, Heather took pity.

"I'll dial if you talk," she said and rapidly clicked keys.

"Hello. Potter speaking," said a thin voice.

"Is that cutie legs Potter, the scientist?" asked Clarissa.

"It is."

"Clarissa Hartwin here. I want to ask you something, dippy doo."

"Hi, pink rabbit. How did your life restoration experiment work out?"

"Oh softie paws, I only brought a couple of people back from the dead and then the caretaker told me to leave the graveyard. Something to do with local council regulations."

"Bad luck, chubby cheeks."

"Listen, bubble head, I'm phoning to find out what you're doing now."

"Clandestine stuff, darling. Sworn to secrecy, you know."

"You can tell another scientist, dearest."

"Well, sweetie, all I can reveal is that I'm in town working for a guy called Velpronov but I just can't say more. That would undermine his trust in me."

"I understand, lover boy. Nice to banter with you."

"You also, kissy lips. Bye."

The call ended.

"What was all that cutie, sweetie stuff? I thought you didn't know him well," asked Heather.

"I don't. You obviously don't attend many science conventions. That's the way we scientists normally talk to each other."

"Oh right. At least we've confirmed he's working for Velpronov."

"At least and at most. That's all we found out," remarked Philip morosely.

"He told me more than that," said Clarissa.

"What?"

"I can't tell you. He said it was a secret."

"You've got to tell us."

"Shan't. So there."

Clarissa picked up the gargantuan book and staggered to the door. Then she dropped it on her foot.

"It's okay. Just cracked a couple of bones. I've created an ointment for that. Be fine in five minutes," she called and picking up the huge volume, limped from the room.

"She's a great girl," remarked Philip as the door closed.

"Yes dear. What do we do now?"

"A stake out. We park near the house and watch like hawks."

The next morning Philip was dozing peacefully in the passenger seat when Heather nudged him.

"Something happened?" he asked blearily.

"Only another convoy of building supplies and machinery. He could be creating a stadium in there."

The air was bruised by constant sound of hammering, drilling and motorised equipment.

"Hello, that's the mad scientist. I recognise him from his photos."

Philip pointed to the roof of the house. A young man had emerged from the skylight and was standing near the edge, staring down. Suddenly, a section of wall on the top floor began to disappear. Bricks were rapidly being removed and after eight minutes, the complete side of a room was revealed.

A short time later, a steel platform was being pushed outwards. It extended the full width of the opening and two thick steel wires connected the end to metal rings on the wall. Further and further it came out until it extended some 15 metres from the house.

"See what it overlooks!" cried Heather.

The new platform now reached out over the open roof of the jewellery store.

"Someone could sit at the end with a fishing line and make a very good catch," observed Philip.

"Absolutely. Or suspend ropes from it and climb down headfirst, using a motorised pulley. Then they could pick up any item of jewellery and send it back up by means of a high velocity vacuum tube. The jewellery would be grabbed at the top by a leather suited accomplice who then raced down to a motorcycle, ready to go with engine running. A high-speed trip to an airport and off to some foreign country to fence the goods. Back to the plane with the money, stopping off to deposit it in a Swiss bank. Then collect another batch of jewels and go again."

Philip paused for a second before responding.

"Perfect except for one thing. What if the upside down person on the rope didn't let go in time under the vacuum tube? Their arm would be sucked upwards, pulling the body to an uncomfortable horizontal position. A tricky decision then. Should the person release themselves from the rope to be sucked upwards or turn off the vacuum and risk all the pieces of jewellery within the tube falling on his or her head?"

"Good point. I hadn't thought it through."

"The principle is still sound. The objective must be theft from the jewellery store and I believe it is planned for tonight."

"I'll tell Inspector Foxhole to send a group of officers round," declared Heather.

"We'll return this evening. I think we will bring Clarissa this time."

"Is that wise?"

"She knows Potter and also has martial arts skills."

"Oh, very well."

Evening. The trio stood patiently next to their car. It had taken some time to Clarissa to escape from the rear seat as the door handles appeared to be a complete mystery to her. After several minutes pushing and pulling, Heather eventually clambered into the back to release her.

"I'm so excited," gushed the girl.

Philip raised the hand of leadership.

"Everybody listen. You can just see the new platform from here and it overhangs the jewellery store. Now, Clarissa, we've told you what they intend to do and the only question is how. I favour fishing rods but Heather is still sticking to the hanging from rope theory."

The girl pressed her lips together and jumped up and down.

"I wish I could tell you, I really do. But I can't break the Soporific Oath that all scientists have to observe. I've brought a high velocity night sight rifle so I can shoot everyone who appears on the platform, if you like."

"We're not killing anyone," Heather said firmly.

"Why? One or two won't do any harm. I was runner up in the National Blindfold Shooting Championship last year. The target was a matchstick so no problem to hit a big thing like a human body."

Heather shook her head.

"No killing. We want to capture the criminals in the act."

"May I talk to you privately, Clarissa?" asked Philip and they moved away from Heather for a whispered conversation, returning just as Inspector Foxhole approached.

"So here you are. I've stationed men all around the house and the jewellery place. Hello, looks like someone's coming out."

A figure had emerged from the top floor and was now standing on the platform. Others followed, pushing large objects.

"Quick, into the jewellery store!" exclaimed Heather.

They rushed inside the building to be greeted by a woman in a gold dress.

"Hello. Welcome to our first late-night opening. Every woman visitor can have a gold bracelet free tonight. It's our special welcome offer."

Heather and Clarissa stopped immediately and began to examine the selection while Philip and Foxhole rushed to the centre of the room. Bad news, the roof was open.

The manager approached.

"Such a lovely night. I thought it would be nice to see the stars," he announced.

Clarissa rushed up, holding her bracelet. Then dropped it, picked it up and dropped it again. The manager quickly recovered the errant article and handed it to her.

"Hello, how old are you?" she asked.

"36," he replied.

"Then I can't accept the bracelet. Sorry."

Heather joined them and looked up through the open roof. Considerable activity now on the platform and she could distinguish Virginia amongst the throng. Then two thick metal cables were lowered from the edge of the platform, directly through the open roof. More activity above as something was attached to the cables.

"I do believe they're creating an elevator," whispered Philip.

"It's a Caxton-Luponskry system based on laser propulsion," commented Clarissa.

The attachment was now descending rapidly towards them.

"They're not being very secretive about it," Heather remarked.

Philip shrugged.

"Why should they be? They're not planning to do anything criminal," he responded.

"What?"

He didn't answer, walking forward to the cables. The attachment was two seats, finished in white with a delicate ornate design in gold and green. At first, it appeared abstract but on closer inspection represented a panorama of animals. Lions, tigers, giraffes all exquisitely printed on the bars of the seats. Somewhat reminiscent of the 19th-century artist Lovan Namminal. Heather found herself drifting into visions of great works of art when Philip grabbed her arm.

"Up we go, dear," he said.

She sat next to him and they began to rise. At the top a few seconds later.

"Would Madame like to take a seat?" asked the waiter, offering them a cocktail and vol au vent.

Velpronov stood near the door with Virginia alongside. Two small sofas, a person on each. One was Burg Stonewall and the other a youngish man with long, prematurely grey shaggy hair. Potter, the mad scientist.

"Welcome to my little moving in party. I see more guests arriving," announced Velpronov with a smile.

Clarissa and Inspector Foxhole had just left the elevator and walked across to them.

"Hello, winkie poos," Clarissa called to Potter.

He rose to his feet, face wreathed in smiles.

"Ducky lucky! Great to see you!"

"I notice you used a Pychelyson arrangement to stabilise this platform, toffee eyes."

"Absolutely, dimple legs. I meant to ask you before. How did your origin of the universe research go?"

"Oh, disappointing, diddle toes. I disproved all the current ideas and then found the answer. Named it the Little Pop theory and jotted down 17 pages of objective proof. Then I spilt coffee on it. Had to throw it away."

"Shame, loopy lips. Going to rewrite it?"

"If I get time. I'm trying to resolve the crustacean world domination problem first."

A silence as Potter's brow furrowed. Then Clarissa clapped her hands over her mouth.

"Oh, I am sorry. Meant to say fluffy ears."

Potter relaxed and grinned. Then Victor Velpronov stepped forward.

"So Mr Caldrock, you came here with the police believing that I was about to steal a few trinkets from the jewellery store. You are sadly mistaken."

He spoke loudly, with a degree of assumed superiority but Philip appeared nonchalant.

"Very disappointing," he murmured.

"I'm sure it is. Never mind."

"I am disappointed that a person with your apparent intellect could think I would believe such a thing. I am already revising my rating of your abilities, Velpronov. Downwards."

"Then what do you believe?"

"That you purchased the property because of its location."

A gasp from Virginia before Philip continued.

"You were told by this man Potter that a gigantic deposit of Zazak was located beneath this house and you wished to ensure your continued monopoly."

Victor's face contorted with anger.

"Well, it's too late now. I've got the property and it all belongs to me."

"That is why we have Inspector Foxhole with us. This area was specified as 'a prohibited for anyone to mine zone' in a statute dating back to 1322."

"My legal people checked. That was rescinded in 1824."

Now Clarissa moved forward.

"They are incorrect. That decision was overturned on appeal and subsequently confirmed in the Wilson-Jones case of 1827 and the Whitney-Bayview case of 1829," she declared firmly.

"Damn lawyers," muttered Victor.

Potter had now risen to his feet, face like thunder.

"You revealed this information, viper mouth. Broke the Soporific Oath," he accused.

Clarissa pursed lips.

"I most certainly did not, parrot face. That oath is sacred to me but I do have bad news for you."

"What's that, piggy feet?"

"You were incorrect, beetle neck. There is no Zazak under this house. I did my own analysis of the geological structure and I can see where you went wrong. The mistake was in inverting the beta particle configuration in a triple helix."

"Oh my god, pookie paws. I can see it now you make that clear. My humblest apologies to you in your capacity as senior representative of the Universal Science Foundation Body."

"Well, don't do it again, sugar fingers."

"You're sure there's no Zazak here?" asked Heather, trying to catch up.

Clarissa nodded.

"Absolutely certain."

A furious look on Victor's face.

"You may have beaten me this time but we will meet again, Mr Caldrock," he hissed.

"The battle is only just beginning," added Virginia.

"A battle is like the rising sun. One never knows what the day will bring," mused Philip.

"The hours of the day are but grains of sand on the beach of destiny," responded Victor.

"Destiny has a mask with two faces and Evil wears both while Justice has but one."

"Time to go Philip," said Heather, dragging him back to the elevator.

"The mask may obscure vision as a cold mist conceals the truth," yelled Victor.

"The sword of truth cuts disdainfully through the intricacies of deception," shouted Philip but they were already descending.

Victor's voice came faintly after them.

"Deceit is like the high card in a game of poker…"

The rest was lost to the heavens.

"Card?" asked Heather.

"I would have said that it plays its hand at the oasis of understanding," responded Philip.

"Shall we not do the verbal wrestling next time?"

"He started it."

"Philip, sometimes in life we don't always have to have the last word."

"The last word is like a raft on the ocean of confrontation," he responded but she had already put her hands over her ears.

"So Clarissa told you the solution in that whispered conversation?" enquired Heather as she drove Philip to the office the next morning.

"Not exactly. I suggested that Zazak could be under the house and she confirmed that was what Potter had researched after I reminded her of the COCOSO rule."

"The what?"

"Capture Of Criminals Overrides Soporific Oaths."

"Does that rule really exist?"

"Not until I instituted it yesterday."

The next morning, they arrived at the office to find Clarissa with a towel on her head.

"I expect you're wondering why I got a towel on my head," she remarked.

"Not really," Heather responded.

"I was experimenting with my antigravity machine last night and tested it on a jar containing a chemical solution. As it floated over me, I reached up and it slipped through my fingers. Ampolydroxpolyisanbridge. Tipped all over my head. Makes all your hair fall out immediately and I had just 26 minutes to discover an instant hair restoration formula otherwise the condition is permanent. I managed it in 21 minutes but it takes 7 hours 14 minutes to restore completely. So I saturated this towel with the stuff. I can take it off in one hour 23 minutes."

"Well done, Clarissa," Philip declared absently.

"So have we finished with Victor Velpronov now?" asked Heather.

"Not at all. This man is undoubtedly an evil mastermind. One whose hands pull the strings of the common criminals. He has temporarily retreated to tend his bruised ego but he will be back with his cohorts. A worthy opponent."

Clarissa looked up.

"Oh, that reminds me. I found a couple of men waiting to ambush you when I arrived."

"What happened?" asked Heather.

"I only broke their noses."

"Good."

"And a couple of legs."

"Yes, right.

"Plus one shoulder blade and two arms. Then I called the police."

"Anything else?"

"Not really. Spent a few minutes over tea in designing a fuel free car. Only problem is it can't go over 150 miles an hour."

"Sorry to hear that," Heather responded sympathetically.

"You've done very well, Clarissa," Philip announced vaguely as he walked to his office.

9 THE WEREWOLF OF BUMPSTON WOODS

A fresh, late summer day. The sun crawled lazily into the cloudless skies and rubbed the redness from its eyes to beam down serenely. The town of Mapleton shuddered into life, everyone awaiting the exact time to ensure the streets were clogged with cars. Old gentlemen meandered in their gardens, watering plants and the first sounds of bitching were heard as women took their seats in the cafes.

The premises of P. Caldrock, Private Detective appeared peaceful. Philip and Heather in their offices while Clarissa was emptying a bin full of broken teacups. Suddenly the tranquillity was shattered as a young woman rushed in, her face a picture of terror. A faint moan came from her and then she fell to the floor. Clarissa moved swiftly, removing her shoe and placing her foot over the woman's nose.

"What is it?" asked Heather as she rushed out of her office.

"She's not dead," said Clarissa with some disappointment.

"Has she fainted?"

Clarissa shrugged with disinterest.

"I expect so. Why didn't she die? I'm never lucky in these things."

"Can you do something?"

"I'm already relaxing her by using the odours of my foot. The toes emit three distinct tranquillising chemicals in gaseous form. If you insist, I'll get her conscious."

She dragged the woman to her feet with one hand and slapped her with the other. The victim's eyes flickered open.

"You must help!" she cried.

Then Clarissa smacked her again, so hard she lost consciousness.

"That should do it," the girl remarked, allowing the woman to fall again and bang her head on the floor.

Then she sighed and returned to her bin emptying as Philip emerged from his office.

"A new client?" he asked.

"I think so," Heather responded.

"She's unconscious."

"I can dump her in the garbage bin. I'm just going there," offered Clarissa.

"I'd rather you got her conscious again."

"The correct medical solution is to sprinkle water over her face. I'll get some."

Clarissa left the room and returned with a metal bucket full of water.

"You're not going to throw it at her, are you?" enquired Heather.

"Absolutely not. Leave it to the expert."

She picked up the woman and held her upside down, head immersed in the water.

"She'll drown," exclaimed Heather.

"Only if I stay like this for 4.8 more seconds. I'll pull her out after 4.6."

She did that and placed the visitor on her feet.

"I feel so much better now," gasped the woman, water rolling down her face.

"I am Philip Caldrock. Come with me and relate your problem."

Heather followed them into his office and sat alongside the woman in front of his desk as the visitor dried her face with a handkerchief.

"My name is Tracy Smith and I'll try to compose myself."

"A musician?" asked Philip.

"No. I'm the personal assistant to Mr Bubbles Sugalump," she announced and appeared disappointed by the ensuing silence.

"Who's that?" asked Heather.

"Only the richest, most powerful man in the area. Fancy you not knowing him."

"Bubbles Sugalump?"

"Oh, did I say that? He insists all that his employees use that name. Really it's Grant Fetlock."

"Is he a scientist?"

"No, no. He owns loads of property all over the country."

"He's in my comprehensive archives. What is the problem?" Philip enquired cordially.

"I can barely speak of it. Horrible. Unnatural creatures."

"Bubbles is a creature?" asked Heather

"I'd better tell you the full story. Mr Fetlock uses several different offices around the country, all of them in places he owns. He just works for a few weeks in each before moving on. He is a man who likes a constant change of scenery to keep him alert. Of course, he is always accompanied by myself and Angela."

"Angela?"

"She's the cook and general housekeeper. A lovely, large lady unless you interfere with her in the kitchen. She doesn't like that at all. Well, it started two weeks ago when we went to Bumpston House."

"That's a couple of hours drive from here," Philip remarked.

"Yes, it's a lovely building, completely isolated in the centre of Bumpston Woods. Everything was fine for the first few days and then it happened. In the middle of the night."

"What happened?" asked Heather.

"There was a hammering at the door and we could hear someone screaming for sanctuary. It was a stormy night, rain bucketing down. I was first to the door and opened it to reveal a man with desperation in his eyes. He wore no coat and his shirt and trousers were sodden with the rain. He pleaded to be allowed inside and although I had some doubts, I said I thought it would be all right. But he didn't enter and insisted that I must specifically invite him over the threshold. Well I couldn't just leave him standing there so I did that. He came into the hall just as Mr Fetlock and Angela arrived on the scene. I mentioned that she was a large woman and she carried him to a bedroom to dry off. When they came back, he was dry but I noticed that Angela had two red marks on her neck."

"How did the man explain his sudden appearance?" asked Philip.

"He told us he had just flown in from somewhere in Eastern Europe. After landing, he decided to go for a stroll and got lost in the woods."

"There is an airport nearby?"

"Not really. The nearest is 10 miles away. We simply assumed that he had flown in by a hot air balloon or perhaps parachuted down. Well as normal, Mr Fetlock took control and asked for identification but the man told him that a stray dog had taken all the documents from his pocket. It's well-known that criminals use trained dogs to pick pockets in the Bumpston area so it's not unusual."

"Did he speak English?"

"Mr Fetlock?"

"No, the visitor."

"Oh yes. Definitely. He told us his name was Jack Weller and he had just bought the old Manor house on the outskirts of Bumpston village."

Heather still seemed confused.

"Just to be clear on this. This man had walked around in pouring rain for some time, having just flown in from overseas. He had no coat or identification."

"He said the dog had taken his coat as well."

"Please continue your narrative, Ms Smith," encouraged Philip.

"Mr Fetlock agreed that the man could stay that night and there are plenty of spare bedrooms in the house. Strangely, Jack didn't seem hungry and wouldn't eat any food we offered. He claimed that Angela had already given him a snack. He'd also asked her to throw away any garlic she was keeping as it was very bad for us. So we all went to bed."

"The next morning, Jack stayed in his room and out of the daylight," Heather suggested.

"That's amazing! Yes, he locked the door and wouldn't come out. I thought he might be one of those squatters but when Mr Fetlock phoned the Manor house, they confirmed that a Jack Weller had just purchased it. Anyway, we decided to place a ladder against the wall and I climbed up to his window but the curtains were drawn."

"You didn't know if he was there?"

"No. The next night I heard a noise and rushed to Jack's room. The door was unlocked and I entered to find it empty and the window wide open. I looked quickly, thinking he had fallen out but there was no body below."

"Is that the end of your story?" asked Philip.

"Oh, no. Over the next two days, Mr Fetlock and I began to notice a difference in Angela. She kept taking about how she was to become a bride and serve her master. We thought nothing more of it, assuming she was getting married and going to work for a schoolteacher. Then, last night, it happened."

"It?"

"I was visited. I suddenly woke with a start at about one in the morning. There was a man in my bed. I turned on the light and saw who it was."

"Jack Weller?" ventured Heather.

"Yes. I jumped out of bed and asked him what he was doing there. He said he'd left the building for an evening stroll and got lost in the woods again. He climbed up a tree to get some idea of his location and then fallen into my room."

"There is a tree outside your window?"

"Yes, about 10 metres away."

"And he fell from this tree, almost horizontally from that distance?"

"Well, yes. There was a strong wind that night and it could easily have blown him sideways. My window was open a little."

"How little?"

"Just a small gap. A bird or other flying creature could easily come in. Like a bat, for example."

"But a man?"

"Jack's quite slim. If he exhaled completely, he could probably just squeeze through."

"So his story was that he'd fallen from the tree, got caught in a gust of wind and was blown horizontally at the exact level to pass through the narrow opening?" Heather summarised.

"Absolutely. I'm sure it happens all the time. Anyway, I asked him if he'd like something to drink or a bite to eat. He readily agreed but then gave a shout and reeled backwards, pointing at my garlic necklace."

"You were wearing a garlic necklace?"

"Yes."

"In bed?"

"Yes, certainly. It's the new fashion, haven't you heard? Natural jewellery? Oh dear, you have missed out. I've already got a parsley bracelet and cabbage earrings. It's called Vegelry. A green bean pendant would really suit you."

"Right. So he didn't like the necklace?"

"Apparently not. From his reaction, I assumed one of the pieces of garlic had been nibbled at while I was asleep. Armadillos, you know."

"Armadillos?"

"They're very partial to garlic, that's why I kept the necklace on in bed. I'd already seen a couple of the animals near the house and didn't want the creatures eating it. But there's always a chance that one could have got to my room during the day and hidden somewhere, waiting for the right moment."

"Have you fully recovered from Clarissa's treatment?"

"I feel completely back to normal now."

"What next?"

"I checked the necklace was okay in the mirror and when I turned back, Jack had gone. He must have climbed out on the windowsill, waited for a suitable gust of wind and jumped back to the tree."

Philip was growing impatient.

"So you're asking us to investigate this strange person?"

"Oh no, I'm just giving you the background. Now I'll tell you why I'm here. This morning, Mr Fetlock called me to his office and I'll remember what he said for as long as I live. 'Good morning, Tracy. Lovely day. I think there's a full moon tonight'. Well!"

She sat back, her words reverberating around the office.

"But it was a good morning today," remarked Heather helpfully.

"Oh yes, lovely. But the full moon. I don't need to tell you what he was implying. And that's not all. In a state of some shock, I looked closely at him and saw hairs on his face."

"His chin?"

"Yes, all round his chin and above the top of his lip. Small hairs but they hadn't been there the night before. They had appeared on the day of the full moon!"

"What did you do?" Phillip enquired with a sigh.

"I plucked up the courage to ask him about this strange growth. All he could do was mumble some ridiculous story about an electric shaver being broken. Yes, I'm here to tell you that Mr Fetlock is a werewolf!"

A silence as Heather looked at the visitor, lost for words while Philip spun his chair round to look out of the window. At that moment, Clarissa entered with a tray. She stumbled and cups flew everywhere. The tray shot forward to impact on the base of Tracy's head.

"Would everyone like tea?" asked Clarissa.

Phillips swivelled round.

"That would be very nice. Well done."

"I'll just get some then."

"You appear to have rendered our visitor unconscious," remarked Heather.

"Excellent. Perhaps she's dead."

She rushed hopefully to the woman who was now slumped forward in her chair. Lifting her head up by the hair, Clarissa began the slapping again.

"Shame. She's only suffering from Contusionary Trayitary Clumpus. Quite common. It helps if you do this."

Gripping the woman's nose she twisted it violently from side to side for several seconds. Consciousness returned.

"Sorry, I must have fainted again but I feel great now," Tracy said contritely.

"I have considered your case and conclude that you are a crackpot," Philip announced gravely.

"The correct medical term is Absolus Lunita," remarked Clarissa.

"And we will therefore take the case," added Heather unexpectedly.

Philip looked nonplussed but Tracey leapt up with delight.

"Wonderful! I'll expect you tonight then. Plenty of spare rooms. You'll probably want to kill Mr Fetlock so I'll get a big polythene sheet ready for the body.

With these words she rushed from the office, humming cheerfully.

"If you're going to murder someone, can you bring back a bit of his brain? Just stick it in a paper bag. I'm desperate to run a new experiment," pleaded Clarissa.

"What do you know of vampires and werewolves?" Philip asked.

"Absolutely nothing."

So shocking was this reply that Philip and Heather could only gape for six seconds.

"Then I'm dependent on you, my dear as you appeared so keen to take this case," said Philip, looking at Heather.

"I have my reasons," she responded mysteriously.

It was nearly seven in the evening when Heather and Philip arrived at Bumpston House. A bleak, rainy evening. As they walked towards the entrance, she heard a flapping sound as an indistinct flying creature descended behind a bush. A few seconds later, a thin figure emerged.

"You must be Jack Weller," greeted Philip.

"Yes, that's me alright. Just dropped in for a bite."

Heather looked behind the bush.

"What happened to that bird I saw land here?" she asked.

"Bird? Oh yes. A bird it was. I ate it."

"Raw with feathers?"

"Yes, lovely. Yummy. Must be going."

He disappeared down the back of the building.

"Vampires are known to take the form of a bat when desired," remarked Philip.

"Wait for me by the front door. I just want to look around," responded Heather.

Philip reached the entrance porch and the door opened immediately.

"Who are you, sir?" asked a small, grey haired man.

"Philip Caldrock. I am nemesis, Mr Wolf."

"Wolf? No, sir. My name is Fetlock, Mr Nemesis."

Tracey rushed up to the door and he turned to her.

"Strange fellow outside. Philip Caldrock Ian Nemesis," he said gruffly.

"I invited him and his assistant," Tracy responded as Heather rejoined Philip.

"Very well. They can stay in the Orange Suite. I noticed you were preparing it earlier. Fortunate coincidence."

"Yes, Mr Fetlock."

"Well, Nemesis, don't just stand on the doorstep and bring that young lady with you."

"My name is Heather."

"Yes, yes. That's what they all say."

"What?"

"Now hurry along. Dinner at seven sharp."

Just time to dump their small case in the room and freshen up. When they reached the dining room, Fetlock and Tracy were already seated.

"Sit by me, Heather and you over there, Nemesis," the old man instructed.

They took their places just as a massively obese woman that had to be Angela, clumped through the door, bearing a large silver tray. Blood was running from two large red marks on her neck.

"Right, m'dears. Get stuck into that," she boomed, placing the tray on the table.

"My favourite. Roast pomegranates in Cheshire sauce," exclaimed Fetlock.

He filled his plate and began eating ravenously.

"So, Angela. Do you use garlic in the recipe?" asked Philip.

"Oh no, my dear. My boyfriend wouldn't allow it."

"I saw him outside. Said he was coming for a bite."

"Oh yes, he had that all right."

"You have two marks on your neck."

A hesitation before she replied.

"Those are caused by the frozen salmon. They leap up and nip you in the throat."

"I see," Philip responded gravely

Heather strained to engage in subtle conversation.

"So Mr Fetlock, I understand it's a full moon tonight."

He stopped shovelling pomegranates into his mouth and looked critically at her.

"A strange thing to say," he muttered.

"You don't like the words full moon?"

"No, you said understand. Most people would have used the word believe. Is there something wrong with you?"

"I expect so."

"Good, good. Then tell me how a young woman like you got mixed up with that strange Nemesis man."

"I'm his wife."

"Wife is it? That status, my dear girl, requires a ceremony universally known as marriage."

"Yes, we had one of those a long time ago."

"Right. Did you know that I'm a very rich man?"

"I've heard that."

"Herd? Like a herd of sheep, no doubt."

"Flock."

"Of birds? Or even bats?"

As he spoke, Angela dropped the tray of chocolate cake she was carrying to the table.

"Oh no!" she screamed and ran from the room.

Fetlock grabbed the cake from the floor and tore off a large chunk that he stuffed into his mouth.

"Fancy a piece?" he asked cordially.

Heather demurred.

"A group of bats is known as a colony but wolves hunt in a pack. Normal wolves, that is. A werewolf is always alone," she remarked educationally.

"A loan? Rented out, you mean? I suppose there could be a demand for them."

Heather changed the subject.

"You made your money in property?" she asked.

"Absolutely. Property only. All legal. No need to get the police involved."

"It's almost a licence to print money."

"What? Who issues this license? Where can it be obtained?"

"Merely a figure of speech."

"I see," he responded solemnly.

Heather looked across at Philip and Tracy who were talking quietly while Fetlock shoved another handful of cake into his mouth. Angela returned pink faced with a tray of tea.

"So sorry, my dears. I thought I heard someone say rats. I hate them. Can't even speak their name. I've never said the word rats since I was five years old. If I hear rats in a conversation or on TV, I have to run. Rats is a horrible word. Rats, rats, rats everywhere."

"Lucky that you stopped saying it then," remarked Heather.

"What? Rats? Yes dearie, rats are horrid."

She placed the tray on the table.

"What if I said vampires?" asked Philip.

"Those bloodsuckers that bite women's necks, dearie? Oh, they're all right. It's rats I can't stand."

"I'm interested in werewolves," remarked Philip, staring intently at Fetlock.

The little man gulped the cake down.

"A figure of speech, Mr Nemesis?"

"What? No, I mean real werewolves. Those that change from human to wolf on the night of the full moon!"

"You mean change into a wolf outfit for a costume party?"

"No, I mean physically change. Their body hair growing into a fur, hands changing to clawed paws, face into an evil fanged creature."

Fetlock paused.

"Are you a loony, Nemesis?"

"Loony from lunatic. Derived from luna, the moon."

"You're not carrying an axe with you, I hope?"

"We will see what transpires, Mr Fetlock as this night darkens and the first shafts of moonlight beam down upon you."

Fetlock turned to Heather.

"Has he had his pills today?" he enquired.

"We are all on the borderline of sanity," she responded.

"Border of sanity? No, that's Wales you're thinking of. Just an hour away from here."

Philip rose to his feet.

"I suggest it's time to retire. One may predict a disturbed night ahead of us."

"Disturbed knight? There are titled people locked up with you, Nemesis?" asked Fetlock.

"Oh lawdy. All this talk about rats, the things I cannot speak the name of. I'm going to bed," declared Angela and disappeared from the room.

A loud hammering at the front door and Tracy departed to open it. She returned with a sodden Jack Weller.

"I got lost again. I just need to go to Angela's room. That will give me my bearings," he announced.

"What?" cried Fetlock, striding across to him.

"What what?"

"Bearings, sir. Bearings. Never heard the word. Little bears, do you mean? Answer me, sir and be straight in your response."

"Supports or guides for moving parts in a machine. Also directional indicators."

"I see. Off you go then."

Weller rushed up the stairs.

"Don't mention rats to her," Tracy shouted after him

A faint scream came from above.

An hour later, in their room, Heather was dressing in dark jeans and jacket.

"Going somewhere?" asked Philip.

"Yes. I think you will solve the case tonight.'

"Then perhaps I should join you. I must say it seems a very normal household to me. Of course, that Weller chap is a vampire and old Fetlock probably a werewolf but every group of people has a couple of eccentrics."

"Yes Philip. I phoned Clarissa earlier and she'll be waiting outside the front door."

"I hope she's not bringing tea."

"We'll let her in and then you will expose the culprit."

"Excellent. Do I need a gun with silver bullets?"

"No."

Clarissa was sitting outside the front door, scribbling in a notepad.

"Oh hello," she said, jumping up.

"Composing a new theory of relativity while you waited?" asked Heather.

"No, a shopping list. I need two crates of tea cups and a communications satellite."

"Well done," murmured Philip.

The trio returned to the hallway and he started up the stairs but Heather pulled him back.

"This way," she said and led them to a door at the end of the hall.

A humming sound as she opened it to reveal a flight of steps leading down. They descended carefully, Clarissa dropping her notepad only a couple of times. Another door at the foot of the stairs, this one apparently soundproofed. It was secured by a combination lock.

"Can you open it?" asked Heather.

"Obviously yes. It's one of my designs. There's a triple sequence for extra protection," responded Clarissa absently.

She didn't move.

"Would you like to open it?"

"Yes, certainly I would. It's so gratifying to unlock a door and it only takes two seconds."

"Please open it," Heather said patiently.

"Oh, thank you!" exclaimed Clarissa.

She pressed the keys in a blur of movement and the door swung open. They were in a large, brilliantly lit basement, full of equipment. Two large machines, working at full pace.

"Money!" exclaimed Philip as he reached them.

A massive pile of currency notes was being churned out and several cardboard boxes full of cash stood nearby.

"What's all this noise?" came a voice from the door.

Fetlock entered followed by Tracy, Weller and Angela who had rivulets of fresh blood running down her neck.

"Philip solved the case so quickly that he disdains to explain it to you. He delegated me to do that," said Heather, noticing her husband nodding in sublime ignorance.

"This room is full of money. I demand an explanation," demanded the old man in a demanding tone.

Heather smiled.

"Very simple. A modern printing press to forge banknotes. There's probably a million pounds in this room."

"Then who is responsible? Did Nemesis construct this equipment during the night?"

"That would have been impossible."

"I could have done it," remarked Clarissa but Heather ignored her.

"The critical clue was armadillos. Not common in England and Tracy said she had seen some in this area."

"I don't understand," responded the woman.

"No, I'm aware of that. Fortunately I happened to study the creatures as part of a course last year."

"I cannot associate a flock of these animals with a printing press," declared Fetlock.

"I know! I know!" cried Clarissa, raising a hand and jumping up and down.

"Then you tell them," offered Heather.

"The Armadillo has one compulsive weakness, known only to people who have studied them intensively. It is irresistibly attracted to Puncollital Oil."

"An oil that is used only in the manufacture of currency notes," added Heather.

"Look, there's one now!" cried Clarissa, pointing at a small window near the ceiling. An armadillo, nose pressed against the glass.

"So I was wrong about the werewolf but Mr Fetlock is a forger," remarked Tracy.

Heather nodded.

"No. You are. Grab her, Clarissa!"

Tracey had produced a submachine gun from under her skirt but Clarissa was much too fast. A flying Rik-Sen kick impacted on the side of the woman's skull and she fell unconscious to the floor.

"Darn it, she's still alive. That kick kills 95 percent of the time. Just my luck again," Clarissa complained.

Philip had maintained his posture throughout and now gestured wearily to Heather.

"You'd better tell them how I knew it wasn't Fetlock," he murmured dismissively.

"Bearings. I realised as soon as he revealed the word was unknown to him. Every forging machine has a multitude of bearings. That's what the oil is used for. The whole purpose of Tracy's ridiculous tale was to get rid of Mr Fetlock. He was beginning to suspect her and she put on a great performance to convince us that he was a werewolf. Her hope was that we'd get him locked up or kill him. Unfortunately for her, she mentioned seeing armadillos, not knowing the significance of their presence."

Fetlock beamed.

"When the convoy of lorries arrived, loaded with big crates, I did ask her about it. She said they were machines for mincing nuts to feed the local squirrels. Very sweet, I thought. I'm impressed, Nemesis. Very impressed. In time, you could be as good as that other chap, Philip Caldrock."

"Indeed I could and my assistant will now collect a fee from you."

Heather drove Philip back without hurry. Clarissa was travelling in her own car, hoping to stop off at a couple of morgues to filch some chunks of brain tissue. She already had the paper bags ready.

"Of course, it was obvious from the beginning," Philip remarked, leaning back in his seat.

Heather glanced at him.

"Absolutely, dear. You haven't yet asked about Jack Weller."

"No, I haven't. You may as well tell me to see if it coincides with my findings."

"Everything he said was completely true. When Tracy had first seen him, he had lost his way and he did eat that bird. I asked Clarissa about him falling from that tree and into Tracy's bedroom. She worked out a wind velocity gravitational curve in her notebook and demonstrated a 68 percent probability of it being true."

"And Angela's neck?"

"Not related. It really was caused by the bites of frozen salmon. She developed a sort of fetish for the experience and kept some of the fish under the bed in her room to continue these strange pleasures every night. I believe Jack was attempting to stop her before she moved on to cod. Our receptionist revealed the correct medical treatment for the condition. Apparently the relevant part of the body has to be removed."

"The neck?"

"Yes. Afterwards the head is sewn back directly onto the shoulders. Clarissa said she could do the operation in a few minutes without need for an anaesthetic but I talked her out of it. By the way, Angela really doesn't like rats."

"Well done, Heather. You've explained my conclusions exactly."

"Thank you, dear."

10 THE EMERALD ANT OF KOLVANIA

A quiet morning at the Caldrock offices until three men entered, just before lunch. Two were large and muscular while the other was slim and much shorter. The pair of heavies stood by the door, eyes darting around while the third man approached Clarissa.

"Hello, you're from Kolvania. Has there been a murder there?" she asked in welcoming tone.

The man gazed down at her for a moment, manicured hands running across his jaw.

"No murder, lovey. How the hell did you know the country we're from?" he responded in a vague accent.

Clarissa was unusually surprised.

"You don't sound like a Kolvanian, more the Nimswich district of north London but you're carrying a bag with the Kolvanian government crest."

"Right you are, ducks. Learnt me English from my wife who does come from Nimswich. Come to see this guy Caldrock. King wants him. I'm the first Minister, Ziglint Zkavsky."

"Now hold on a minute. Just because a King wants something, it doesn't mean that we're going to drop everything and come like a flock of sheep. We're all equal nowadays, from a King to the poorest tramp, lying in the gutter and guzzling cheap whiskey whilst verbally abusing women who walk past at the same time as ferreting in his pocket for a dry crust that he took from the garbage at the back of a restaurant as it was not consumed by a recent customer who was almost certainly a King."

"Right you are, darling. So is he in or not?"

Clarissa smiled.

"Ordinarily I would have said he wasn't available but no woman can resist a man who calls her lovey and darling," she said, clicking on the intercom to speak to Philip.

Five minutes later, Zkavsky sat facing Philip with Heather on a chair to one side.

"Now, squire. I'm not one to mess around here. Us Zkavskys get right to the point. No flannel, no bull, just tell it like it is. You'll never accuse me of waffling on about everything apart from the subject in question. Come straight out with it without all the fancy jargon and legal speak. If it needs to be said, then I'm the man to say it. You won't hear me…"

"The king asked you to come," interrupted Philip.

"Yep. Old crownhead himself. A proper gent if ever there was. And you know the best thing about him?"

"He gets to the point?"

"You've nailed it, old son. Yer a smart 'un. Yes, he's like me. No faffling, just gets on with it."

"Mr Zkavsky. The next words you speak will relate the reason for your visit. Otherwise you will leave immediately."

A pause.

"Sorry guv. King's prized possession, emerald ant stolen during night 48 hours ago. Taken from his office. No suspects. No ransom. Not offered to dealers."

"I suppose that there are few that will not have heard of the famed Emerald Ant of Kolvania but I am one of them," Philip responded and noticed Heather shrugging.

"Seen it once. Fantastic and it's actually a life-size representation."

"I will take this case. When can I visit?" asked Philip.

"Now, guvnor. King's private plane waiting at airport. Urgency essential."

"Then my assistant and I will come with you forthwith. Do we have bags packed, Heather?"

Zkavsky looked dubious.

"Assistant? A woman? Not sure about that, old mate."

"Why is that?" Heather enquired coldly.

"King don't allow no women in his chambers. Excepting the concubines, of course."

"Concubines?"

Heather's voice had raised a tad.

"Nine of 'em. Lovely bits of stuff."

"I insist that this lady comes with me," declared Philip.

"Okay then but I don't know what the King'll say."

Heather always kept ready packed cases in the office and they were soon en route. Now she was a woman on a concubine liberation mission, utter determination on her face. Four hours later, they were in Kolvania, entering the royal palace. Zkavsky left them in the care of a man with a gold braided uniform, who showed the way to a vast reception room.

"Rather indulgent for my taste," remarked Philip.

Heather's expression remained grim.

"You realise that I will speak my mind to the king regarding this equality issue?"

"Absolutely."

Two more servants entered, bearing trays of coffee and biscuits. One was female and Heather approached her immediately.

"It doesn't have to be like this, you know."

"The coffee?" enquired the woman.

"No, this grovelling obedience to a man. Instead of being some royal harlot, you could have a career. Perhaps a scientist, financier or a doctor."

"I am a doctor."

"What? Then it's even more disgusting. One who could be out there healing people reduced to a simple toy for the king's pleasure."

"Actually, I work every day at the hospital."

"But then return to the king's bed every night."

"Yes, I have to admit I do."

The male servant looked at her.

"Except when you stay out all night at the operating theatre. Well, hello folks. I'm King Gynist and this is my wife."

Heather took a backward step.

"What? This woman is not a concubine?"

"What's that?"

"Concubines? There are women who are kept as bed servants for the king."

"You mean wash the sheets and pillows?"

"No, no. To sort of, you know, do things at night."

Royal puzzlement was manifest.

"Sorry, don't understand. Anyway I'm the King but you can call me Your Highness. This is my wife Debby."

"Ooops! I've just realised," exclaimed the Queen.

"What is that, dearest?"

"Did Zkavsky tell you the concubine stuff?"

"Yes," replied Heather.

"Then that's it. He's a compulsive liar. Does it all the time. The same families have been in this royal household for generations. For some genetic reason, all of them sufferer a serious deficiency in one of the human qualities. In Zkavsky's case, he rarely speaks the truth."

"That can't be true!" expostulated the king.

The Queen's sighed.

"Can you repeat what I just said?" she asked Philip.

"That Zkavsky compulsively lies?"

"My word, you're absolutely right Mr Caldrock," responded the king.

"My husband's deficiency is that he disbelieves everything said by a woman. It is caused by a complete lack of the CQV84 chromosome."

"This case is going to be hard work," Heather whispered to Philip.

The king raised his eyebrows.

"What's that? You think it's easy, do you? Well we'll see about that."

"Your Highness, we are here to investigate the theft of the emerald ant."

"What?"

"Zkavsky lied about the theft as well?"

"No, a precious royal treasure has been stolen but an ant? What a stupid idea. What would I want with a piffling little ant? A ridiculous notion."

"Then what has been stolen? A ruby spider, perhaps," asked Philip with some sarcasm.

"Ant, spider? I'm not impressed by your investigative abilities, Mr Caldrock."

"From your amazement at the possibility of a small creature, I deduce the real thing is large. An elephant perhaps?"

"Amazing," said the Queen and Philip smiled smugly.

"Don't believe her," the king declared, shaking his head.

Now Heather showed impatience.

"For goodness sake, will one of you tell us what has been stolen?"

The king looked at her cautiously.

"What devious trick do you play now?" he asked.

Philip joined Heather.

"Come, we will leave. I cannot work without the facts," he announced.

"It's a diamond beetle!" called the king as they turned for the door.

"At last," said Philip and returned to the sofa.

"Now your Highness. I need to have the details of the stolen item and view the location of the theft," he continued.

"I'll show you," said the Queen.

She led them through a door and into a large closet.

"In here?" asked Philip.

"No, sorry. My deficiency is that I have absolutely no sense of direction. Let's try the next door."

Another closet.

"Of course, she's lying about the sense of direction," muttered the king.

Phillip shrugged.

"Although the interior of your cupboards are in themselves fascinating, I fear that my deductive powers may be blunted by interminable visitations."

"I think it's the next door," said the Queen hopefully.

The king gave her a look of disbelief.

"You stay here. I will show our guests the way. Follow me."

They left the room and crossed the hallway to enter a much smaller chamber.

"My study. This is where the crime took place."

Bookshelves on every wall and a large mahogany desk near the window.

"And where was this bejewelled insect kept?" asked Philip.

"In this box on the desk."

"That's a matchbox," exclaimed Heather and received a sharp look from the king.

"Your deceitful ways will not distract me. This receptacle was handmade in cardboard by my finest craftsmen."

Philip took the box from him.

"I deduce that the diamond beetle was no more than an inch long. May I suggest that a cardboard box, lying on your desk was a rather insecure location to hold such a treasure?"

"Yes, you may. When it is recovered, I will have a wooden box made."

"When did you notice the disappearance?"

"I was sitting at his desk at 9.30 in the morning and I opened the box then. The beetle was certainly there at that time. Then I went through the mail with my secretary and was just having tea and biscuits when I felt the desire to look in the box again."

"And the insect was gone?"

"No, it was still there."

"What was the time?"

"Exactly 11.08. After that, I dictated some letters, drank more tea and then decided to go out shopping. Just before I left, I checked the box again."

"Yes?"

"The beetle had disappeared."

"When was that?"

"Precisely 11.27."

"How can you be so sure of the times?"

The king pointed.

"That large clock on the wall facing me. I look at it regularly."

"Then the solution should be simple. We are left with a time span of just 19 minutes. Who was in the office during that period?"

"Only my secretary, Zizi and the girl who brought the tea, Klepta. They are both liars but otherwise reliable."

"Right. Did you notice either of them touching the box?"

"No but I frequently dictate while standing in front of the window, looking out over my kingdom."

A pause and Heather whispered in Philip's ear.

"Ask him if the letters were typed correctly."

"What untruths is she telling you?" asked the king.

"Just an aside, your Highness. May I ask if the letters you dictated were accurately transcribed?"

"Now you mention it, one of them wasn't. She got the dear sirs and yours faithfully bits okay but nothing in between."

"Then I wish to see this Zizi, if I may."

"Very well. You stay here and I'll send her in."

As soon as he departed, Philip sat at the desk.

"I feel most comfortable," he remarked.

"I really don't think that kingship would suit you," Heather responded.

A woman entered. Large and square shaped. Jutting jaw and an aggressive expression.

"What you want?"

Phillip waved an arm.

"Merely the truth about how you stole the diamond beetle."

"Stole? Don't you accuse me of that! I did no such thing!" she said vehemently, moving to stand over him.

He cringed under the verbal assault and Heather wedged herself between them.

"Ms Zizi, please take a seat. You are in serious trouble here and we will not be deterred in our quest for the solution."

"Oh, right. Sorry about that then."

She moved to a chair as Heather continued.

"The diamond beetle disappeared from this office during the time you were here, taking dictation. You failed to note any of the contents of one letter. What were you doing at that time?"

"Yes, I remember. I think I dropped off to sleep for a few seconds."

"That really doesn't sound very plausible, Zizi."

"It's true. I must have just dozed off."

"Have you ever done that before?"

"No, never. It's just like that time never existed. A total blank in my memory."

"Did you meet anyone prior to entering the king's office?"

"Only one person. When I arrived, I spent an hour with Mr Zkavsky, the senior minister. Then I went directly to the king."

"May I ask what you did with Mr Zkavsky?"

"Not much really. I remember him staring at me with his strange eyes. Then he showed me an absolutely gorgeous new pendant he had bought for his mistress, a lovely sparkling ruby. Just swung it back and forth in front of my eyes. Back and forth, back and forth."

"And after that?"

"I'm afraid it's a complete blank. Next thing I knew, I was going to see the king."

"But you insist that you didn't steal the beetle?"

"Don't you accuse me of that! I did no such thing!"

"Those were exactly the words you used before. It's as if you'd been programmed to say them," remarked Heather.

"Hypnotism. Does that word mean anything to you?" asked Philip.

"I know nothing whatsoever about it and that's the absolute, honest truth."

"You're saying that you know nothing about hypnotism?"

"I know nothing whatsoever about it and that's the absolute, honest truth."

"Thank you Zizi. You may go now."

After her departure, Phillip resumed his seat.

"Just about wraps it up, I think. We just need to apprehend Zkavsky. He hypnotised Zizi and directed her to take the insect while the king was looking out of the window. No doubt he is currently offering it confidentially to a number of international buyers."

Heather sat in front of him, expression firm.

"Philip. It is rare that I contradict you but in this case, a woman's knowledge is critical. Zizi did not steal the insect from the desk."

"Really? There is some clandestine female fund of knowledge in the field of mesmerism?"

"No, in the field of jewellery. I'm sure the word 'WODJA' means nothing to you."

"A town in Poland?"

"No. It stands for a condition well known to psychologists. Womanus Omylordus Desiderous Jewellerius Avidantum. It's a desperate craving for any piece of jewellery a woman is unable to obtain. You can see evidence of it at any time by watching the window of a jewellery store. A constant flow of women with this condition will press their noses against the glass."

"A strange addiction."

"Every female is born with it but most of us can keep it under control to a degree."

"I remember you looking at a diamond necklace once and I offered to save up and buy it for you. Then you told me not to be silly because you'd not put it on very often."

Heather laughed.

"INGATWI. I'd never go anywhere to wear it. It's a recognised side-effect."

"Then I believe this condition must also apply to clothes."

"Absolutely. That's another version of wodja."

"So how is this relevant to the present case?"

"Zizi wasn't hypnotised. When she saw the pendant she suffered a wodja attack. One symptom is that the mind goes blank afterwards whilst the subconscious churns through a series of images of them wearing the item of jewellery."

"After seeing that diamond necklace, your brain did seem elsewhere for the remainder of the day."

"The rest is simple. Zizi would have been in no condition to steal anything and the king couldn't be responsible. Only one person left."

"Klepta? The one who brought the tea?"

"She has to be the thief."

"But what evidence do we have?"

"None. That's the problem."

"Then I will institute a subtle strategy."

15 minutes later, Phillip was sitting alongside the king when Klepta entered. A slim young woman with narrow eyes.

"You called for me?"

Philip nodded.

"I have a simple question. Did you steal the diamond beetle from this desk?"

"No, of course not," gasped the woman.

His Highness jumped to his feet.

"What! You admit it then. One of my own employees transformed into a treacherous viper that nestles in the not insignificant bosom of the Royal household."

"No, I mean I did take it. Yes, it was me. Definitely."

"An outright confession then. Who told you to do this, Klepta?" asked Philip.

She burst into tears.

"I did it for love. My fiancée asked me to get it for him."

"Then who did?" enquired the king.

"Your Majesty. Her last statement was a lie," said Philip.

"I see. So who is this man?"

Klepta continued to sob.

"We only met a week ago. He stopped me in the street and said he would definitely marry me on condition that I brought him the diamond beetle. That was so romantic and I had to agree. I ran back here to take it before he could say another word."

"Is she telling the truth?" asked the king.

Philip shook his head.

"No, your Majesty. Now, Klepta. I assume you have given the insect to the man by now?"

"Not yet. It's safe in my room."

"My partner is searching it at this moment. The name of your husband to be?"

"Victor. Victor Velpronov."

Philip nodded.

"Just as I suspected. His fingers insert themselves in so many orifices. His brain is like the clockwork motor of nefarious activity throughout the world. I must tell you, Klepta that this man already has a regular female companion."

"That's okay. I don't mind sharing."

"But Velpronov is the greatest criminal mastermind on the planet."

"A mastermind? Really? I love men with brains."

Heather entered holding a small box.

"Found it in her room," she announced, placing the box in front of the king.

He opened it to reveal the minute diamond creature.

"Not in her room? Then there was it?" he asked.

Heather sighed.

"It wasn't hard to find. Klepta had pinned a sheet of paper over her bed. It said 'the diamond beetle is in my bedside drawer'. And it was."

"I had to put up that note. I can never remember where I've put things," admitted Klepta.

The Queen entered and the King called out to her.

"My dear! Our investigator has solved the case. The diamond beetle is back in my possession. You will be receiving a large sum for your services, Mr Caldrock."

Heather smiled at Phillip in his moment of triumph but he shook his head.

"Ah, but the case is not yet closed. Heather, please take the Queen to another room and search her thoroughly."

"What?"

"Do not question my reasons, dear."

Very well," added Heather and guided the protesting Queen out of the door. The king rose from his chair, pink cheeked.

"What is the meaning of this? I ought to send you to the dungeon for interfering with a royal personage."

"I ask only that we await their return. If nothing is found then you are welcome to consign me to the lowest, foulest chamber of this palace."

"Good, good. I'll look forward to that then."

Eight minutes before the women returned. Heather walked over to Phillip with a baffled expression.

"What did you expect me to find?" She asked.

"The item you are holding behind your back."

Heather produced a closed hand. She opened her fingers to reveal a diamond beetle.

"What is this? Two of them?" cried the king.

Philip regarded him with a smug expression.

"Just this one, your Highness. If you inspect the insect found in Klepta's room, you will discover it to be a fake."

The king summoned his jewellery expert and they moved to a corner where they examined the treasured item. Then the king returned.

"I am told that Klepta's beetle is plastic. What does this mean?" he asked.

"I will tell you. This scheme was the work of Victor Velpronov. He formulated a simple strategy. To trick a young employee here into believing he would marry her in return for stealing the beetle. However, being a rather simple girl, Klepta ran back to the palace before he could tell her the complete plan."

"Simple! That's a lovely thing to say. Are you married?" enquired Klepta.

Phillip ignored that and continued.

"Victor rightly assumed that the girl was unreliable and sought another target. I can't say exactly where and when he met the Queen and how she succumbed to his silken tongue that no doubt proposed everlasting love to her."

"He found me wandering round the town, trying to find my way back to the palace," the Queen interjected glumly.

"This time he was able to describe his plan in full. He gave her a box containing a fake plastic insect, almost identical to the real one. At some time prior to the reported theft, the Queen switched the boxes. No doubt she would have given the real insect to Velpronov soon afterwards but I speculate that she was unable to find her way out of this palace. The real beetle has therefore been in her possession ever since. Soon afterwards, Klepta carried out Velpronov's instruction and committed the theft, not knowing she was stealing a fake."

A silence as the information was absorbed.

"Amazing!" declared the king.

"Fantastic!" added Klepta.

"I have to admit, you did well," admitted the Queen.

"Phillip, that was brilliant," Heather said softly and moved to stand alongside him.

"I'm doubling your payment," the King announced.

"What won't happen to the women?" asked Heather carefully.

"Oh, I'll give them both a royal pardon. Can't bear grudges, even against compulsive liars."

Back home in Mapleton the next day.

"Just one thing puzzles me. How did you know that Velpronov had seduced the Queen? It could have been Zizi," asked Heather.

"Tuli Hews Sam," responded Philip.

"Pardon?"

"The Unmistakable Look In Her Eyes When She's Seeing Another Man. Every human male is born with the ability to recognise it. I saw it immediately when we first met the Queen."

"I see."

"However I must counsel that this is a man's secret and I have to trust you never to reveal it to another woman."

"Absolutely, Phillip."

11 CALDROCK'S CLAN

"Urchins," said Philip suddenly.

"Really? Well done, darling," Heather responded absently. She was engrossed in a thick volume, 'Penguins in Ancient Sumerian Literature'.

"Wincepole's urchins. You know, that bunch of youngsters who roamed the streets and reported back all sorts of criminal activity."

"Yes?"

"That's what I need."

"But we don't know any children like that."

"A good point. I'll ask Clarissa."

Just at that moment, the receptionist entered. No tray but carrying two metal cubes. She dropped one and laughed mockingly as she picked it up.

"Problem solved. No more spilt tea," she declared, placing the cubes on Philips desk.

"The tea is inside these cubes?"

"Yes and the heat is maintained. I shall name my invention the spill free beverage consigner."

"Vacuum flask?" asked Heather.

"What?"

"A vacuum flask."

"Never heard of it," announced Clarissa.

"How does one imbibe the liquid inside?" enquired Philip, examining a cube.

"I sealed them completely to prevent leakage. All you need to do is to direct a laser beam into the top, thus producing a convenient aperture for the tea to emerge."

"Do you have a portable laser beam?"

"No. I haven't got time to design one. Anyway, you've got the tea safe and sound."

"Excellent, Clarissa. Well done. Now I want to ask you something. Do you know any groups of young people?"

"Yes."

"I want them to volunteer to help in our investigations."

"Yes."

"Are you able to confide any details of the potential candidates?"

"Yes."

"What is the identity of this group?" Heather asked.

"Oh, my sister and a couple of friends. They're always out and about."

"Ideal. When can they come and see me?" enquired Philip.

"Eight minutes 31 seconds after I phone her."

"Then please phone her now."

"Yes," responded Clarissa and she departed.

Seven minutes 48 seconds later, the door bell rang. Then rang again. Heather moved to the outer office to find Clarissa checking a stopwatch.

"7.58, 7.59, 8.00, 8.01…"

Another ring and Philip emerged.

"Someone at the door?" He asked.

Clarissa shook her head and continued counting. The ringing continued for another 15 seconds. Then the knocking began. Suddenly Clarissa was out of her chair and opening the door.

"The eight minutes 31 seconds exactly," she announced as three people burst into the room.

Not what Heather expected. A smartly dressed girl with two suited young men. They stood in a line, looking expectantly at Clarissa who made the introductions.

"Mr and Mrs Caldrock, this is my sister Elizabeth and her friends Angus and Alistair," she announced.

"Pleased to meet you, sir and madam," they said in unison.

"How old are you?" Heather enquired and Elizabeth responded. A slim girl with long dark hair.

"I'm 18 and the two boys are 19, madam."

Philip chortled.

"Well you young scamps. Fancy a bit of detective work, do we?"

"Actually, that would be rather good. Angus and I have got some time on our hands now that our company is up and running," replied Alistair, a tall academic looking youth with smartly groomed brown hair.

"The boys have been establishing a computer software business and just appointed a manager to run it. How many do you employ now, Angus? 300?" remarked Elizabeth.

The thickset, bespectacled member of the trio responded.

"Don't be silly, Elizabeth. It's only 284 and that includes us."

Philip was ebullient.

"Jolly good. Well, why not start straight away? What I want is to hear of any unusual goings-on. Anything out of the ordinary you find as you wander this great town of ours. I may also have special assignments for you."

"Sounds absolutely perfect. May we communicate via mobile phones?" asked Angus.

"I suppose so although crumpled scraps of paper hold great appeal. I'll be happy to give you a few pennies for every report, if that's okay."

"No need, sir. Knowing the taxation system as I do, I'll write it off as expenses against agency work in one of our offshore bank accounts."

"Very well. You know where to find me so be off with you, little scamps."

The trio beamed in its gratitude and just before leaving, Elizabeth moved close to Heather.

"Don't let Clarissa make tea," she whispered and then departed.

"Well done. An excellent bunch of little rascals," said Philip after the door closed.

"I get on well with my sister. We often spend some time together in the laboratory, working on nuclear fission," responded Clarissa.

"It seems that the boys have found a bit of work to do. What about Elizabeth?"

"She's a bit lazy. Spend a lot of time in the laboratory and likes music a little. She conducts a few orchestras around the world, does some concert pianist work and biological research but not much else. And she's hopeless at brain surgery."

"Well, I feel much better now I've got my little band of young ruffians. I will call them Caldrock's Clan."

The new employees phoned several times over the next few days but Philip simply passed the information on to Inspector Foxhole. International smuggling organisations, plots to take the Crown Jewels and the like held little interest for him. Then, on the fourth day, it happened.

Philip answered a breathless call from Elizabeth.

"Found an envelope, Mr Caldrock."

"Really?"

"And it has your name on it."

"That is intriguing. Where did you find it?"

"In your letter box. I saw it sticking out."

"Where are you now?"

"Outside your office. Angus and Alistair are off tailing a government spy and I was just walking past when I saw it."

"Right, I'm coming."

Philip called Heather and they left the building together. Elizabeth was waiting.

"From the angle it was inserted into the postal aperture, I would say the one who left it was a muscular male, about 32 years old with Secret Service or Armed Forces training," she announced.

Philip beamed.

"Well done, young lady. If you go inside, I'm sure your sister will provide you with a mug of hot soup."

"Yes. Thank you, sir."

"Her description fits Burg Stonewall perfectly," Philip remarked as she disappeared inside.

"The bodyguard of Victor Velpronov?"

"I'm afraid so. We have not heard of the master criminal for some time. Not for him the trivialities of smuggling, corporate fraud and crown jewel theft. He is cunning, this man as is his attractive consort, Virginia Incent. Between them, they control a veritable web of minor miscreants but always at the centre, sit these two spiders, watching, waiting for the moment to strike!"

"Attractive?" said Heather frostily.

"What?"

"You called that Virginia woman attractive."

"Yes. Is that a problem?"

"It's not important. Why don't you open the letter?"

The envelope was cheap manila, sold only at every stationery shop in the world. Only the words 'Philip Caldrock' were written on it. A single sheet of paper inside and he read the text aloud.

'Think you're so smart at detection

Then try and take the right direction

North, East, West, no! You must start then finished finish

But take a chair, ungreeted

It cost much to buy, how much to charter?

Great amount of years

Hurry, find the next link quickly

Your feeble brain can not match mine and you'll feel sickly'

"Ah yes. Most definitely the work of Victor Velpronov and his delectable accomplice," Philip announced.

"Please do not mention that woman's appearance again in the future," insisted Heather.

"He can't even write a good rhyme. The last line is desperate."

"The question is, what does the text mean?"

"It seems pretty logical. If not the other directions, one must go south. Then find a chair, avoiding being seen by the owner. Subsequently one negotiates a price, spreading payment over several years."

"I'm not sure that's the right answer. It says we need to hurry to find the next link. That implies a series. Perhaps we have to solve a number of clues."

"I've had a thought. It may be a person or company called South that sells chairs. A furniture store."

They returned to the outer office as Elizabeth was leaving.

"Ah, my dear. Did you get some hot soup?" asked Philip.

"Actually, Clarissa and I shared some caviar with a Petrus red wine but nearly the same."

"Excellent. Now run along and jolly well done."

"Thank you, Mr Caldrock," she said as she closed the door.

Heather gave the message to Clarissa and asked her to make photocopies. She took the paper and scanned it quickly before inserting it into the copier.

"Hmmmph," she muttered.

"You've seen something in the text?" asked Heather.

"Childish clue. Too simple."

"And do you know a furniture vendor named South?" enquired Philip.

"No I don't."

Heather grimaced.

"What does the message mean?" she asked.

"Pathetic. Too trivial."

"And the meaning?"

"Pathetic is derived from the Greek pathētikos, meaning sensitive. Trivial is from the Latin, Trivialis, which comes from Trivium, crossroads and that is made up of Tri and Via, meaning three ways."

Heather paused, phrasing her question carefully.

"Clarissa, can you tell me what the words written on that paper mean?"

"Yes I can. However, I don't want to spoil the game for you."

"We need to know."

"Then it's a matter of morality. I need to meditate on that for one hour 22 minutes 19 seconds. During that time I can continue to operate normally while my subconscious is occupied."

Philip continued to his office while Heather moved closer to her.

"I really hope you meet a man soon. Of the correct age, of course," she said with forbearance.

"If I don't, then I'm going to build one. I've already sketched out a design."

"Perhaps that would be best."

Heather entered Philip's office to find him behind his desk sucking from a tube. He twisted a valve near the end and looked up.

"Tea. Clarissa created this system last night. The beverage is pumped through a tube directly to my desk. It's very eco-friendly. The power comes from a dish on the roof that picks up energy from the flapping wings of passing birds."

"Impressive."

"I've just run a check. No furniture supplier called South in the town."

"Clarissa seems to know the answer. I think we should wait."

Heather returned to her office to continue a study of ancient Mongolian flora. She returned some time later to find Philip had turned his chair to face the window.

"Are you asleep?" she asked.

No reply and she shook his shoulder.

"Hello dear, just deep in contemplation," he said muzzily.

"It's nearly time."

Just then, Clarissa entered, holding a stopwatch. Her lips were compressed tightly together. A minute passed and then she looked up.

"That's it. 82 minutes and 19 seconds," she declared with some joy.

"And the answer?"

"I formulated a new principle of human moral values that correlates to the individual's DNA structure. Previous theories haven't included one important factor. It's a negative polarity complex!" she declared triumphantly.

"Well done again, Clarissa," commented Philip.

"And the message?" asked Heather.

"Oh that silly little thing. Obviously, I know what it means. Would you like tea? I'll bring a tube for you if you do. Just need to solve the biscuit question now."

Heather rose from her chair and gripped the girl's shoulders.

"Clarissa. You're a lovely young lady and very intelligent but I'm losing patience. What does the message mean?"

"Go to the Eric Tindo used car showroom and look under the seats of the one priced at 1,215 pounds."

A silence as Philip wrote it down with a puzzled expression. Then he raised his head.

"Exactly correct, Clarissa. Excellent," he said.

Heather looked across at Philip as they drove to the Tindo establishment.

"So you'd worked it out, Philip?"

"Absolutely. Smart of Clarissa to do the same."

"Want to explain?"

"No time now, we're just arriving."

A typical used-car business. Rows of vehicles around a central office.

"We need to find one priced at 1,215 pounds. I'll cover this side," said Philip, walking off to the left as Heather moved right.

She found it in the second row. A small Puntro Sabillo. Large card on the windscreen indicating the price with a sticker across it marked 'Sold'. A man approached. Slicked back hair, sharp eyes and a suit. Heather's heart sank. A car salesman.

"Good morning madam."

"Hello. I'm just looking."

"I don't blame you. Nothing worse than being pestered by some suited man with greasy hair."

"Yes."

"I wouldn't buy anything here. Most of the cars are patched up rubbish. We just make the bodywork shine to catch the mugs."

"Right."

"And the prices are a rip-off. Who on earth paid all that money for this one? Anyone can see the chassis is warped. Won't last more than four weeks. That's why no guarantee was offered."

"Yes."

"Still, there's always some stupid person who'll buy it. Give a speech about it being a great little vehicle and you can con them every time. We had one yesterday that wouldn't even start so we put the customer in the driving seat and pushed it along while making engine noises. They bought it."

Philip walked over to join them.

"Buying a car, dear?" he asked.

"I certainly hope not if she's got any sense," responded the man.

"Right. Can I look inside this one?" asked Heather.

"It's already sold but you can if you like. Don't bounce up and down in there. Probably collapse if you did."

"Thanks. Would you mind going back to your office to 30 minutes while we look at it?"

"Not at all. Just leave when you've finished. And remember not to buy anything from this place."

"Thank you," Heather called as the man disappeared towards the office.

It was under the front passenger seat. Another coded message.

'The library but rush

And find the right book

You of all people

Should know where to look'

"Have you got a favourite book?" Asked Heather.

"Yes, of course. The Wincepole series."

"Perhaps Victor or that little vixen of his found out."

"He has a fox?"

"The obnoxious viper that's always with him."

"A snake as well?" asked Philip sharply.

"Doesn't matter. I suppose we'll need to take the message to Clarissa again."

"I think you're right. Always good to see she agrees with my interpretation."

"Yes, Philip."

They arrived back at the office to find the receptionist buried in a textbook.

"I'd like to know how you solved the first clue," remarked Heather.

"That? Anagram of direction is Eric Tindo. You must start means letter 'u' first followed by 's' for south and 'ed' is finish of finished. Chair without greeting 'hi' is car. Charter is Magna Carta signed in 1215."

A pause.

"Right. Can you tell us what this means, please?" asked Heather, handing her the paper.

"No."

Heather sighed.

"I don't think I could stand another conscience resolving wait."

"It's not conscience."

"Then tell me."

"I can't."

"Why not?"

"Because I don't know. No, wait. If I translate it into Egyptian hieroglyphs, then transpose the equivalent Tibetan symbols, I get a completely new message."

"Yes?"

"It says 'The wise woman always eats her bananas'. I think that's as true today as it ever was."

"Absolutely," agreed Heather.

42 minutes later Philip and Heather stood in the local public library. The traditional layout with computer monitors appearing incongruous on old oak tables amid ancient bookshelves.

"Anything inspire you?" asked Heather.

"No."

"It says 'You of all people' so it must be something you can relate to."

"I feel no relationship."

Heather wasn't listening. Relate to. Relations. A name. Philip's name. Of all people. Book of names. Find him there. She hurried to the nearest librarian.

"I need a dictionary of surnames please," she pleaded.

"Reference section, third block, second shelf down," he responded.

Reaching the area, she found three possible volumes and chose the thick, old one. Turn pages to Caldrock. A tiny slip of paper inserted there. She read it quickly and handed it to Philip.

"It's just a row of numbers," he said.

"I recognise the code. It's a mobile phone. Let's go outside and try it."

Out of the library and back to the car. Heather prepared a notepad and pen before putting her phone on loudspeaker. Then she dialled. A recorded message and she recognised the voice. Virginia.

'We have Alistair. He is suspended above a vat of acid and will be dropped in it at 19.28, Tuesday. But where will he be? Sounds like a woman would know.'

The message finished.

"That's awful," exclaimed Heather.

"Yes, no rhyme this time and no help at all. What's the time?"

"Eight minutes past five or 17.08. Just over two hours to save him."

She quickly dialled Alistair's mobile phone. Unobtainable.

"We need to hurry. Clarissa has to tell us what the clue means this time."

A surprise when they reach the office. Angus and Elizabeth in reception but no Clarissa.

"Good afternoon," they said in unison.

"Where is she?" asked Heather.

Elizabeth shrugged.

"Oh, got called out to London for a bit of brain surgery. No one else in the country could do it. Lucky thing."

"So we're acting as emergency cover under the European regulation 4852 subsection 33," added Angus.

"I'm afraid I've got bad news. A master criminal has captured Alistair and he's hanging over a vat of acid. He'll be dropped in it unless we can get to him in two hours."

"Really? What acid?" asked Elizabeth without emotion.

"I don't know."

"It's not very convenient. Our primary bank account in Switzerland requires a retina scan for both of us," remarked Angus.

His companion put a hand on his arm.

"Don't worry. Clarissa will create a replica of his eyeball in a few minutes. You can keep it in your pocket."

"A good idea but there will still be a lot of paperwork to sort out. Company ownership, list of directors and the like. Jolly inconvenient."

Elizabeth sighed.

"Well, I suppose we'd better save him then. Is there a clue to his location?"

Heather handed her a transcript of the recording and she scanned it quickly.

"That's easy. We'll be there in 10 minutes. Plenty of time for a chess game, Angus."

"Jolly good," he remarked.

Before Heather could react, the game had started. She attempted to interrupt but received severe looks and fingers on lips. Eventually she followed Philip back to his office.

"It seems Clarissa's whole family have the ability to irritate," she remarked.

"Little scallywags are forever up to something. Always scrounging a crust of bread from the bakery or playing football in the street."

"Yes, Philip."

An hour passed and more. Heather returned to watch the game, looking as irate as she could. Finally, Elizabeth dumped a knight on the board and called for Angus to resign.

"Oh dear, forced mate in nine more moves. Super game," he declared, knocking over his king.

They rose from the desk as Philip emerged from his office.

"Well, my little scamps. Are we ready?" he called.

Elizabeth nodded.

"Yes, let's go. I've only got the sports car today but Angus has a six seater. Plenty of room for my weapons so we'll use that."

"Weapons?" enquired Heather.

"Just a pair of laser rifles and a few pistols. And a couple of stun guns. Plus the grenades, of course."

Angus drove steadily, listening to a Mozart CD. The huge car would have graced a king and the others sat in the plush rear seats.

"So where are we going?" asked Heather, looking at Elizabeth.

"Clue says sounds like. The words where and be sound like wear and bee. Clothing reminiscent of a bee. Black and gold stripes. Only one shop selling dresses like that in this town. Dina's Fashion. That's why a woman would know."

"Just what I thought," Phillip said unconvincingly.

"Now I've got my guns here, I suggest Angus and I enter and shoot everyone we see while you go to the back room, basement or whatever to rescue Alistair."

"No," Heather said firmly.

"Well, what's the plan?"

"I'll go in and pretend to be a customer while you three look round the building. There's sure to be a back entrance."

Elizabeth grimaced.

"If we must. I was hoping to surprise Clarissa with a nice chunk of brain tissue."

Dina's Fashion was in a secluded street away from the town centre. Very exclusive. Heather had to ring a bell to gain entry. The door opened and a young woman eyed her frostily.

"Yes?"

Her dress was long and loose fitting. Gold and black stripes.

"I'd like to look at your latest designs."

"Are you very rich?"

"Yes, absolutely."

"Are you sure? The cheapest dress is forty thousand pounds."

Heather gulped.

"That's less than I usually spend," she replied bravely.

"Oh very well. You can come and look."

A long rack of dresses against the wall. Long, short, low and high but each had exactly the same gold and yellow stripes. Heather looked at them quickly and reached a door marked 'Private'.

"Is this the dressing room?" she asked.

"No and you haven't chosen a dress yet."

"This one," Heather responded, grabbing the nearest from the rack.

Ignoring the cubicle next to her, she tried the 'Private' door.

"It's locked," said the girl.

"Can I go in?"

"I don't have the key. Actually, I've never been in there since I rented the premises. Don't know why."

"Right. In that case, I'll be going."

"Hold on. I think I saw a key somewhere. Maybe in this cupboard."

She opened a large wooden cabinet and an avalanche of packets fell to the floor. Packets of chocolate covered honey bars.

"It's my snack store," explained Dina.

"I don't see a key."

"No but I've remembered where it is. In the beehive."

"What?"

The girl moved to the back of the shop and opened a window. A massive beehive directly outside.

"If you just reach in, you can feel it," said Dina.

Heather hesitated.

"But I could be stung."

"Yes, certainly. These are Uruguayan Predator Bees. One sting kills instantly. And they hate humans, especially women. Something about the female body scent drives them to savagery."

"Uruguayan Predators?"

"Yes. Would you like to buy a dress before you're killed?"

"Quiet. I need to sing."

Heather began to croon a gentle lullaby and slowly extended her arm inside the hive. Yes, something metallic. She pulled it out quickly, still singing. Dina looked disappointed.

"You're not dead then," she observed accurately.

"I happen to have studied Uruguayan insect life. Not many know that a children's lullaby, sung at a certain pitch, will send the Predator Bee to sleep."

"Are you going to try the key now?"

"I am but there could be danger behind that door."

"Bees?"

"No, a ruthless gang of criminals."

"Don't think I'll bother then."

The bell rang and Dina left to welcome a new customer. Heather unlocked the door and pushed it open. A dimly lit room. In the centre was a huge metal bowl full of liquid with a thick wooden beam running directly above. A rope was looped over it and fitted with a timing device. Every second, the rope dropped a fraction.

Alistair hung upside down, one ankle tied securely to the rope. He was reading a pamphlet.

"Good afternoon, Mrs Caldrock," he called pleasantly.

"Hello, Alistair. Are you okay?"

"To be honest, I'm bored. Luckily, I found this leaflet about how to start your own airline in my pocket."

"Don't worry, we'll get you out."

"We? Don't tell me you've got Angus and Elizabeth with you?"

"Yes."

"Oh no. They'll laugh their heads off."

"I'm sure they won't."

The noise of shooting from behind the far wall. The door flew open and Elizabeth entered, pistol in each hand, followed by Angus and Philip. She burst into laughter and Angus joined her, rolling on the floor with mirth.

"Silly old Alistair," she yelled.

"Told you," he called to Heather who didn't join the merriment.

"Stop all that and let's get him down," she said firmly.

Elizabeth moved forward to dip the corner of her handkerchief in the bowl. A frizzly noise and she pulled it out minus the corner.

"Wow! From the fibre decomposition, it must be Bandycleric Acid. Eats through anything instantly, including flesh and bones."

"What's the bowl made of then?" demanded Heather.

"Oh, I use the word anything in the Chemical Reaction 2003 regulatory sense. It means less than four exceptions. The bowl must be Yobydilium. The only other things not affected are parrot feathers and brown bread and it's obviously not made of those."

"Obviously. Shall we release Alistair? I think he'll go into the acid in about 30 seconds."

"Easy. I'll shoot through the rope and at the same time, Angus will leap across the bowl and push him to safety."

Her companion seemed keen.

"Fine. Let's give it a try," said the chubby youth.

Heather nearly closed her eyes as Elizabeth raised her pistol and shot twice. Meanwhile, showing surprising agility for one so chunky, Angus took a running jump over the bowl. He struck Alistair in the chest and carried him past the far edge to fall to the floor.

"That's bad luck. I think I've broken my watch," observed Alistair.

Philip had observed the scene in silence but now moved forward.

"Right, now you youngsters have finished playing, we need another clue."

"There's a sign on the wall," remarked Angus.

There was. Over to the left. Just three words. 'Clue in acid'.

They gathered round the bowl. At the bottom was a loaf of brown bread.

"Has anyone got a parrot on them?" asked Elizabeth.

Surprisingly, no one had.

"Why not tip the acid out?" enquired Philip.

Elizabeth shook her head.

"It would bore a hole down to the very central core of the planet and cause molten rocks to gush to the surface. A massive eruption that would probably send the whole country under the seas. Unless it hit a vein of bread on its way, of course."

"There must be some means to get it," said Heather.

"Obviously the acid can be neutralised but we've no chance of finding the correct material to do that."

"We could try. What is it?"

"Honey. Preferably covered in chocolate as that helps to give consistency to the chemical reaction."

"Wait!" cried Heather and rushed back through the door.

"Hello, anything interesting in there?" asked Dina.

"No, nothing at all. I just need a one of your chocolate bars."

"Help yourself."

Heather returned to her companions and handed the bar to Elizabeth.

"That's absolutely amazing. Which pharmaceutical company made this?" she gasped.

"It's confectionery."

"Don't know then. Anyway, now for the hard bit."

"Let me do it, Elizabeth" pleaded Angus.

"No, I must take the responsibility."

She pulled at the paper wrapper. And pushed. And twisted. And bit.

"Let me try," insisted Alistair.

Now the girl's expression had turned grim and her eyes were blazing.

"No! I will do it. Just got to keep calm."

More pulling, twisting and biting. The wrapper remained intact. Now she was talking to the confectionery.

"Right, you rascal. I'm getting the laser rifle. You'll be sorry then, won't you?"

Heather stepped forward and wrestled the bar from her.

"I'll open it. Look, Elizabeth, you just hold it with both hands at the end and pull in opposite directions, like this."

No effect. The shiny wrapper remained in its virgin state.

Elizabeth pulled out both pistols.

"Just hold it up. Away from your body might be best. It needs to be taught a lesson."

"For goodness sake, look how easy it is," cried Angus, grabbing the bar from Heather. He pulled a gleaming meat cleaver from inside his jacket and sliced the wrapper neatly with a horizontal slash. Showing astonishing dexterity, he caught the bar as it fell.

"That's how it's done," he announced proudly, handing the bar to Elizabeth.

"How do you make it react with the acid?" asked Heather.

"It's a chemical process called Irrandominus Immersus."

She threw the bar into the bowl.

"Can be a little tricky but I've managed to pull it off," she added with satisfaction.

The liquid foamed slightly and then subsided.

"Is it safe now?" asked Philip.

Elizabeth nodded.

"Completely safe."

He reached a hand towards the liquid.

"Subject to the usual variances," she added.

He stopped.

"Variances?"

"Well, obviously. The reaction works 83.924 percent of the time."

"In that case, I would like to test it first."

He took a coin from his pocket and tossed it in the bowl. It clattered to the bottom and now Philip reached in and pulled out the loaf of bread.

"You were lucky. All currency coins have a minute amount of ground parrot feathers in the alloy, so they're not affected," remarked Elizabeth.

"Thank you," Philip responded and began to examine the bread. Words were embossed on one side.

'The next clue tells you where we're robbing

Better hurry or you'll be sobbing

Big bang at ten

It's time on your side?

Old mother hen

Consoles those who tried.'

Heather wrote it down carefully.

"Victor is a pathetic poet," said Philip, looking at her.

"It's just his way of giving the information. It should be the last clue as it will give us the place they are planning to rob. The rest needs thinking about. Has anyone got any ideas?"

"No," responded Elizabeth in the same style as her sister.

"I can probably help if it's related to international company law, stocks and shares or corporate marketing," offered Alistair.

"When is Clarissa back?"

"I'll phone her and ask," offered Elizabeth and dialled on her mobile phone.

"Hello, big sis. How's the surgery going?"

A pause and she put her hand over the mouthpiece.

"Just in the middle of her fourth operation now," she whispered.

A pause.

"Lovely. So you've collected a few bits of brain then. If you have any scraps spare, can you let me have them? I want to try dropping them in a few chemicals to see what turns them pink."

A pause.

"When will you be back?"

Another pause.

"Okay, you need your hand free to stop a bit falling out. See you later then. Bye, Sis."

She clicked off and then started for the door.

"What did she say?" called Heather.

"Who?"

"Clarissa, your sister."

"She's going to try and get some brain bits for me."

"When is she coming back?"

"Tomorrow or the next day. Or two. The hospital has just received a batch of ears and there's a queue waiting for aural replacements. Don't worry, I'll do the reception job while she's away."

"Right."

Back in the office and cups of tea. No spillage.

"The boys have popped over to Washington for some meeting at the White House but you can depend on me," Elizabeth announced.

"The tea is first class. Well done, young lady."

Heather turned to Philip.

"I have an idea," she said.

"Does it involve a bomb and a clock?"

"Well, yes."

"The town hall has a large clock in its tower. The original mechanism was recently replaced by a new, state-of-the-art electronic version. This has a huge LCD screen that shows a chicken alongside the digital time display. On the hour, the bird goes into an animated sequence, laying one egg for each hour of the day. That is the time and mother hen part of the clue."

"Yes Philip."

"Big bang at ten obviously indicates that the bomb is programmed to detonate at that time. That just leaves 'consoles those who tried'. My best guess is that there is a console somewhere in the tower that controls the clock. Presumably that's where we'll find the bomb and also the clue."

"I'm impressed."

He waved a hand.

"Mere triviality. We just need a bomb disposal expert."

"I can do that. Simple little job," offered Elizabeth.

"We have just 50 minutes before ten. Shall we go?" Heather asked.

"I'll just finish my tea," remarked Philip.

30 minutes later the trio were climbing the winding steps of the town hall tower. Not a tall construction and they quickly reached a small chamber at the top. One person there. A middle-aged woman sitting in front of a screen.

"Hello," she greeted them cheerily.

"Have you just arrived?" asked Heather.

"No, no. I'm here all the time, if you'll pardon the pun. Someone has to make sure the clock's working correctly."

"All the time?"

"Yes, 24/7. I only leave my position for toilet and washing purposes. People bring food to me here and I doze in the chair at night. It's not a bad job at all."

"And that keyboard in front of you controls everything?"

"Yes. We call it a console and I can check whatever I want on the screen. It even has a camera view of the clock face outside."

"Isn't it all automatic?"

"It is but you never know with these electronic thingies."

"How many times has it failed?"

"None so far but I've got a feeling this could be the week."

"Has anyone been up here recently?"

"Before you three came? Just the man to service the clock. He was here a couple of days ago."

"What did he look like?"

"Chunky and muscular. Looked like ex-army. He said his name was Burg Stonewall."

"What exactly did he do?"

"He opened up the console and put a new box underneath it with a little timing mechanism attached. I remember he said I'd get a big surprise at 10 tonight. That's just eight minutes from now."

"It was a bomb!" Heather affirmed.

"Really? What does that do?"

"A bomb? It explodes in a big burst of light, fragments everywhere."

"Lovely. Can't wait to see it on the screen. That stupid hen is driving me mad."

"No. A real bomb."

"Oh, right."

A four second pause and then the woman gave a scream and raced down the stairs yelling "Bomb! Bomb! Bomb!"

"Over to you then, young lady. Just three minutes before it explodes," Phillips said calmly.

Elizabeth held up a small case.

"Everything I need is in here. All my tools, wiring, gloves and masks. Another section for biscuits and fruit juice and there's even a separate compartment for cosmetics. And it's real synthetic leather."

She held the case up proudly.

"Time is passing," Heather remarked.

"Oh, yes. The thing here is not to panic. Don't worry about the seconds ticking away to certain death. Just stay calm and get the job done quietly."

"Yes. So when are you starting?"

"I've disarmed a few bombs in my time. Even trained Clarissa to do it but she kept dropping the screwdriver. I think she's better at brain surgery."

"I suggest you start now."

"Okay then."

Elizabeth fumbled in the bag and produced a biscuit. She shook her head and put it back. Then out came a screwdriver. Another shake of the head. Third time, she was satisfied she had the right tool. A heavy duty builder's hammer.

Her first swing smashed the console in half. Further blows reduced it to fragments.

"I see it now," she said.

Underneath the shattered panel was a small black box with a timer on top. Back to the bag for a pair of tweezers that she used to carefully remove pieces of console from the timer to expose it fully. Heather could hear it ticking and saw the display counting down. 14, 13, 12…

"Now the tricky bit," announced the girl.

She grabbed the hammer again and struck with ferocity. The box cracked but kept ticking. 9, 8, 7…

"Right, that does it," Elizabeth shouted and a violent attack ensued, hammer blows raining down like incredibly heavy snowdrops with psychopathic tendencies. 4, 3, 2… and the most violent strike of all that made the whole tower shudder. The timer was no more. Just a twisted, battered wreck.

"There you go. Some are a bit trickier than others but you just need to be firm with them," announced Elizabeth.

Philip brushed perspiration from his brow.

"Well done. You young rascals certainly pick up a few things on the streets."

Elizabeth grinned.

"I used to when I was a kid. Bottle caps, mobile phones, old shoes, lost rabbits, cars, wallets and all that sort of stuff. Most of all, I kept finding paving slabs. Loads of them out there. I remember bringing one back every day until the seventh garage was completely full. Then daddy built me a workshop with a laboratory inside so I stopped. The things you do when you're 11."

"There should be a clue on that box somewhere unless it's been beaten out of existence," remarked Heather.

Elizabeth fumbled around and produced another envelope.

"Taped to the bottom. It's a lovely bomb. Shame, it would have made a great hollow where the town centre was. We could have filled it with water for miscellaneous aquatic pursuits, such as rowing and synchronised swimming."

Heather opened the envelope and read the message aloud.

'Panting with excitement

They go forth from the hall

Where are they going?

To us of course

So now I've revealed all

A bit of it makes sure

A bit of it says all'

"That's a bit childish," exclaimed Elizabeth.

"Then what does it mean?" asked Heather.

"Well, I'm not a child, am I? I'm a grown woman of 18. It's bad enough battling through to adulthood without snide remarks like that. Don't you remember when you went through it? All those changes from being your natural self to a living object of partnership potential. All the men and women assessing you, judging if you're right for them. Well, I'm not ready yet and I don't care who knows it!"

"So you don't know," said Philip.

"As I'm not a girl, I can't help."

He nodded sagely.

"Then I must again turn my considerable brain to the task. A critical conundrum from one of the finest master criminals the world has ever seen. A challenge I must not fail with so much depending on me. The citizens of this fine community look for a saviour, one who will lead them away from the morass of crime and subterfuge. I stand alone but I stand proud and erect. The burden must and will be borne, even though the cesspits of wrongdoing will I carry it."

Heather sighed.

"Excellent, dear. What is the answer?"

"I'm not sure yet."

"The opening line, 'panting with excitement' is unusual and incompatible with the remainder," she suggested.

"It could be a circus, cinema or similar popular entertainment. The clue mentions a hall of some sort."

"I used to go to cinemas and circuses when I was young. Can't do it now though, not now I'm a woman. All my friends love parties and if I go with them, they spend all the time gossiping, dancing and doing the cuddling thing. Really boring. It's so hard being a woman," Elizabeth observed morosely.

Heather ignored that.

"What about the last part about a bit of it saying all? A bit of a movie?"

Elizabeth made a 'hmmph' noise.

"If I was a child, I could tell you but I'm not."

"You know, don't you?" asked Heather

"Childishly simple."

Heather gathered patience.

"Elizabeth, inside each of us adult women is a child, bouncing with youthfulness and vitality. We need to let her out regularly otherwise she gets bored and miserable. I do it all the time. Only this morning I was playing with my skipping rope."

"You were?" Philip exclaimed.

"Absolutely. It's a great feeling. Men don't do it so much, which is why they're often grumpy and frustrated."

"You mean a woman can be like that sometimes?" enquired Elizabeth.

"Certainly. Try it now and you'll feel much better."

"I could tell you the answer to the clue."

"Yes. That's a good idea."

"Well, 'a bit of it' is literal. The first letter of it is 'i'. Insert it in panting to give painting. With excitement describes the Post-Trauma School of artists. Forth is a homonym of fourth. So it's the art gallery where they currently have a Post-Trauma exhibition. Hall Four contains the most valuable pictures. Those are the ones they're going to steal. Wow! I do feel much better now!"

"It's another secret to be kept strictly between women," advised Heather.

Philip put a finger to his forehead.

"The Art Gallery. Just as I suspected," he remarked.

They descended the steps and left the Town Hall to find a huge crowd gathered outside. The terrified woman was scampering around the area and still yelling. An army bomb disposal team ran up to them.

"Where is it?" asked the officer.

"The bomb? Our colleague deactivated it," responded Heather.

He saw the girl behind her.

"Hey guys. It's her! Elizabeth Hartwin!" he yelled, pushing past Philip and Heather.

The men surrounded her, begging for autographs. Many had her photograph and pleaded for a message to be written on it.

"You used the big hammer, no doubt," said the officer as the hubbub subsided.

"Well, of course," she responded.

"A great pleasure to meet you. Every man in our battalion has your picture on his locker. If only you'd agree to date one of us."

"The only reason you all want to date me is because I'm a young and unattached woman."

"Well, yes. And attractive too."

"Listen, guys. It's not easy for me, being a woman. I get an average of 216 date offers a day. What am I supposed to do? And not one of them wants to take me to watch laser beam experiments. I'd do anything to be invited to one of those."

All the men scribbled on notepads, glancing shiftily at each other as Elizabeth rejoined the others in the car.

"Shall I come with you?" she asked.

"It could be dangerous," said Heather.

"That's why I offered. You might need a bodyguard and I've got a couple of Witzman 473 pistols and some other stuff in my bag."

"Jolly good, you young scamp," said Philip.

The art gallery, reposing in serene tranquillity amid a backwater of the oldest part of town. A tree-lined arc of buildings that simpered dreamily far back from the main thoroughfares. People walked more slowly here, wallowing in the near lost world of social consideration.

Three cars drove slowly to the parking area, secluded within a leafy perimeter and twelve occupants emerged slowly. On a break from a business meeting perhaps? Eleven men and women in smart grey and blue suits gathered round the leader. Burg Stonewall, the merciless, murdering, mercurial mercenary muttering meaningful mandates. The team nodded dutifully as he issued instructions.

Heather drove to the gallery with concern. Also Philip. And a fighting machine in the rear seat. Elizabeth, bulging with weapons. A pink bullet-proof jacket, two rifles on her back, pistols in every pocket and a selection of knives scabbarded at various parts of her anatomy. She was humming cheerfully.

"I got this kit on vacation in California this year. It was an adventure holiday where we fought the Puce Porcupine gang."

"Who?" asked Heather.

"Just a mob of criminals who set up a base there for drug smuggling and robbery. Like a fortress with about 600 fighters stationed there."

"You're not one to be on the beach, tanning yourself."

"What's the point in that? Holiday was great but I hadn't bothered to rent the optional weaponry package, so in the first big battle, I was still in T-shirt and shorts. Still, the squad I was leading were a good bunch. Followed me everywhere. I still remember the laugh we had when we charged down the slope towards the base. A couple of them hadn't even learned how to dodge machine-gun bullets. Can you believe that?"

"No."

"Well, I didn't have weapons so had to rely on my martial arts. I made a silly mistake though and nearly spoiled the vacation."

"Yes?"

"I got split from my team when we were inside the base. I was looking for the ladies toilets and opened the wrong door. It was a guard room with 16 armed men inside. I can joke about it now but I was really embarrassed. Anyway, after I'd knocked them all out, I went through a door and found the ladies. Then I rejoined my team and they all laughed at me. Was my face red."

"Yes?"

"My T-shirt was covered in blood. A couple of the men I'd been fighting had got broken noses and stuff. Went all over me. I had to go out and buy a new T-shirt afterwards. A blue one. It's really comfy and I still wear it sometimes. You just never know when you're going to pick up a bargain on holiday."

"It sounds an interesting break."

"Yes, that first week was fun. Then I did a quick trip up to the North Pole before the shark hunting hunting in Australia."

"Hunting hunting?"

"Hunting the shark hunters. Pity it was just three days. I only had time to sink six boats."

"Did you go with Clarissa?"

"No, she just likes boring things. This year all she did was a space flight and solve the Bermuda Triangle thing. Still, to be fair, she only had four days off."

"Don't you want to go to clubs? Dancing with boys?"

"That's such a chore. Takes me three solid days to get the make-up on. Isn't lipstick a pain to get right? I usually allow 12 hours for that. It's one of the few things where I'm like my sister."

Heather nodded understandingly.

"Well, we're here now."

The art gallery, reposing in serene tranquillity except for the four armed figures in grey and blue suits near the door.

"Great! I'll mow them down," yelled Elizabeth, eyes alight.

"We don't want to kill them," advised Heather.

"I wasn't going to. I want to try my new truth serum out later. From the position of the trigger fingers and the slope of their shoulders, I can tell they've only been using weapons for less than eight years. I'm guessing that you two don't know how to dodge bullets?"

"That is correct, young lady," Philip declared gravely.

"I can see four guards by the door. The classical armed robbery protocol indicates that there will be eight inside, not including any criminal masterminds who may be present. Come on, let's go then."

"You want us to come with you?" asked Philip uncertainly.

"Yes, no problem. If they try to shoot you, I'll just jump in the way and take the bullet in my jacket. I designed it myself, you know."

"Are you sure?" Heather enquired cautiously.

"Of course. Off we go."

They followed the girl towards the entrance. A mass of armed police surrounded the building at some distance. Another delay as the officers crowded round for Elizabeth's autograph. Then they stood back to allow her through, Philip and Heather following with trepidation.

"Hello everybody!" Elizabeth called as they approached the entrance.

Four guns were raised.

"Go back. We don't want to kill you," shouted one of the gang, a blonde woman.

Just then Heather heard a call from behind them. Clarissa was strolling up the path.

"Shame. She'll want to get involved now," muttered Elizabeth.

Her sister joined them, looking fresh as a koala.

"Just finished the brain surgery. 16 hours, working through the night. I flew the helicopter here so I could change my book at the library. Then I saw the police cordon."

She held a slim volume entitled 'Kissy Smoochie Love Story' by Bellesugar Sweetielips.

"I haven't read that one," Elizabeth remarked.

"I found it hard going but it's worth persevering with."

"She also wrote 'Cutie Darling Meets Her Handsome Prince'. I loved that one."

"Yes, I borrowed it after you, remember? I think they've got her new one in now. Simply must read it. Hello, I see a few people with guns here. Are you going to shoot them?"

"No. New truth serum to try."

"Okay. Shall I help? Don't want you getting blood on your shirt again."

Elizabeth groaned.

"Everybody reminds me of that. It wasn't a big stain."

"Get out of here before I start firing," called the woman with the gun.

Clarissa turned angrily.

"Do you mind? We're talking."

She sprang forward and kicked up into the blonde's stomach a fist clipping her on the jaw as she fell. Clarissa grabbed the gun. The other three began to shoot and Elizabeth moved in a blur, taking all the bullets in her jacket.

"Right," she said with determination.

The three men were down before they could move. Noses cracked, jaws hammered and necks thumped. Clarissa burst into laughter.

"You've done it again!" she cried.

Elizabeth looked down. A banged nose had spurted blood on her fresh pink bullet proof jacket.

"Not fair. Why does it always happen to me?" she wailed.

Clarissa took a couple of pictures with her phone camera to show to Angus and Alistair later.

"I think I should take the lead," Philip declared and entered the building.

The girls dutifully stood back and joined Heather in the rear. No one outside the closed door of Hall Four. Without hesitation, Philip opened it and led the others inside.

A semicircle of weaponry faced them. Machine guns, laser rifles, anti-tank guns. About 14 barrels altogether. Holding the artillery was Burg Stonewall with seven others. Victor Velpronov and Virginia behind them.

"Well, well, what have we here? Our two detectives and a couple of girls," greeted Victor.

Elizabeth looked frosty.

"I'm not a girl. I'm Elizabeth Hartwin, an 18 year old woman," she announced.

"Elizabeth Hartwin? And this is your sister?"

Clarissa nodded.

"Yes but I've grown out of the girl-woman thing. I understand now that the word girl does not always imply an attempt at superciliousness and actually has eco-friendly values in saving one syllable compared to woman. It also has the benefit of not being derived from the word man, with connotations of an inferior class."

Burg dropped his two guns.

"Everybody surrender. It's the Hartwin sisters. Both of them."

Gasps of horror and weapons clattered to the floor. One woman stepped forward with a notepad.

"I'd really like your autographs, if you don't mind."

Elizabeth shook her head.

"No. I'm not happy now. I brought my guns along specially. Doesn't anyone want to fight?"

"Honestly, you're like a spoilt 13-year-old sometimes," remarked Clarissa, hand on hip.

Now Stonewall moved forward.

"In all my 33 years, I never thought I'd meet you two together."

"And how many days?" asked Clarissa sharply.

"What?"

"33 years and how many days?"

"I'm not sure. I was born on April fourteenth."

Silence while Clarissa stared, open mouthed.

"Do you like looking at brains under a microscope?" she asked dreamily.

"Sure I do. How did you know that?"

"And calculating the correlated particle spectrum of water molecules whilst watching a red sunset over water?"

"Amazing. I do that every time I'm near the sea."

"Oh my goodness."

Elizabeth began to giggle.

"Clarissa's got a boyfriend! Watch out Burg, she's after you."

The look of disbelief in the man's face.

"You must be joking. Clarissa Hartwin wouldn't be interested in someone like me. The only thing I'm good at around the house is carrying teacups and stuff although I also get a kick out of picking up things that people have dropped."

Clarissa was feverishly flicking through her diary.

"Here we are. I've got a timeslot in 87 days at 17.36 GMT in Hawaii. One of my patients gave me a couple of ocean cruisers and I can fit in the marriage just before I try out my new mini submarine design. I'll pick you up at the airport, Burg and then fly us over. E-mail you with complete time schedule."

"Can we sit on the cruiser and do the sunset thing?" he asked.

Clarissa closed her diary and looked at him.

"Only if we do the kissy, cuddly thing as well," she declared with enthusiasm.

Victor seemed a mite frustrated by events.

"This is just a hollow victory for you, Caldrock."

"Perhaps the hollow needs a little filling," added Virginia, raising her pistol and shooting immediately.

Philip froze as inevitable death approached. Then a blur in front of him.

"I can't keep doing this. I'll have to teach you how to dodge them," remarked Elizabeth casually.

"Thank you, young woman," he gasped.

"Can I kill these two? Then the day won't be a complete waste."

"No," Heather said firmly.

"Just cut out a bit of brain then? A wedding pressie for Clarissa?"

"No."

Victor was becoming frustrated by lack of attention.

"As the greatest master criminal of our time, I give you this warning. A wave of robbery and violence will sweep over this town such as never before has been not been ever seen in history previous to it occurring," he declared tortuously.

Virginia smiled.

"And I am recruiting the most evil, dissolute gang of ruthless thugs who will undoubtedly be the most violent and horrific bunch ever to have entered the conurbation before the present time and almost certainly in any future time although one may never predict that which is to come with any certainty."

"On second thoughts, Elizabeth perhaps it is best if you shoot them," remarked Heather.

The girl raised her pistols but Clarissa walked in front of her, having completed the marriage arrangements.

"A Carnforth- Singleton. Notice the distribution in the blue spectrum?"

Elizabeth grimaced.

"Now you've spoilt the joke."

"Sorry."

Phillips looked confused.

"What?"

"It's a hologram of Victor and Virginia. I wanted to shoot to give you a shock but Clarissa ruined it," Elizabeth responded with some displeasure.

"Ah yes. Obviously I knew that. Carnforth -Simpleton system, I believe."

"Carnforth -Singleton."

"Absolutely. Well done team."

As he spoke, the images of Victor and Virginia disappeared.

12 THE ROYAL RABBIT

The morning it began, Heather was sitting in Philip's office, attempting to interest him in Etruscan hairstyles, her latest study. Clarissa entered with a huge stack of papers, dropped them, laboriously picked them up, dropped them again and finally deposited a scrambled heap on the desk.

"Important e-mails," she announced.

Heather took a stack from the top and shuffled through.

"We seem to have won several lotteries and have exclusive offers for a large number of enhancement drugs. Also we can purchase a number of qualifications and have various young ladies who wish to offer their services. Then there are a number of opportunities to receive several million pounds from various accounts that only require us to pay an amount of expenses to obtain the windfall."

Clarissa nodded.

"Yes, I thought you should take action immediately before someone else gets in first," she said.

Heather looked at her.

"Clarissa, do the words fraud, swindle or deception mean anything to you?"

"No."

"All of these are invented stories to obtain our bank or credit card details and use them to rob us."

"Oh, I see," the girl responded.

"I suggest that when you're married, you let Burg do all the financial housekeeping."

"Right. I'll put it in the contract."

"Contract?"

"Oh yes. Every woman needs one when they enter a legal marriage partnership. I'm writing it myself, of course. Let me show you."

She left the office and returned quickly with another huge stack of papers that she handed to Heather. The first sentence wasn't promising in addition to being apparently interminable.

'In so far as I, Clarissa Hartwin, hereafter named the first party, being of sound mind and of the correct DNA structure, will agree to cohabit on specific occasions that are defined in appendix 38, subsection 431 and notwithstanding any corrections made solely by the first party within the context of appendices 52 to 84 inclusive, hereinafter named 'Changes of Mind', will, without prejudice and solely, without the exceptions that include but are not limited to those specified in clauses 102 to 138 of the appended section entitled 'Definition Of Functions Of The Second Party' may or may not prohibit, refuse or otherwise concur, this concurrence limited strictly to written, signed and dated documents that are in the sole possession of the first party and remain…'

"Does Burg know this is coming?" asked Heather.

"Oh no. He's got to sign a global agreement that ensures his legal compliance with any contracts I had deposited with the delegatory lawyer that I use."

"So you want him to sign a paper without knowing what he's agreeing to?"

"Of course. Every woman needs that security."

Heather sighed and Philip finally emerged from his post Etruscan ennui.

"So what other missives have reached us in addition to these critically important e-mails?"

"Just a couple of letters. This one's interesting. A mysteriously lost one pound coin."

"The mystery?"

"The man is certain he had just that one coin in his pocket. He checked it was there during dinner. When he went to bed, it had disappeared. He hadn't gone out so the only rational explanation he can offer is invisible aliens. It just so happens that I'm working on an invisibility formula at this moment. One could hypothesise that the entities landed their invisible craft in his garden and slipped in through the door when he opened it."

"They knocked?"

"That would be silly. It presumes that the social protocols of humanity are also adopted by an unknown civilisation, thousands of light years away. No, our man opened the door when his neighbour called."

"A visitor."

"He didn't enter the house. Just came to collect a pound that the man owed him."

Heather returned to her Etruscan book and even Philip grimaced.

"The other letter?"

"Just some King or other. Doesn't sound interesting."

Heather looked up.

"King? A real King?"

"Yes, King William of Anmonstien, that little country in Europe. Anyway, these invisible aliens may have some knowledge that I need for my research. Perhaps it would be safer if I checked it out. Better someone with my scientific knowledge."

"Good idea. You do that, Clarissa while we handle the mundane matter of the King."

A beam of delight crossed the girl's face.

"My first solo investigation! Perhaps I'll invite Burg to join me."

"He's not with Victor Velpronov now?"

"No, he's given up all that criminal stuff. I think he's planning to become a monk."

"That may not be a good portent for the marriage," remarked Heather.

"Why not?"

Heather paused.

"When we've sorted these current cases, I think we need to have a little talk, Clarissa. Woman to woman."

"Fine but I could be invisible by then."

"Right."

After Clarissa had departed, Heather picked up the second letter. The envelope bore the Royal seal of Anmonstein and the letter was printed impeccably.

'The King hereby requests the presence of Philip and Heather Caldrock to resolve a matter of state importance. Flights and hotel bookings enclosed.

Lots of love, all the best.

His Royal Majesty, King William of Anmonstein.

PS King Gynist of Kolvania recommended you.'

"Another Royal request. Your reputation is certainly growing," observed Heather.

Phillip's hand waved disdainfully.

"It is of no import to me whether pleas for my help come from the highest or lowest orders. When do we start?"

"The flight is this evening."

"I presume you are in a womanly tizzy, wondering what clothes to wear, whether you need to curtsy, what you should say and the awesome prospect of meeting a royal presence?"

"No."

"Right. Then we'll pick up a few things from home this afternoon on the way to the airport."

"That's fine. I'm interested to learn what could be so important to a King."

An uneventful flight with limousine and chauffeur waiting at the airport. Luxurious five-star hotel. A message bearing the Royal Crest was waiting when they arrived in reception.

'Glad you could come. I'll send one of the lads round to pick you up at eight for a spot of dinner. Dress how you like. See you later, King William.'

"Seems a friendly sort of chap," observed Philip.

"I read up on him during the journey. He's very much a man of the people and always out and about. Unlike most countries, King William still retains the final veto on all decisions of the state assembly and he often submits new regulations for their approval. They usually approve without a vote but I see there's a lot of fuss over the one he proposed just last week."

"Why?"

"It was a bill to allow rich foreigners to live in the country tax-free and without any check on their suitability. Anyone who has five million US dollars or equivalent would be able to come and stay in Anmonstein."

"That seems a bit unusual."

"Absolutely and the King has also allocated a large area of his own land for these rich newcomers to build their luxury mansions."

"He must have a reason."

"The report says that he believes the move will bring new wealth into the country."

"That could be right."

The limousine pulled up outside the hotel just before eight and they were approached by a man of about 40, wearing jeans.

"Mr and Mrs Caldrock?" he asked.

"We're here in response to a summons from his Majesty the King," responded Philip.

"Yes, sure. Have a good trip?"

"Fine, thank you. May I ask...?"

"We're delighted to meet you, your Majesty," Heather interrupted.

"Call me Bill."

Phillip quickly repositioned.

"This is a great honour," he declared.

"Come on in the car. Want a drink?"

15 minutes later, inside the palace. Three of them sitting in a massive lounge, the size of a concert hall. Glasses of orange juice.

"You wish us to resolve a problem?" enquired Heather.

She studied their host. Average height, average brown hair and a friendly but average face.

"The details after dinner. After King Gynist mentioned your name, I studied your exploits and you have a record of getting results. I have been disappointed by another detective who has achieved little since he came a week ago."

"Another detective?" asked Philip, somewhat irked.

"Stesky Petrov. You know of him?"

Heather knew. The Servatvian Sleuth. A master of immense self aggrandisement. His publicity agents had promoted his favourite expression 'The truth will upcome' to generate oceans of media coverage and even used it as the title of his biography.

"I've heard of Petrov," she responded with a smile.

"He is dining with us tonight but leaving tomorrow."

Heather noted the steely glint in Phillip eyes and began to feel less comfortable about the repast to come.

The dining room, just a little smaller than the lounge. The first course was being served when Petrov entered.

"I am here! Amongst you I honour with my presence," was his opening shot.

A small, wiry man with jet black hair brushed back and a lean, sharp nosed face. Phillip rose from his chair to tower above the newcomer.

"I trust that the honour is mutual. I am Phillip Caldrock."

He strung out the name like a statement of intent.

"Caldrock? Reminds me of shopkeeper in Belgium. You shop keep?"

A lost point for a direct answer and Phillip didn't give one.

"Ah yes, retailing. I have considered establishing a chain of quality stores throughout Europe but the demands for my services as a detective make it impossible."

Petrov's expression hardened a little.

"I say only that the truth will upcome," he announced and paused for a response to the much hyped phrase.

Philip smiled.

"I'm so pleased you agree with me, Mr Petrov."

To retain the final word, he turned quickly to the King.

"May I say that your palace is most impressive, Bill."

"Thanks. No more talk while we stuff ourselves with food. The meals are pretty good here."

Another lounge after the meal and unlimited coffee supply. Petrov had remained, much to Phillip's discomfort. The King leaned forward in his chair.

"Now I will tell you about this matter. Stesky is already aware of the details but all of you must treat it as completely confidential."

"Of course," responded Philip.

"A letter has gone missing. A very important document. To be exact, it is 50 percent of a two page letter that has disappeared. By this I mean the second page."

"A single sheet of paper?" asked Heather.

"Yes, exactly but this sheet, or the words thereon, could threaten the stability of this whole country."

"Can you reveal the contents?"

"I cannot. All I can say is that it is an unfounded libel against myself. However, in the hands of the less scrupulous members of the media, it could result in an upheaval affecting not only this country but all of Europe."

Petrov raised a hand.

"A cataclysmic event, my friends that I shall prevent by biting off the layers of the tearful onion until I find the essence of this matter. The truth will upcome!"

The King shrugged.

"Sorry Stesky, you haven't made any progress after a week so Phillip and Heather are taking over."

"I wait only for the first two or three murders. Then secrecy veils removal will be just exposing all to the little squirrel thingy that is my brain."

"Are you a loony?" asked Phillip cordially.

"This is not known word. Means genius?"

Heather moved on.

"So we are looking for half a letter. One sheet of paper."

"That is correct," said the King.

"What size is it? Is it written by hand?"

"The simplest response is to show you the first page."

The King reached into his pocket and pulled out a single sheet from a writing pad, folded in half. He handed it to Heather who examined it closely. Standard, cheap white paper and the message was laser printed.

'Page one of two.

This letter is very secret and must be read only by the Chief of Police who personally sent me to spy on certain high-ranking persons on an undercover sort of basis. Not undercover in the sense of covering my head with something that obscured my vision. That would render the whole assignment pointless as I would not be able to view any misdemeanours. No, the word is used in a more abstract sense to represent a secret spying assignment, which is what it is, as I said earlier.

Anyway, I now have something of great importance to report. When I say great, I mean it. It is so enormously significant that I can barely find the words to express myself. My message is very simple and can be contained in one sentence. Yes, just a few words will tell you all you need to know and the words are… (continued on page two of two, meaning the second page of this letter).'

She handed it to Phillip who read quickly.

"I have already made one deduction. This was composed by a simpleton, if not an outright loony. Did you write this, Petrov?" he asked.

The little man looked affronted.

"On the contrary wise, those words illuminating I found. A word outstands to my squirrel's brain. The word is 'secret'."

"Yes?"

"Ah but fortunately I recognise a little detectivity tricking. I say to you 'ee'."

"Would that be the squirrels talking?"

"No, no, my sad Englishman. The unconsidered letter of 'e' but twice that add to the secret word. But not anywhere, silly like. I put them like so!"

He scribbled quickly on a notepad and held it up.

"See Crete?" Heather enquired.

"Now you understand, my little angel lamby. Mystery have we begs for answer. And where to find? See Crete! Say I no more."

Philip smiled.

"Excellent. You have ceased talking. Your Majesty, the message mentions a Chief of Police. Have you contacted him?"

"Yes, I phoned and asked if he had any unknown people on spying missions. He was most emphatic in stating that he probably hadn't."

"Where was the letter stored?"

"It was kept in the drawer of my desk in this very room. Unlocked of course."

"I see. And who has access to this area?"

"Myself, my friends, government officials, other officials, any citizens who call, tourists, vagrants and servants."

"Then it is fortunate that you summoned me here. I will have your answer in 48 hours."

"Really? Super. I'll write you a letter of introduction that will allow you to see anyone."

The King scribbled a note on headed paper and gave it to Phillip who took it with a scornful look towards Petrov.

"Your Majesty has experienced the work of those blessed with squirrel brains, now you have the finest in Europe."

Back at the hotel.

"So what do you think?" asked Heather.

"I really don't know."

"But you said you'd have the answer in 48 hours."

"Necessary to stop that Petrov fellow boasting. Virtually anyone could have taken it so our only lead is the Chief of Police. He was mentioned in the letter."

"What did you think of the King?"

"A splendid fellow."

"Yes but something strange. I need to check on the internet."

After breakfast the next morning they were asking in reception for directions to police headquarters when a limousine pulled up. The same car as the previous night and same chauffeur. He presented them with a card that displayed just a few words.

'The Prime Minister asks if you would visit urgently.'

Another short journey to a large building in the centre of the capital. They were taken to the office of a short, unshaven man of about 50 with random brown hair.

"The detectives? Come in and sit," he greeted them.

They waited while he ran a hand over his bristly jaw.

"Right you two. Here's the plan. You look only for the missing letter page, got it?"

Philip nodded.

"Yes. Is there something else that needs resolving?"

"No, nothing. Absolutely nothing at all. You are not permitted to look into any of my business. That includes my documents and any contact I may make with any other people."

"Yes."

"You've got it then. No poking around in this office at all. If you do, I'm not answerable for the consequences. So just don't do it."

"Very well."

"Good. That's understood then. Have a lovely stay in our country."

Back to the limousine and they asked to be dropped off at the Police Chief's office. Not at all as expected. Just a small, ground level building of rough concrete. A rudimentary office inside, cheaply furnished with battered old desk and chairs, filing cabinet with a drawer missing and walls that were covered with various documents, fixed by sticky tape. Another surprise was the man himself. Tall and no more than 30 with dark hair and an immaculate uniform.

"Hello, I'm Ricardo, Chief of Police," he said in a deep, rich voice.

After introductions, they sat during coffee.

"Do you realise that the page of this missing letter, held by the King, mentions you specifically? It indicates that it was written by a spy that you assigned," declared Philip.

"I didn't know that. His Majesty didn't tell me."

"And do you know that the second page of the letter is fixed to the wall behind you. We both saw it immediately we entered."

Ricardo laughed.

"Everyone who comes here says that. The King, the Prime Minister, other ministers and plenty of others. They invariably point and say 'here it is'. It's so funny."

"Why?"

"Well, as if I'd keep a letter from a spy stuck on the wall where everyone can see."

"The typeface is identical although I can't read it from here."

Another laugh.

"Ridiculous."

"So where did it come from," persisted Heather.

"Oh, I don't know. It simply appeared there some days ago."

"You haven't looked at it?"

"Of course not. Why bother?"

"Can we read it?"

"No, I'm sorry. Everything on these walls is confidential police business."

Heather sighed.

"Then can I ask about the King? Have you noticed anything unusual about him recently?"

"No. Unless you include the prisoners."

"Prisoners?"

"Yes, the King asked us to pick up a miscreant from the palace and lock him up. He instructed me to put him in the old dungeon."

"Where's that?"

"It's below this building. The door on your right as you came in leads down to it."

"What was his crime?"

"I don't know. The King didn't tell me."

"What is this prisoner like?"

"Hard to say. He was wearing a rabbit mask."

"Didn't you take it off?"

"Impossible. It was a moulding of two halves around his whole head. The pieces were welded together."

"An iron mask?" asked Philip.

"That would be silly. No, it's plastic of some sort. Good likeness of a rabbit, though."

"You questioned the man, of course?"

"We're not allowed to speak to him on the King's orders. All we do is bring food to him. For documentary purposes, he's recorded as Mr Bunny."

"You said prisoners."

"Yes, an almost identical situation. Call from the King to take someone else to the dungeon. An important difference though. This one had a gorilla's head. Also it's a woman. She's down below as well."

"Can we see them?" asked Heather.

"No, sorry."

She paused in frustration.

"Have you seen the King writing anything recently?"

"Oh, probably."

"I looked at pictures of him from last week. Then he was holding the pen in his right hand but yesterday I saw him write left-handed."

"Maybe he's ambidextrous."

Another pause as Heather gathered patience.

"Ricardo. Let me describe a little fantasy to you. A small European country, led by a Prime Minister with criminal connections. He forms a plan to kidnap and lock away the King, subsequently replacing him with an impostor. Under instruction, this puppet proposes a law that allows the Prime Minister's sleazy associates to live in the country. A safe haven for them. A police spy sees what is happening and tries to send a personal message to his boss. The criminals intercept the first sheet but he somehow manages to stick the second page of the message on the wall of the Police Chief's office. Then he is then grabbed by the Prime Minister's people and they send him to join the real King in the cells. When the conspirators read the message, they realised the second page was missing and recruited detectives to find it. I expect this all sounds very silly."

"Ridiculous. What country would be that stupid?"

"Nevertheless, I think that is exactly what has occurred here," Heather declared in a formal tone.

"Are you a loony?" asked Ricardo.

Now the explosion as Heather rose to her feet.

"I have been very patient to this point. Now I'm going to take that letter from the wall and read it. I will become very violent if anyone tries to stop me."

"Is she always like this?" Ricardo enquired of Philip as Heather moved to the wall and took the letter. The same laser printed text as on the first page.

'Page two of two.

This is a continuation of the letter that started on page one and I emphasise that the contents of this sheet are just as secret as the words on the previous one. Some could argue they are even more so. In fact, measured on a scale, this second page could easily merit a nine and certainly no lower than eight. I say this because it contains the most important part of the message, the very crux of the matter, a revelation of earth shattering importance, I can tell you. The King is an impostor. In fact, I think it could well merit a ten, providing one is using a scale of one to ten because if not, it would be something different. Anyway, I must be going now and my good wishes to everyone. With the very best regards and yours sincerely, the Spy'

"Now who is the loony?" demanded Heather, still icy.

Ricardo studied the page.

"I deduce that this is a message typed on a Wartstrimp keyboard and printed on a Casungson mono laser printer in a modified Holvasica font. It was written by a woman of under 30 years of age. The text itself contains intriguing numerical references. Page numbers are laboriously defined and the scale of one to ten mentioned when other comparisons could have been used. The conclusion is elementary. A young female mathematics teacher who has been recruited as a spy."

"Jolly good," remarked Philip but Heather wasn't so impressed.

"Do you have any spies matching that description?" she asked.

"I've only got two. One of them is Ted Jones, a retired gardener but his identity is a total secret and I cannot reveal his name to anyone. The other is Marcia."

"Marcia?"

"Yes."

"Is she young?"

"Yes."

"Does she by any chance teach mathematics?"

"Yes."

"Well?"

"Ah, I see where you're driving to, as they say in America. You think there may be some connection between Ted or Marcia and this mysterious spy. That's a line of thought I hadn't yet travelled on, although I certainly journeyed on many other mental routes in this veritable maze that represents the human imagination. Far have I ventured and oomph…"

The soliloquy was castrated by Heather clutching his collar and pulling him forward to almost touch her nose.

"Ricardo. Do not test my patience further. Marcia wrote the letter to you. The letter states that the King is an impostor. Do you recall what I said earlier?"

"About becoming violent?"

"No. My little fantasy."

"Yes indeed. But then you referred to the police spy as 'he' and that doesn't fit with Marcia at all."

"I just assumed that it was a man."

"Are you going to let go of my collar now?"

"Not until you agree to take us to talk to the two prisoners."

"The rabbit and gorilla?"

"Yes."

"This jacket is the most expensive I own."

"I don't care."

"In that case we will see the prisoners together."

Heather released her grip and followed him out of the office with Philip trailing behind. Through a battered wooden door and down a winding concrete staircase. Down and down. And down. Eventually they reached a flat area with a single door, nearly completely rotted and fitted with a lock that had long since rusted away. It was hanging open from the last remaining hinge and Ricardo pulled it to one side.

Heather walked in, not expecting the unexpected sight that was far outside her expectations. A spacious chamber, smartly decorated with double bed, sofa and large screen TV. An adjoining bathroom, beautifully appointed. Two people in the bed, both sleeping soundly. A rabbit and a gorilla.

"They look so peaceful. We'd better leave them," observed Ricardo.

Heather gave him a look and moved to the rabbit, shaking its shoulder gently.

"Meal time already?" came the mumbled words.

"I'm sorry to wake you, your majesty but we are here to set you free."

"Who's that?" asked the gorilla, sitting up in the bed. Definitely female.

"And you are Marcia, the police spy who wrote the letter."

"We can't hear a word you're saying. These masks cover all over the ears. Just getting a mumbling sound," said the rabbit.

"Let me see if I can remove it," Heather responded, moving round to the simian side of the bed. The back of the mask had a red clip clearly marked 'open here'.

"Didn't you see this?" she asked Ricardo.

"No, I only saw them from the front. However, I suspect that it may well be a method of removing the animal head covering from these people. If you're going to open it, then I must leave. The King expressly forbade me to look at the prisoners. I'll wait upstairs for you."

With these words he left the chamber.

Heather immediately pulled the clip on the gorilla head. The mask opened to reveal a young woman with short brown hair.

"Hello! Wow, was I a gorilla? Great! My favourite animal."

"Your free now, Marcia," Heather announced with satisfaction.

"Don't be silly. That rabbit is a man," said the woman.

"I mean you."

"I mean you what? No harm? That's good then."

"Having read your letter, I shouldn't have expected much, I suppose."

"You've read my letters? That's a terrible thing to do."

Heather ignored her and unfastened the other mask.

"Your majesty. First you can get cleaned up and then I will accompany you to recapture your rightful throne," she declared to the bearded figure inside.

"What's all this your majesty stuff? I'm not in the spotlight now. Hey, who's this?" he exclaimed, seeing the brown haired woman.

"I'm Miss Gorilla."

"Really? Fantastic. Let's go for dinner tonight."

"I liked you as a rabbit but this is even better."

Now Philip stepped forward.

"Well done, dear. You've completed the first part of our plan. Of course, we knew that you two people are thespians who somehow displeased the King with your performances."

"What?" exclaimed Heather.

The woman smiled.

"We're both actors who performed for the King. For some reason he ordered us to be captured and sent here."

"Why the masks?"

"He said I acted with the ability of a gorilla."

"And that I performed like a rabbit," added her companion.

Back at the hotel and now Heather was asking.

"Can you explain what's happening?"

Philip nodded.

"No, I can't."

"Well, I'm totally lost now. I thought I had the answer but didn't expect to find two actors under the masks. It seems that they had displeased the King by their performances although it seems a bit excessive to send them to a dungeon. Still, I think the rabbit man did resemble the King under his beard."

"Let us return to the facts. We were summoned to locate part of a stolen letter. The Prime Minister threatens us not to look into his affairs. The Police Chief has the missing page on his wall. The letter states that the King is an impostor. It appears simple enough."

"Yes?"

"But I'm completely baffled."

"You've never admitted that before, Philip. I suggest we sit here and work it out between us. I don't care how long it takes, we'll resolve it."

"That's exactly what Pongo Wittler would have said to Wincepole."

"Then I'll try my best to do a Pongo."

She found a large pad of paper and joined Philip at the table. All the facts were listed and each character described on a separate sheet, starting with the King. During the next hour, papers were moved around the table innumerable times, new notes written, theories proposed and coffee consumed.

"I think we've reached a conclusion," announced Philip eventually.

"To call Clarissa?"

"Yes."

Heather pulled out her phone and dialled quickly, switching to speaker mode. The call was answered within a second.

"Caldrock Investigations. Don't continue this call unless you wish to talk about a really interesting crime," said Clarissa.

"It's me, Heather."

"You could be lying."

"Well, I'm not. I'm phoning from Anmonstein."

"Anyone could say that."

"Listen, Clarissa. It is me and I want to know something."

"Oh yes, I'm sure you do. Expecting me to reveal all sorts of secrets about our Agency, I suppose. Well, hard luck, whoever you are."

Philip leaned forward.

"We don't have time for delay," he said.

"Oh, Mr Caldrock. Yes, ask me anything. I think I should warn you that the woman you're with is pretending to be your wife."

"I know that. Now I'd just like to tell you of the events here since we arrived."

He spent some time describing in detail.

"Yes, Mr Caldrock."

"Heather suggested that it would assist in developing your investigative potential if we find that your thoughts coincided with my own conclusions."

"But I'm not in your class."

"Nevertheless, I would like you to try."

"My ideas would sound silly to you. It's like asking a cavewoman to compare herself to Socrates."

"Inside every cavewoman is an unreleased intellect. Although it may never reach my Socratic level, it is certainly worth hearing."

"I think I should stick to brain surgery and nuclear fission. I'll never be as good as you."

"Clarissa, please tell me your theories immediately."

"It's too embarrassing."

A pause while Philip ruminated desperately.

"I need your deductions to offer them as a diversion to the King whilst I pursue the real solution."

"Oh, right. You should have said earlier."

"Yes?"

"Earlier means before the current moment."

"The question was aimed at eliciting your theory and you will now recount it to me."

"Prime Minister criminal. He kidnaps and locks up King, replacing him with impostor. False King proposes law for Prime Minister's sleazy associates to live in country. Police spy sees this and writes message. Half message taken but spy manages to stick other half on police chief's wall before grabbed by criminals and sent to join King in dungeon. Both prisoners in animal masks to avoid recognition. When conspirators find second page of message missing, they recruited you."

"That's exactly what I said," exclaimed Heather.

"Listen lady, any more interference from you and I'll fly over there. You'll be sorry if I do."

Philip interrupted quickly.

"Don't worry Clarissa, I have this woman under control. Your theory is interesting but how do you explain the fact that the two prisoners say they are actors and not the king and a female spy."

"Easy. They're lying."

"An interesting idea. Why would they do that?"

"Because, during the incarceration, they found their DNAs matched and this caused what is known in science as a 'relationship' to develop."

"They fell in love?"

"What does that mean?"

"It doesn't matter. So why did this DNA relationship cause them to conceal their identities?"

"Because they plan to move elsewhere under new names and form a contractual arrangement, known as marriage to the layperson."

"Well, I think that's a good enough diversionary explanation. It should mislead everyone whilst I uncover the real truth."

"It is a bit feeble but may convince the King. Can't wait to hear the real solution from the master sleuth."

"Yes, right. However, it could be that certain confidences make it impossible for me to ever reveal that to you, Clarissa. I must be going now. Goodbye."

"Bye."

Philip put down the phone and looked across at Heather who shrugged her shoulders.

"That seems the right answer to me," she remarked.

"Possibly, possibly. I think we should return to the dungeon."

Ricardo's office, 15 minutes later.

"The letter has gone," remarked Heather.

He nodded.

"Oh, yes. The King popped in and took it. He said he was collecting all useless pieces of paper to feed the poor of our country."

"I didn't think he was so altruistic. I'd suggest that he sells it for pulping to some paper company that he owns."

"No, no. There is no opportunity for anyone to make money out of it. 100 percent direct to the people. All the paper is placed in a big heap and the poor can take all they want to eat. A dictionary will feed a family for a week."

Heather didn't pursue.

"We are here to visit the prisoners again."

"They've gone. The King took them as well."

"What for?"

"His Majesty mentioned that he planned to execute them. Decapitation. It's a royal prerogative to do that."

"Then we must save them. Where are they?"

"In the Palace, I would imagine. There's a special head chopping room there"

Heather laid a hand on his shoulder.

"Ricardo, I must tell you something. The real King was kidnapped and he was the one in the rabbit mask. The other was your own spy, Marcia."

"What!"

"I did try to tell you before," she added.

"But this is terrible. My own spy to be executed. One who looked up to me as her boss, trusted me to ensure she came to no harm. I must have coffee to console myself."

"But we can still save her."

"What! Save her? Can this be true? Has the shock sent me into exclamatory question mode? How?"

"Come with us to the Royal Palace."

Minutes later, they were entering the Palace. As before, no guards on duty and Ricardo was now in saviour mindset, pistol in hand and jaw jutting as he strode forward. Philip and Heather followed him through a series of rooms and then down a flight of stairs. A corridor with a door at the end marked 'Chopping Room'.

Ricardo burst into the chamber.

"Cease the activities that are currently occupying your bodies and minds. Or both. In addition, provide no indication of physical movement in any direction, including upwards!" he declared.

The chamber was small and fully tiled in a pleasant cerise colour. Drainage in the centre to make hosing down a very simple and efficient operation.

Five people there, not including the three who had just entered. That made a total of approximately eight, assuming that each of them was counted as one and they certainly were, as the hypothetical aggregator was most definitely a firm believer in total equality amongst humans. However, if a dog had been present in place of one of the people, then the total would have been between 7.28 and 7.41, dependent on the breed of dog and condition of its fetlocks.

That may well appear unfair to some dog lovers but it must be remembered that the average number of legs per capita would increase as would the combined potential for fetching sticks and dead rats.

The trio saw five people in the chamber. The two prisoners, masked again and on their knees. The King standing over them, large axe in hand. Next to him was the Prime Minister and in the far corner, an old man reading a newspaper.

"Who is that?" yelled Ricardo, pointing at the latter.

"Don't know," replied the King.

"Nor me," added the Prime Minister.

"Venerable but scruffy person, who are you?" Ricardo called.

The old man looked up.

"A vagrant of no fixed abode," he responded.

"Abode? What's that? And why is it not fixed? That could be dangerous. Get your abode serviced immediately."

The man nodded dutifully, picked up his paper and left.

"An innocent bystander," remarked Heather.

"I think not. Bystanding is a criminal offence in this country."

"Then I will change that law. By definition, all bystanders are innocent," announced the King.

"Okay, well said. Right, we'll be going then," responded Ricardo.

"No, wait," Heather shouted.

A silence as everyone looked towards her.

"My associate is requesting a cancellation of the 'we'll be going' plan and replacing it with a 'rescue the prisoners' strategy," said Philip belatedly.

The King looked at him.

"Ah, Mr Caldrock. I think your services are no longer required. I have recovered the missing page of the letter."

Heather moved forward and the men cringed slightly.

"I must now say words that I never thought I'd speak after the age of four. You are an impostor and this rabbit is the real king!" she declared, finger pointing at the long eared figure.

The King shook his head.

"No it isn't."

"And you were planning to decapitate him, as well as the police spy who revealed your subterfuge."

"No."

"You sold yourself to a bunch of criminals and are just a pathetic puppet."

"No."

Now Heather's offensive was losing impetus.

"Well, you should be ashamed of yourself."

"No. I feel quite good, actually."

Philip had been deep in contemplation but now whispered two words to Heather.

"Diamond Beetle."

She turned with a puzzled expression but he was already taking centre stage.

"My assistant's cleverly constructed accusations have given me all the evidence I need. You are correct in saying the case is finished, your Majesty. Their destination is perhaps South America? And the proposal withdrawn?"

The King grinned hugely.

"Yes and yes, Mr Caldrock. I trust you have enjoyed your stay and a very significant fee has already been transferred to your bank account."

Philip hustled a reluctant Heather from the chamber to find a large group of people milling outside the door.

"Anyone here not an innocent bystander?" he yelled.

Murmur of negatives but then one woman came forward, arm raised.

"I'm not one yet but I'm studying hard. Should qualify next year," she said.

"Then carry on," Philip instructed and guided Heather out of the Palace. The royal car waiting with their packed bags already inside. A short trip to the airport and on board the Royal plane.

"Now explain, Philip," demanded Heather as they settled in their seats.

"Like the Diamond Beetle of our previous royal investigation."

"Victor Velpronov was involved?"

"No. You and Clarissa were nearly correct. The King was kidnapped by a gang with a substitute put in his place and the impostor proposed a new regulation to permit criminals to reside in the country. A police spy wrote a letter, exposing the fake."

"What about the Prime Minister?"

"He wasn't involved."

"But he told us not to investigate his office."

"The whole thing was conducted by an outside criminal organisation and its leaders were seeking a country where they could reside without fear of arrest."

"So why did we let them get away with it?"

"This all occurred some days ago. The real King was freed with help from the Prime Minister. He captured the fake King and put him in a rabbit mask to ensure no one could think he was the real Monarch. It was only then that we were summoned."

"Why?

"To recover a letter stating that the King was an impostor. If that was found, the people could think that the real King was a fraud. That is why the Prime Minister warned us off investigating his office as he didn't wish the events to become public. Also he was wary that we could have been planted by the criminals."

"So that's why he wanted it. But what about the woman in the gorilla mask?"

"She was Marcia, the spy who wrote the letter. When the King resumed the throne, he found that she had formed one of Clarissa's close DNA relationships with the fake King. I believe she asked to be incarcerated with the impostor and whilst in the dungeon, they formulated a plan to go away together under the assumed identity of actors."

"But the King was going to execute them!"

"No. He just wanted to ensure the fake would be too scared to allow himself to be employed in the same role again."

"So your last questions to the King were asking what he would do with the pair and would he withdraw the new law allowing criminals to reside in the country."

"Eventually, it turned out to be very simple but I suppose that genius will always be the conduit of the great deductive magnifying glass of simplicity when it is directed by a master sleuth at the complexities of criminal deception."

"Sorry, can you say that again?"

"I don't think so."

13 THE NEEDLE IN THE HAYSTACK

"I need your help and I need it now," Inspector Foxhole declared.

Heather sat alongside him while Philip relaxed back in his chair and shuffled papers on his desk..

"In what manner may I assist?"

"I have to identify a murderer. Two days ago, an old farmer called Scrog Earthworm was found dead in his cottage. He lived in the village of Pugwurdle, just 15 minutes from here. After painstaking work to identify his killer, we've narrowed it down to one group of people. My men are getting them together now and I'm going to go in to face them, sort out which one it was and arrest them on the spot."

"So why do you need Phillip?" asked Heather.

"Well, to be honest, I haven't got much of an idea what to ask these people."

"When is the confrontation?"

"In about 25 minutes."

"Then we will accompany you and I will listen to your description of the events during the journey," announced Phillip.

10 minutes later they were travelling to Pugwurdle. Foxhole in the rear alongside Phillip and Heather. Fortunately, another officer was driving. The Inspector began his account.

"I'll give you the facts, Caldrock. Cold, hard facts. No dithering."

"All you've told us is that a man called Earthworm has died," interrupted Heather, fearful of a continuation.

"Right. The facts. Earthworm was seen entering his cottage at 11.34 in the morning. Just over two hours later, at 1.42, his neighbour, Mrs Cesspot found him dead as a brick."

"And what makes you suspect it was murder?" enquired Philip.

"Ah, a grim business. His face was covered with scratches, like the claws of a giant hound. Or lion. Or one of those big, hairy, fierce creatures. You know."

"Gorilla?" offered Heather.

"No, antelope. Anyway, he didn't die from the scratches. Oh no, it was suffocation said the medics. Probably caused by the black polythene bag that was tied around his head. Yes, Caldrock, a bag just like the garbage sack of a huge, vicious bear."

"Anything else?"

"Oh my word, yes. The worst of all. Old Earthworm's hair had turned completely white! As white as the fangs of the dreaded vampire bat of the Hundjong Andes! What sort of perverted creature could have performed this disgusting act?"

"A vampire bear hound?" sarcasmed Heather.

"Good point. One of those is kept as a pet by the lady who runs the village store. However, we checked and it has a waterproof coat for the time in question."

"Waterproof coat?"

"Did I say that? I meant alibi. Always getting them mixed."

"Allow me to summarise, Inspector. The indications are that Earthworm was attacked by some clawed creature and the shock of its appearance turned his hair white. Subsequently, his attacker tied a black polythene bag over his head and suffocated him."

"You've got it! Now, I'll surprise you. I deduced that the murder was committed not by any crazed, horrific creature from hell but by a human!"

"Because only humans can tie plastic bags," observed Heather.

"Well, yes. I think that's correct. So I gathered together the possibles in the human category and now we will see how they react to a face-to-face. Right, here we are."

They left the car and entered a building that was ringed by police officers. A large building, the village hall. Crowded inside. Not crowded, packed. People crushed together in the large chamber. Foxhole forced his way through the throng to reach a small, raised area with Phillip and Heather following the difficulty. Three steps up to the stage and they reached it as the Inspector began to address the crowd. From this vantage point, Heather estimated there were in the region of 186 people in front of him.

"Listen everyone! The murderer of Mr Earthworm is in this room today!"

He looked around for reaction and got several.

"Can't hear you!" yelled voices from the rear.

A few minutes and one megaphone later, everyone could hear very well, the ones in front pressing hands over their ears.

"Now, I want you to get into groups. The ones who will say nothing without their solicitors in the far corner on my right. Those who just want to babble on about meaningless conversations that have no relevance to the murder should go to the back left corner."

The turmoil of movement and police officers moved in to form a line around the two sections. 28 in the back right and 157 in the back left. Just one person left, a pleasant faced woman in her mid-twenties who smiled benignly.

"Now we're getting somewhere. Who are you?" Foxhole boomed through the megaphone.

She tried to speak but her voice was drowned by a babble of conversation from the back left. Loud discussions about how they'd never liked her, always found her a bit odd, didn't like the way she dressed, thought she mixed in bad company and a series of wild allegations regarding her relationships with every celebrity on the planet.

Foxhole turned to Phillip.

"I don't think I'll be needing you. My subtle questioning has produced the criminal immediately," he remarked.

"May I suggest that one of your officers removes the woman's ear phones before proceeding," Philip responded.

Foxhole gestured to one of his men and he confiscated the offending item.

"Sorry, did you want something?" asked the woman.

"We are investigating the murder of Mr Earthworm."

"Oh, well. I was talking to my friend Tilly the other day. You know, she's the one who makes cakes at home. Lovely they are and no one knows what her recipe is. I think the chocolate one is the best but my friend Annie says…"

Foxhole raised the megaphone.

"Please join the group at the back left," he boomed.

She wandered into the throng who now crowded round, telling her how they always knew she was a good sort, a pillar of the community and how terrible it was that the police could even have suspected her.

Now Phillip stepped forward and took the megaphone.

"My name is Phillip Caldrock, private investigator."

He paused for gasps of admiration and wasn't disappointed.

"Now I will ask some simple questions. You will respond truthfully as I am able to detect even the slightest form of deceit."

Dutiful and expectant nodding from the multitude.

"Those that did not know Mr Earthworm, leave the hall now."

24 people pushed through to exit the building.

"Now I want the people who are unable to tie a black polythene bag to depart."

It took several minutes for 148 men and women to jostle their way out. Just 14 left and Phillip descended the stage, dispensing with the megaphone.

"Please hold up your hands," he instructed.

"Good plan, Caldrock. Nail inspection," muttered Foxhole as he joined the group.

Nine more dismissed, leaving a group of five. They looked somewhat uncomfortable, surrounded by the 26 police officers recruited to control the original crowd.

Three women and two men, all with sufficient fingernails to scratch a face. Three of them had an unbreakable alibi. They had been performing lunchtime lap dances at the local cafe throughout the time of the attack. Philip dismissed the pair of women and the man. Just two suspects remaining as Heather joined him.

"Can we talk with the Inspector privately?" she asked.

"Is that necessary? I'm down to the last two."

"I think we need to. I've been thinking."

"Very well."

She led Foxhole and Phillip to the far corner.

"Inspector. First question is, was the body found in the bathroom?"

"Well, strangely enough yes. How did you know?"

"And you said Earthworm's hair had turned white?"

"I did."

"A final question. Did you find any recently used containers in the bathroom? Bottles of liquid, perhaps?"

"Right again. An empty bottle of something near the wash basin. Can't remember what it was."

"Excellent. Could you excuse us for a moment?"

"Certainly. I'll get back to the suspects."

"What's all this?" asked Phillip after Foxhole had departed.

"The solution. Earthworm wasn't murdered. It was accidental death."

"How could he have been attacked by accident?"

"I know what happened. He was attempting to restore his hair colouring, no doubt strands of grey were appearing and he was desperate to regain a youthful look. He used the colourant but it failed. Not just that, it turned his hair completely white. Imagine how distraught he would be to see himself in the mirror. He clawed at his face, desperate to rid himself of the ghastly reflection. Unable to bear the sight, he pulled a black polythene bag over his head and tied it tightly. What a relief as he no longer had to look at his image. Unfortunately, he forgot that he was also cutting off his oxygen supply and thereby perished."

A silence.

"Heather, you have surpassed yourself."

"Thank you, Phillip."

"Surpassed even your previous most esoteric visits to the fantasy universe."

"Sorry?"

"I can only surmise that you attempted to apply the inherent vanity of a photographic model to some old chap living in a cottage. Why on earth should he care if his hair was grey? And severely scarring his face would be of no assistance in correcting the appearance of hair follicles. I cannot even begin to conceive why he would subsequently cover his own head with a plastic bag. However, it is correct that the bag was there to conceal the wounds."

"Very well. You have another theory?" Heather responded knife edgingly.

"Yes, I've just realised what must have occurred. I just have to ask the two suspects more questions."

They returned to the pair in question. The woman was chubby, fortyish, nicely dressed with long dark hair. The man alongside was a different shape. Tall and lean with a bony face and long fingers. A tight fitting suit only served to accentuate the emaciated look.

Philip approached the woman.

"Your name, madam?"

"Cynthia Rosebush."

"Rosebush? You have an affinity with the produce of the Earth?"

"I do indeed. My husband and I spent lots of time in the garden. The true glory of nature is a wonderful gift. Is there anything better than seeing the first green shoots come forth in the spring?"

"Absolutely. I can imagine you relaxing on the veranda after a day's pruning, consuming tea and cake."

"How could you know we did that? Amazing, Mr Caldrock. I sit with Henry and the dog and we feel the warm arms of mother nature encircling us in fond embrace. I make my own cake. You must try some."

"What sort?" asked Phillip sharply.

"Fruit cake, of course. Lots of currants and raisins. Lovely and crumbly."

"Have you ever visited Australia?"

"No. Do you think I should?"

"It is perhaps unimportant. Thank you, Mrs Rosebush."

No Phillip turned to the man.

"Hello Sir. I trust you don't find the delay inconvenient?"

"Groat," the man responded in a deep, hoarse voice.

A short pause.

"Ah, you are Mr Groat. What is your employment?"

"Teach."

"A teacher? At a local school?"

"No."

"Where do you teach, Mr Groat?"

"Training college."

"And what subject?"

"Public relations."

"And your wife?"

"No wife. Had cat. It died. Live alone."

"I see. Do you also like flora?"

"Girl in pub? No."

"Plants and flowers, Mr Groat."

"No."

"And have you visited Australia?"

"Once. Gave lecture."

"Thank you, sir."

Phillip returned to Heather, deep in thought.

"Australia? A koala bear gone bad?" she asked quietly.

Phillip returned from his musing and smiled at her. Then he turned.

"No case is too complex for Phillip Caldrock and this one is simple in the extreme. I will now describe the events of that tragic day when Mr Earthworm met his sad demise."

The crowd gathered around. A horde of police officers, the two suspects plus Heather and Foxhole. Philip looked around imperiously before continuing.

"Mr Earthworm returned to his cottage at 11.34 and perhaps 10 minutes later, he had a visitor. A neighbour who asked to be given something. Milk or sugar perhaps, Mr Groat?"

"Sugar," responded the lean man.

"I suspect that Earthworm attempted to have a pleasant conversation about the weather or similar subject but found Groat his usual self, the most dour and unsociable person in the area. Eventually, he handed over the sugar and thankfully, Groat left. Then another knock at the door. Upon opening it, Earthworm was attacked. Jumped upon by a massive creature that raked his face with its claws. The shock of the sudden assault turned his hair white."

"Creature? A feral wildebeest?" enquired Foxhole.

"No. The dog of Mrs Rosebush. From the width of the marks, I believe it is an Icelandic Corgi Hound, fortunately of the herbaceous strain."

A sobbing sound.

"He couldn't help it. Just being friendly," blubbed Mrs Rosebush.

"Dragging the hound away, you then escorted Mr Earthworm to his bathroom where you attempted to assist him in treating the bloody scratches with a bottle of some antiseptic liquid. After making your apologies, which I am sure were accepted, you left the house while he was still tending to his wounds. Meanwhile, the hound, filled with remorse for its overzealous greeting, had crept back into the cottage through the rear door. It found Earthworm in the bathroom and offered its own canine apology, no doubt crouching down and looking upwards at him whilst whimpering softly."

"I didn't know that but he's always been such a polite and helpful doggie."

"Too helpful, I'm afraid. The hound perceived the distress caused by its actions and sought for a method to compensate. As everyone will know, dogs frequently have bald patches on their bodies as result of fighting, scratching or simple old age. They conceal these areas by taking spare hair from another dog, cat or other creature and fixing it over the bald space by licking it. The dog's saliva contains a strong adhesive which is activated on contact with its skin. Thus the repair is usually permanent. This is the reason why one never sees a bald dog."

"The dog glued some of its hair to the old man?" asked a puzzled Foxhole.

"No, no. That would be ridiculous. The hound would know that its saliva does not become adhesive on a human skin. It therefore conceived another plan, another way to hide the scratches. Dashing to the kitchen, it grabbed a black polythene garbage sack and return to the bathroom. It took just a second to leap up and pull it over Earthworm's head and then the dog knotted it firmly using paws and teeth. Pleased with its actions, it scampered outside to rejoin Mrs Rosebush and continue the walk."

"I was in the street, calling it," came a sob.

"Why didn't Earthworm remove the bag?" asked Heather.

"Two reasons. First, the dog had knotted it firmly at the back and out of reach. Second, he was one of the vast majority that find tying and untying polythene bags virtually impossible."

Now copious tears were rolling down the face of Mrs Rosebush and onto her clothes.

"He's such a good doggie. Never caused any problems since he eat the postman by accident."

"When was that?" Heather enquired.

"Last week. I'm afraid he was a little rascal before that. Always up to some mischief like biting off legs and arms. But he's settled down now."

Foxhole nodded.

"It was certainly a kind and noble act to cover up the marks of the attack."

"What is the name of this dog?" asked Heather, unconvinced.

"We named it Vicious Killer but everyone calls it VK. He's great around the house. Always helping to bite open chocolate bar wrappers and the like, providing he gets the sofa of course."

"Sofa?"

"He took a fancy to it when we first had him. Henry used to sit there but VK made it clear it was his place. Luckily, my husband is left-handed so it wasn't too important."

"Sounds like a really helpful dog," remarked Foxhole and the surrounding officers nodded agreement.

The newspapers were full of Phillip's latest triumph although the dog took centre stage. Various photos of it chomping reporters demoted the detective to a supporting role.

14 THE CASE OF THE MAN WHO ENTERED A HOUSE AND WAS NEVER SEEN AGAIN. EVER.

"This case seems a bit too trivial for you, Caldrock," remarked Inspector Foxhole.

He sat in Phillip's office with Heather alongside. All three were sipping from tubes connected to a large metal cylinder positioned against a wall. Clarissa's latest invention provided hot tea on a 24/7 basis and was powered by a mini nuclear reactor in the base.

"One may find the most fragile strand in a forest only to discover that it is part of a gigantic web, spun by a spider of a size never before witnessed by mortals," commented Philip.

"I may as well tell you then."

"My tentacles of attention are waggling in your direction," responded Philip but noticed Heather wincing at his words.

"Seems straightforward enough on the surface. A man walked into an empty house and disappeared. I'm sure the explanation is either spontaneous human combustion or a simple alien abduction."

"Describe the events in detail, if you would."

"It was six days ago. A Mr Connue was looking to buy a new home and the estate agent was showing him two houses that day. He viewed the first but didn't like it and then travelled to the second. They were in separate cars and the agent was there first. Connue arrived some time later and by then, the agent was in a rush to get to another appointment. He suggested that the client went in the house by himself while he remained in his car to telephone the people he was meeting and arrange a delay."

"Could he see the house from his car?" asked Heather.

"Oh yes, the property is close to the street. Connue took the keys and the agent saw him enter the house before making his call. It took a while to get through and about 15 minutes had passed before he finished. He assumed that the man would be out at any second and so decided to wait. Then he had a telephone call from his office. By the time that was completed, Connue had been in the house for nearly half an hour."

"Didn't the agent suspect something?"

"He said he wasn't concerned. People often take some time when looking at a new home, frequently taking a bath, making toast or having a lie down in a bedroom. However, he decided to go and fetch the man as he was now overdue for his delayed appointment. He entered the building and visited all the rooms. No sign of humanity anywhere."

"Did anyone see Connue?"

"I need to tell you the position of the house. There is a narrow communal alley on each side that separates it from the adjoining properties. It has a lawned area at the back encompassed only by a waist high hedge. This is surrounded by the gardens of the adjacent houses, one on each side and one at the back."

"So the garden would be clearly visible if the neighbours were in?"

"Yes and they were. During the whole of the time in question, there were people in each of the three adjoining gardens. On one side was a garden party for eight members of the 'Society of Honest People'. On the other, a group of ten nuns were holding an outdoor reunion. At the back a retired vicar and his wife were having lunch outside. All of these neighbours insist that no one had appeared in the garden. In fact, they had seen no signs of anyone in the house at all."

Philip nodded sagely.

"So the back of the building was under observation by groups of people but we only have the word of the estate agent regarding the front. Additionally, you mentioned that he was involved in a telephone conversation and I'm sure he could not have maintained continuous observation."

"True, Caldrock but just as the man entered the building, a touring coach broke down just next to the agent's car. All the occupants got out to stretch their legs. Every one of them saw the man go in and all were absolutely certain they saw no one leave the house."

"Reliable witnesses?"

"I think so. 34 police officers on a day's outing. After the agent had looked in the building, he told them the story and they all searched thoroughly. Every room, every cupboard was examined. Not a sign of anyone."

"This case intrigues me. When can I visit?" asked Philip

"Right away. I've had four men stationed around it and I can guarantee that no one has entered or left the building since the disappearance."

The door opened and Elizabeth entered, balancing a tray of teacups on one finger. She pulled the finger away, caught the tray safely in her hands and placed it on the desk with a satisfied smile.

"There we are. Can't have you sucking from tubes, can we?"

"Very good, young lady," remarked Philip.

"Shall I meet you at the house in say 30 minutes?" enquired Foxhole as he moved to the door.

"Yes indeed, Inspector," replied Philip.

Heather turned to Elizabeth after Foxhole's departure.

"Is Clarissa not in?" she asked.

"Gone away for a couple of days. I think she's still drawing up a contract for her fiancé to sign. Alistair and Angus are in China, negotiating some international trading agreement so I'm the substitute. Hope you don't mind but I brought an electronic keyboard with me. Just need to compose a couple of new concertos for tonight."

"You're giving a recital?"

"Nothing special. A place in London called the Royal Opera Hall or something. Just a few government people and the Royal family and hopefully Angus and Alistair will fly back in time to see it. I'm playing a bit of Mozart but the royals requested that I compose one or two concertos especially for the event. That shouldn't take more than an hour or so."

"The Royal family?"

"So I'm told. They seem to enjoy my music but it's a bit boring for me now. I'd rather be working on my chemistry or out on the firing range."

"Your mother and father must be delighted."

"We're a very close family. Clarissa and I fly over as often as we can."

"Where do your parents live?"

"In the Caribbean. They bought an island there. I find it a bit tedious though. They spend their time lying about on the beach, swimming and celebrity parties every night with all those stars from music and films. I'd rather be in the lab and Clarissa's the same. Still, Mum and Dad love the party scene."

Now Philip looked impatient.

"Very interesting. Now we have a case to solve and I'd like you to be involved, Elizabeth."

"Great!"

"I will drive and Heather can tell you the details during the journey."

They arrived at the house to find Foxhole waiting outside.

"This is the place," he announced.

"I was expecting something bigger and older," remarked Heather as she scanned a modern, compact construction with a narrow alley on each side.

They entered the house and explored. Not a long tour. Downstairs comprised two reception rooms and a kitchen-diner. A door on each side led to the alleys and one at the back to the garden. Upstairs, two bedrooms, bathroom and a small box room. A hatch in the ceiling of the upper hallway.

"The attic," said Foxhole, pressing a button on the wall. The hatch opened with a hum of electricity as a flight of steps slid down. Heather climbed up quickly but was disappointed to find only a compact chamber with white painted walls and murals of blue sky and clouds on the ceiling.

An empty, modern house.

Foxhole led them back downstairs.

"As I said, it seems pretty straightforward. I favour alien abduction over spontaneous combustion as there's no sign of any residual ashes. I believe that the entities were already inside the house and captured the man immediately. They then loaded the body on their spaceship, switched on the invisibility blanket and zoomed off to the outer limits of the universe. Either that or they used time travel."

"Were any of the windows open?" asked Philip.

"Not when it was searched and anyway, one of the neighbours would have noticed someone climbing out."

"Tell me more about this disappearing man."

"Mr Connue. He's 31, average size and good looking with a black beard. Works at the big bank in the town and they say he's an ambitious sort."

"Any criminal record?"

"Not really. He used to run a company that offered signed pictures of the British Royal Family, all forgeries of course but nothing could be proved. Then he made a lot of money selling tickets to fly to the moon on a new English spaceship. Even told customers the craft would stop off at their homes to pick them up."

"Who would be stupid enough to fall for that?" asked Heather.

A rueful look from Foxhole.

"Well, I managed to get my money back but most weren't' so lucky. Still, Connue was found innocent on some technicality. He claimed he was suffering from legal loopholes and they dismissed the case."

"Is that it?"

"Yes apart from the auction he held in Texas to sell the city of London."

"What, all of it?"

"No, that would be silly. Just the central area to include Buckingham Palace, Tower Bridge and the Houses of Parliament. A pretty good investment, if you ask me."

"But he didn't own it."

"Ah yes, that was the drawback. He claimed it was his property, even had a handwritten note that said it all belonged to him that was signed by the Queen, Prime Minister and American President ."

"What happened?"

"The auction went ahead and London was sold for 42,000 dollars."

"That seems a few billion dollars too cheap."

"True but most of the buyers were put off as the area hadn't been repainted for a while. Anyway, just as the auction closed, the FBI moved in."

"Connue must have been jailed for it."

"No, he was freed again when he claimed diplomatic immunity as a citizen of Atlantis. Even had a handwritten note to prove it."

"A not he wrote himself, no doubt."

"My word, I hadn't thought of that! No one bothered to check his credentials with the Atlantis government."

Heather was about to pursue the subject when Philip held up a hand

"This is a tricky case but I have ideas. Will you leave us here to evaluate the facts, Inspector?"

"Of course. I'll be waiting outside in my car."

Philip led Heather and Elizabeth to the kitchen where they sat on benches around the table.

"I'd be happy to listen to your theories whilst I cogitate," he said.

Elizabeth took the bait.

"I can think of several chemicals that could eat up a body completely but all of them would destroy the house as well."

Heather ignored that.

"Perhaps we should summarise the facts. A man entered this property. That was validated by the agent and 34 police officers. There were impeccable witnesses to say that he didn't emerge in the garden. Leaving aside any supernatural explanations, there are just two possibilities. Either he is still here or he left somehow without being seen."

"Or he was seen but not recognised!" exclaimed Philip.

"Not recognised?"

"You recall that the house was searched by this group of police officers. The man could have pretended to be involved with the search and the others believed him to be part of their group. Then he slipped away when they left."

"A good thought. I'll check with the Inspector."

She made a quick telephone call.

"He says all of the coach party were known to each other. Any strangers would have been recognised immediately."

Philip looked crestfallen but bluffed bravely.

"Just as I thought. No doubt you ladies have theories to throw in the pot, as it were."

Elizabeth offered immediately.

"If this man didn't come out, there's a good chance he's still inside. I could plant explosives to blow the place up. That would make him show himself."

"Or kill him," remarked Heather.

"Obviously that's a probability but I could arrange for a couple of helicopters to spray the ground with fire suppressant foam immediately after the explosion."

"That would save him?"

"No but it should preserve the corpse. After he's identified, I can save some bits for Clarissa to experiment on."

"What do you think, Heather?" asked Philip.

"I think you need to ask the Inspector something. Find out if Connue had changed his life insurance," she suggested.

He phoned Foxhole, nodding as he finished.

"Life insurance. Connue had increased the amount substantially just a few weeks ago. The payout is now over one million pounds. That has to be the first crack opening. A small crevice into which I would insert the nimble blade of my intellect to probe for the crannies of revelation."

"Yes, Philip."

"The Inspector also told me the name of the inheritor. A woman called Irna Knightslittle."

"A relation?"

"Connue apparently had no relatives. Originally a hostel for stray ferrets was due to receive all his assets but when he increased the insurance, that was changed to Irna."

"Then we should visit this lady and discover her relationship with Connue."

"I'll get the truth out of her," Elizabeth murmured savagely.

Heather shook her head.

"I need you to do a very important job. Stay in this house and watch for anything unusual."

"Okay. I've got about 170 texts on my phone to answer, most from Army guys wanting a date."

30 minutes later, Heather rang the bell of a flat on the second floor of a small block. It was opened by a woman of 30-ish with frizzy brown hair.

"Are you selling something?" she asked.

"No," responded Heather.

"That's a pity. My name is Irna Knightslittle. Knight with a K. Can you put me on the mailing list for a special offers and sell my address to every company you can think of, especially those with salespeople who come and visit you."

"We're not selling anything."

"You must have some useless plastic bits and pieces or stuff that you say cleans everything but never works and you throw it away after a week?"

"No."

"What about watches? You know, the gold ones that aren't gold but you don't tell me that."

"No."

"Property then! The timeshare for some rundown shack in the middle of nowhere that you got for nothing and are trying to make a fortune out of?"

"No."

"Then you must have come to tell me I've won a fortune in a lottery that I didn't enter in some weird country outside legal jurisdiction and you just want me to give you a payment in cash to cover the expenses of claiming the prize? I'd pay you immediately, if you are."

"No."

"It's got to be double glazing then. You should be ashamed of yourselves, trying to sell new windows to a lone woman. Disgraceful how you confuse and mislead with your smooth sales talk to take advantage of her."

"Shall I call Elizabeth?" asked Philip quietly.

"No, I can handle it," responded Heather, turning back with determination.

"Irna. This is Philip Caldrock, investigator and I'm Heather, his assistant. You are the beneficiary of the life insurance of Mr Connue."

"Who?"

"Connue."

"Never heard of him. No wait, I remember. Yes, we were close acquaintants and his sad loss is severely distressing for me, notwithstanding the fact that I benefit significantly from his tragic demise."

"You knew him well?"

"The previous statement represents my full and complete response under the terms of statute 624, otherwise known as the Witness Declaration About Knowing Someone Act of 1822."

"I understand you could get a million pounds."

"This amount, or any portion of it that I retain, in no way compensates me for the sad and distressing loss, hereinafter referred to as 'the loss of a distressing nature'."

"Any part of? You mean the amount is to be shared?"

A pause.

"Even one quarter, otherwise known as 25 percent, of the amount is a pretty sizeable chunk of cash. I can certainly buy a few timeshares with that, all right."

"Thank you Mrs Knightslittle."

Heather turned to find quite a queue had formed behind them. Smartly dressed men and women, all carrying briefcases and many with timeshare brochures under their arms.

"Where to now?" asked Philip.

"We found out why, just need to discover how."

"You think this Irna was involved?"

"Certainly. Now we need to get back to the house."

When they returned, Elizabeth was in the kitchen, scribbling in a notepad.

"Did you reply to all those men wanting to go out with you?" enquired Heather.

"Men and women. I sent a bulk response to say I was busy for the next 53 days."

"Why do that? You could have found your ideal partner."

"I'm just not ready for it. All that responsibility. I'm a woman now, just emerged from the chrysalis of girlhood and I don't want to be manacled by the chains of marriage too quickly."

"Are you like Clarissa and believe in the DNA partner thing?"

"No, that's ridiculous. I just need to experience a specific chemical reaction when I meet the right person.

"It's called love, Elizabeth."

"Don't be silly, that's only in the novels. Most women just look for the best deal they can get but my system is based on objective chemical analysis."

Heather sighed.

"So why come back here?" Philip asked her.

"Assuming the police outside have kept the place secure, we've come to find out how it was done."

"We've already searched. Anyway, he can't be still in the house after all this time. If nothing else, he'd have starved by now."

"Do you know anything about house construction, Elizabeth?" Heather asked.

"No."

"Do you think there is a possibility of a hidden chamber between rooms?"

"No."

"Would you like to provide more detailed answers?"

"Yes."

"Elizabeth, could a man be hiding in this house?"

"No."

"But we know he didn't leave the building."

"No."

Now the dam burst.

"Right, young lady. Listen carefully. I want you to stop saying yes and no and tell me how on earth it could have happened."

Elizabeth grimaced.

"When one joins the ranks of women, one often finds that the established members of that group are resentful for some reason. This emotion frequently emerges in the form of aggressive language."

"I'm very sorry and I apologise. You are most welcome addition to our community and I'm sure that, in time, you will prove to be a beacon for other women to follow. Now, for goodness sake, what is the answer?"

"Two possibilities. The compact construction of the modern house precludes the concept of any hidden chambers between rooms or floors. Consequently, no one could hide in the house."

"So what are the possibilities?"

"One would be a hiding place beneath the ground floor."

"I checked with the Inspector. There is no basement."

"Not a basement. These type of properties often have Intrasublar Block Foundations. That's like thick pillars underground. So there could easily be a cavity big enough for one person. If this house was constructed by that method, the entrance will be here in the kitchen. It's usually under the cooker or washing machine."

"You said you didn't know about house construction."

"Yes."

"I would rather not have any one word answers, Elizabeth."

"Okay, okay."

"I think I've got it. Do you know about house design?"

"Yes, yes."

"I think we'll check for the entrance now."

Much effort in moving kitchen appliances and floor covering. Elizabeth stamped her foot several times during the operation.

"Just doing an Intersect Impaction Test as specified in Architects Code 483."

"And the result?" asked Heather

"To use an architectural expression, it's a solid as a donkey's bottom. That means a Lateral Cubiboofbar was utilised."

"Yes?"

"Concrete blocks."

"Okay. So no room for a man."

"Not unless they were small enough to fit between the concrete molecules."

"Right."

"You don't approve of me doing this stuff, do you? It's not easy being a woman. Problems to overcome every day. Men find it easy, they can do what they like but for a woman, well, need I say more?"

"I think we all understand by now that you find it hard to be a woman," offered Heather understandingly.

"I don't know what I'd do without my chemical experiments and weapons."

"I really think you should go on a date with one of these hundreds of people who keep asking."

"Yes. Yes, I will. I'll pick one at random and do it immediately."

"And the other possibility, Elizabeth?" asked Philip with some impatience.

"Could have left. I'll pick one now from the messages on my phone. Number 84, I think. Let's see who it is. Here we are. Some man called John Sterling."

"Not the young multimillionaire tycoon?" asked Heather.

"Umm, yes, that's him. He'll do for tomorrow. I'll phone him now."

Ignoring Philip's look of frustration, she dialled quickly.

"Hello. Is that John? Elizabeth Hartwin here. I'll agree to go on a date with you."

A pause.

"Yes, yes. I'm sure it's fantastic, wonderful and all that. No, I'm not getting dressed up or wearing make up. I'm thinking we could spend the night by the river, taking water samples and analysing the chemical composition. Unless you know of any good surgical operations we could go and watch? No? Okay, river it is then. I'll meet you in Riverbank Meadows at eight tomorrow night."

Another pause.

"No, I don't want gold jewellery or flowers. I'll accept an Indonesian Spindle Legged Sea Toad but only if it's the blue variety."

Another pause.

"See you tomorrow. Bye."

"That seemed to go well," Heather remarked wistfully.

"He sounds all right. Said he'd fly back from his yacht in the Caribbean for the date. He's using his private helicopters and planes so I'll expect him to be on time. Promised to get his Indonesian office looking for the toad so I'll give him a bit longer to get it."

"He seems keen on you. Don't you think you're being a bit too demanding?"

"Me? Look, it's not easy being a woman."

She was about to enlarge on the statement once more but Philip interjected.

"Some time ago, did you say Connue could have left?"

"Yes."

"You're saying that someone could have gone out without being seen?"

"No."

"It can't be both."

"Yes."

Heather moved in again.

"Can you provide us with details how this could have occurred?"

"Yes."

"I really hope this millionaire is not easily deterred. Elizabeth, please describe how a man could leave with all these witnesses around."

The one who found it hard to be a woman sighed.

"I proved that he couldn't be in the house so he must have left. First, we consider possible exits. No tunnels and my first idea was that he went by hot air balloon or helicopter but unfortunately he couldn't do that without being observed by all the people in the gardens."

"We also know there was nothing taken from the house such as wardrobes or rolls of carpet," observed Philip.

"Yes, that was my second idea. So he must have walked out through one of the doors."

"There are four of them. One each side leading to the alleys, then the front and back door but he must have been seen by someone."

"Yes."

Now Philip smiled.

"I think I have it. Connue disguised himself as a postman or a worker for the water or electricity company. No one ever notices them."

"A report by the Useless Research On Government Grants Institute showed that is true for up to three people but not for larger numbers."

Elizabeth paused serenely, savouring the hilltop of attention. Several seconds before Philip and Heather spoke simultaneously.

"The Society of Honest People!"

Then Philip continued.

"He was a member of the Society and was expected at a garden party. Maybe he even arranged it for that time. Connue simply left the house, into the communal alley and joined the rest of the gathering. I was always thinking on these lines."

He waited for praise but no sign of that from Elizabeth.

"It's not easy being a woman, you know," she declared.

"You're saying we are wrong then?" enquired Heather.

"What? You think it is easy? Well I'd like to see you trying to construct a laser pistol with some man pestering you to go to a party with him."

"Yes, I'm sure that would be annoying."

"Or some rock star begging on his knees for a date while I'm analysing plankton."

"That must be an ordeal," agreed Heather, painfully aware that Philip was simmering.

"It was so simple being a girl. I could spend all day composing symphonies, experimenting with nuclear fission and feeding my rabbits."

"Of course, a woman takes pride in her abilities. This case, for example. Who else but a woman would know that Connue didn't go to the Society of Honest People gathering?"

"No."

"No?"

"Not because I'm a woman. I just happen to be a member of that Society and I know he's not in it. That's why he dressed up as a nun to join their reunion meeting."

"But he had a beard."

"An attempt to mislead. Plenty of time for him to shave it off. He had the nuns outfit and shaver in his briefcase. I made a quick call while you were out. The nuns didn't know each other, it was for those who had become novices 10 years ago."

"Well done, young lady. I did try not to reveal my conclusions to allow you to express yourself and I'm very impressed," Philip bluffed bravely.

"All the police need to do is follow Irna Knightslittle. At some point she'll go to meet Connue and give him the money," suggested Heather.

Elizabeth shook her head.

"No need. He's hiding in her flat. When I phoned, one of the nuns told me they had given a lift to the one with the deep voice after their reunion. Dropped her off just outside Irna's place."

"Yes, just as I suspected," declared Philip unconvincingly.

"I suppose I'd better get ready."

Heather clapped hand over mouth.

"I'd completely forgotten. You're giving a piano recital. Can you still get there in time?"

Elizabeth shrugged.

"Yes of course. They usually send a royal limousine with chauffeur and police escort. I'll have a quick shower when I get to the Hall and then ad-lib a couple of concertos. A bit of chatting to the Royal family and government people afterwards and then they put me in a luxury suite at some hotel."

"A hectic schedule."

"Not really. I'll lie in until five tomorrow morning and then do a couple of hours on the firing range. After that, I've got to pop over to Spain to collect a few chemicals and then back in plenty of time for my date. Analysing river water! Wow! I'm really looking forward to that."

Heather sighed deeply.

"It's not easy being a woman, it is Elizabeth?"

15 BB

Inspector Foxhole staggered into Philip's office, mopping his brow.

"It's trouble, Caldrock. Big trouble. An epidermis of crime."

"A skin?"

"Yes, asking for your help."

"Epidemic is the word."

"Is there? Well I feel fine, apart from the stress, that is."

Before continuing, Philip glanced at Heather who was taking a seat alongside the Inspector.

"Please provide information on this crime wave."

"The main bank was almost broken in to when the vaults were stuffed full of new gold shipment."

"Almost?"

"Yes, the break-in was at the place next door, a second-hand sock company. Pair of men's grey socks believed to be missing. But it could easily have been the bank. All that gold! Earth shattering!"

"But it wasn't stolen. The next event?"

"The precious stones jewellery shop. Incredible burglary. We've worked out that the criminal parachuted onto the roof from a balloon and then slid down an air conditioning duct to the top floor. There were sensors everywhere but they avoided them by walking on the ceiling with suction pads. Descending by this method to the ground floor showroom, the thief dangled upside down, holding a glass cutter with their teeth. They cut a circular piece from the top of a cabinet whilst pressing against it with a gloved hand covered in adhesive. This held the cut glass circle while they reached into the cabinet with the other hand and took a gold necklace."

"How can you be sure of these events? A CCTV system?"

"No, they've got one of those but it was tuned in to another channel. We pieced it together quite easily. Marks of suction pads on the ceilings, the glass cutter was left on the floor with teeth marks on it alongside a sticky glove attached to a circle of glass."

"A gold necklace? That must have been worth something," enquired Heather wistfully.

"Yes indeed. Those were my exact words to the shop manager. The five remaining necklaces on display were each priced at over a hundred thousand pounds. Incredible. The missing one was worth two pounds."

"Two pounds?"

"It was a gold coloured plastic, just there as part of the display."

"Were there further similar crimes?" asked Philip.

"The gigantic train robbery. A special train with just two carriages. The first held six armed security guards and the second was security sealed and made of armour plated steel. Just a large safe inside packed full of banknotes and gold bullion. We believe the thief jumped from a bridge onto the roof and then forced open the sun window."

"A sun window?"

"Of course. All armoured carriages must have one under the health and safety provisions. It's not permitted to rely solely on artificial light in case of power failure. Anyway, they got in through it and reached the safe with three million pounds worth of gold and banknotes inside."

"I will predict that something went wrong."

"Thanks to the stringent security features, the robbery failed. There were signs that many attempts had been made to open the safe. Chisel marks, scratches and an electronic thingy that helps you find the combination was left behind. Look, here's a photo we took when we arrived."

Foxhole handed over a large print showing a battered, scratched safe. Heather pointed at a large notice, taped to the door. It read 'Combination is 987654321'.

"The combination was displayed on the safe door?" she asked.

"Of course, most companies do that. No one could possibly remember a nine figure number. Actually, it's a very clever code. Reversing the sequence from nine down to one would be impossible to guess."

"Are you saying that the thief didn't notice this sign?"

"Can't have done but it's easily missed."

"It's printed in large text on fluorescent yellow paper."

"Yes, nearly didn't spot it myself."

"So nothing was taken," summarised Philip.

"Oh yes. This cunning thief took something all right. A mop."

"Did you say mop?"

"Yes. Nothing else movable in there."

"Apart from incompetence, why should you link these crimes?"

"Two B's."

"Shakespeare? An unlikely suspect."

"Double B. The letter B in duplicate. A pair of B's. Printed on a business card and left at the scene of each crime. The burglar also wrote a note on the reverse of the card left in the train."

Foxhole produced a business card. On one side 'BB' was printed bold and large. On the other was a handwritten message. 'The safe was too tough for me this time but I'll soon find another one to open. Oh yes, in the pretty near future, everyone will have heard of me'.

"The 'BB' could be initials," observed Heather.

The Inspector mopped his brow again.

"Yes, that's possible or maybe an organisation. 'Brilliant Burglars' or something similar. I need help here. Very skilled robberies but no clues."

"I think there is little point in wasting my efforts by examining the scenes of the crimes. I propose that we set a trap," said Philip.

"Trap? A lure to entice this person or persons unknown to come forth and attempt to purloin some irresistibly valuable item that we place in a position of apparent insecurity whilst surrounding the area with trained personnel, cleverly hidden from view?"

"Not quite. The item must not be in a place of insecurity. One common factor in the robberies is that the target was significantly protected. I theorise that the perpetrator only attempts the challenging crimes."

"And has a 100 percent failure rate," remarked Heather.

"We must allow for that in our plan. Just one other point, Inspector. We are trying to deceive a very skilful criminal and I think it best if your people are not involved. Any sign of a police presence and they will not proceed."

"We could try not wearing uniforms."

"I think not. I am proposing to ask Elizabeth and Clarissa to assist us in apprehending the miscreant."

"My god, man. Elizabeth Hartwin, the one girl army? Her sister is pretty tough but I wouldn't allow any of my officers in the vicinity when either are in aggressive mode. Both of them together? Enough to make a battalion run for cover."

"Good. Then it's settled. Just leave it all to me, Inspector."

An hour after Foxhole had departed. A full-scale planning committee in Phillip's office. He sat behind his desk with Heather in front of him, flanked by

Clarissa and Elizabeth. Having described the background, he was now outlining a plan.

"I propose to plant a story in the media to announce that a van will be coming to Mapleton with a large shipment of gold, jewels and banknotes. The story will specifically state that the van is totally secure and no one could possibly, ever, at all break into it. That should attract this BB."

"I could travel on the roof and mow down anyone who comes near the van. A couple of automatic laser guns would do it," announced Elizabeth.

Clarissa looked at her coldly.

"You're so bloodthirsty. Far better to electrify the bodywork so anyone who touches it is fried to a crisp immediately."

Philip held up his hands.

"Please, ladies. My plan is that Clarissa drives the van, disguised as a guard and Elizabeth hides in the back with the safe. Heather and I will follow the van in our car."

"Hand-to-hand combat! Great!" enthused Elizabeth.

"You could drive with me in the back. I'm better at martial arts," observed Clarissa discontentedly.

"No you're not."

"I am. You're too emotional and always breaking people's arms and legs. I can render them unconscious in under three seconds."

"You can not! Last time, I measured it at 3.84 seconds."

"I've improved since then," insisted Clarissa.

"Me too."

"And I don't get my top covered in blood."

"That's not fair. Cheap shot. At least I can carry a tea tray safely."

"Also cheap shot."

Philip interrupted swiftly.

"Now, ladies, if you will permit me to remind you. I am the master detective and you are both employed by me."

Horrified looks on the sisters faces.

"Mr Caldrock, I am so sorry," grovelled Clarissa.

"And me. I'm even sorrier than she is," added Elizabeth.

"Some time ago, you were outlining a plan, Philip," reminded Heather.

"Ah yes. Clarissa will drive, Elizabeth will be in the back and we will follow in our car."

"When is this to happen?"

"Tomorrow. You can phone the newspaper and local radio stations to spread the word. Clarissa can hire a van and Elizabeth find some cheap imitation jewels to make it look real."

The next day, one hour after midday. Or 1 pm. Or 13.00 hours. Heather sat next to Philip as he crawled along behind the white van. They were two miles outside Mapleton, moving along tree-lined country roads.

"When you think the thieves will make the attempt?" she asked Philip.

"Imminently."

She followed his gaze to the van ahead. It was passing under a row of tall trees and something was visible in the branches. Something dark with flashes of white. With amazing agility, the figure swung from branch to branch and then made an astonishing leap directly onto the roof. The roof of their car.

"Drat!"

Heather heard the word clearly. A woman's voice. Suddenly she saw a head upside down outside the open car window. A black mask across a face with startling blue eyes. Bright, glossy red lipstick. A tight fitting black cap with a broad white stripe running back from the forehead and similar ones from each cheek.

"Terribly sorry to interrupt but I wonder if you could speed up a tad and get a teeny bit closer to that van," asked the woman.

Heather could only gaze with open mouth but Philip responded immediately.

"It would be a pleasure, madam."

He accelerated steadily.

"Thank you so much," responded the masked figure and the face disappeared.

Now the car was about three metres from the van and Heather heard a thump on the roof. Then the figure dropped down, straight legged onto the car bonnet bending knees as it landed. With a cry of 'Uppeeee', it sprang upwards in a forward roll to fly in an elegant curve onto the roof of the van. The woman turned after landing and mouthed the words 'thank you' while giving a wave.

"That was incredible," gasped Heather.

"A very athletic performance from a young lady with an excellent figure."

In normal circumstances, she would have bridled at that comment but she had to admit it was true. The girl wore a skin tight, one-piece black outfit with just the three broad white stripes around the head. Not unlike a fashionable skin diving suit but modified to include a mask across the eyes. Now the woman was crouching on top of the van, using some sort of cutting equipment that had been clipped to a wide belt around her waist.

Heather spoke quickly into her mouth piece. They were all equipped with Clarissa's new headset design that gave crystal clear communication.

"Elizabeth. The thief is on the roof. It's a woman," she whispered.

"Yes, I can hear her. From the sound of it, she's using a Pollak-Chinweld laser to cut out a hole. Are you sure you don't want me to shoot her?"

"Definitely not. Just see if you can capture her without shooting or breaking any bones."

A long sigh.

"Okay then."

"As soon as the girl is inside, tell Clarissa to stop the van," instructed Philip and Heather nodded.

Now the lithe figure had finished cutting and rose to her feet, holding a neat square of metal. It was unfortunate that, at that moment, the van passed under a thick overhead cable crossing the road. It hit the metal square and twisted it horizontally with the woman still holding on. Within a microsecond, she was standing on the square, balancing perfectly with arms spread.

Philip screeched to a halt directly underneath and jumped out of the car.

"Can we start again?" asked the balancing figure above him.

He was about to respond when she began to slide. The cable sloped slightly towards a pylon in the field across the road. Like a professional surfer, she balanced exquisitely whilst gaining momentum. Heather watched her accelerate towards the pylon and then, at the last moment, she jumped upwards in a series of backward flips to land perfectly in the grass with arms outstretched, just like a Bulgarian gymnast.

Philip began to applaud and the girl smiled and bowed. Then she squealed.

"Eeeek! I've landed in something disgusting!"

By this time, the two sisters had joined the onlookers.

"You look great!" yelled Elizabeth and the woman responded with a wave, whilst wiping her feet on the grass.

"I'll be back," she called cheerily and then sprinted off into a nearby wood.

"From her stride pattern and thigh proportions, her age is between 21 and 23," announced Clarissa.

Wasn't she terrific?" asked her sister.

"Her covering was ostentatious, her outfit would elicit positive responses from the subtaminar glands and her movement demonstrated linear synchronisation between neural activators and specific muscular groups."

Elizabeth beamed.

"Yep, you always say that when you see a woman you like."

Now Clarissa grinned.

"She's okay."

"But she's a thief," remarked Heather dubiously.

"That's true and under my duty to the state, I will apprehend her at the first opportunity. However, any future judgements will recognise that her activities have caused no injuries to anyone, including but not limited to innocent bystanders," Clarissa declared laboriously.

Philip broke up the woman talk.

"Now everybody listen. We were unsuccessful this time, not through any failure in my plan but as a result of an unforeseeable circumstance. I am calling a meeting of you all in my office at ten tomorrow morning when I will conduct a brainstorming session."

Heather nearly asked the 'do you think that's wise' question but held back.

The next morning, 10 a.m. Philip had acquired a meeting table with four chairs. He sat at one end, facing Heather with a sister on each side and now opened proceedings.

"Brainstorming. We are faced with a female miscreant in excellent shape. She is clothed in a skin tight black bodysuit with white stripes around the head that serves to emphasise her remarkable figure. However, she is incompetent, despite her outstanding physical assets."

Heather gave him a look, taking exception to the references to the female form. She also had a bad feeling about his brainstorming concept and a glance at the two sisters only reinforced her trepidation. They were tensed, bright eyed and facing each other like gunslingers in a fast draw competition.

Philip continued.

"Now I've been reading up on this. Brainstorming means you shout out any ideas on the subject, however silly they may sound. Do you understand, girls?"

"Yes," Clarissa and Elizabeth responded immediately and in unison but their eyes remained fixed on each other.

"I think they've done this before," remarked Heather.

"Yes."

Same instant reply.

"Count down from three please," asked Clarissa without moving her gaze.

"Very well. Three, two, one, go!"

An avalanche of speech buried the end of his count. Almost impossible to believe that the English language contained so many unique words, and there was excessive use of those not found in any standard dictionary. Perhaps they were only listed in obscure medical or scientific tomes. Both sisters spoke simultaneously, matching each other word for word at a speed that jarred the hearing. Their voices became louder and louder until finally, Philip shouted for silence.

"I scored 1,124 words, two more than you," announced Clarissa.

"No, you repeated 'perspicacious' three times, at numbers 241, 843 and 1,072."

"I did not. I said perspicacious, pernicious and perceive."

"No you didn't. I think your mind's on your marriage."

"It is not."

"Yes it is."

Philip looked at Heather in appeal and she answered the call.

"Stop all that, girls. Let's forget the brainstorming. Each of you will describe your best plan, starting with Elizabeth."

"But I'm the eldest," complained Clarissa.

"Only by chronological measurement," responded her sister.

"Stop!" Heather shouted, a flush appearing in her cheeks.

Silence before she continued.

"Now, ladies. I have spoken to both of you before regarding the responsibilities and techniques of womanhood. When you join the ranks, you must abide by our own methods and protocols that have served us so well since the beginning of time. These are subconsciously communicated to every girl when she becomes a woman but sometimes the message doesn't get through properly. You will know that none of these secrets can be spoken of in the presence of a man and you must remember that Philip is present. I therefore now expect you to behave accordingly."

The sisters stared at her, mystified for a second and then their eyes opened wide in understanding. Suddenly they were adjusting their clothes and tidying their hair. Clarissa even produced a hand mirror to facilitate the operation.

"I'll start, if that's okay with you," offered Elizabeth, smiling at Philip.

His expression matched the girl's initial mystification but in his case, it had remained and even intensified.

"Yes of course. Proceed."

"I'm sure you'll find flaws in my proposal but I'll go ahead anyway. Recognising this thief's gymnastic ability, I suggest that's we draw her into a confined area and drop a large net on her. That should negate her physical prowess and permit a swift capture."

"Yes, that's certainly an idea. And you, Clarissa?"

"My plan can't be as good. Elizabeth is always so much better at pushing her ideas through. I suppose I'm just not aggressive enough."

Philip smiled benignly.

"Not at all, Clarissa. I've always respected your opinions. Please go ahead."

He didn't notice that she had turned her head slightly and winked at Heather, nor Elizabeth squeezing her lips together in an undermined sort of way.

With an innocent glance at her sister, Clarissa continued.

"I don't think we need to invite a robbery. I just have a sort of woman's intuition that this 'BB' is really seeking notoriety. She simply wants to be famous. I'm sure you've already thought of that, Mr Caldrock."

She looked at him, wide-eyed and Philip smiled.

"Indeed that was most definitely an aspect I was considering for exploitation," he lied.

"Well, I was going to suggest that we announce a 'BB' fan club. Either Elizabeth or I could be the founder and dress up in a replica suit. We could rent a hall somewhere and try to get people to join is. I'd be very surprised if this woman didn't come to see her admirers."

Now Elizabeth was reading the game.

"Clarissa will be so much better in the suit. If I wore it, I couldn't have anything on underneath otherwise it would look lumpy on me," she suggested primly.

Heather jumped in as Philip hesitated.

"Very impressive. You have both definitely absorbed at least some of the secrets of womanhood. That was a good comeback, Elizabeth. I thought Clarissa had you beaten."

"I didn't understand that," said Philip with a bemused expression.

"I certainly hope not. Now I thought Clarissa's idea of a fan club was a good one."

"Yes, I was just musing on the problem of Elizabeth's lumpy body suit."

"That was the intention but you can stop now. I'd suggest that both of them dress like this thief and if she comes, I very much doubt if they'll let her escape. We'll have to keep out of sight as she's already seen us close up."

"Good point. What we need is a hall with an adjoining room where we can watch proceedings on a screen."

Elizabeth smiled coyly.

"I know somewhere. Givit Hall, near to Mapleton library. I did a charity recital there and told lots of those rock groups to come plus a bunch of Hollywood film people."

"You had them collecting from the public?"

"No, that's ridiculous. Why should average people be harangued to give their hard earned money? All the celebrities are massively wealthy so when they arrived, I suggested that each gave half a million dollars. They all agreed."

"Suggested?"

"I was wearing a pair of Cortax repeating automatics at the time but that was only because I was going for target practice later. Clarissa was there and she'll confirm it."

Her sister nodded.

"It's true. I collected the cheques while Elizabeth was playing. Most of the guests started asking for expenses so I had to show how giving and taking are like fingers."

"Fingers?"

"Yes. You could only give with your fingers but even if a few of them are broken, you can take in your palm. Anyway, I demonstrated it to a couple of the rich scroungers and they saw it my way."

"So you think we can rent this hall?" asked Heather.

"They said I could use it any time I wanted," responded Elizabeth.

Two days later. Givit Hall. Clarissa behind a desk inside while Elizabeth encouraged passers-by to enter. Significantly encouraged by physically shepherding women inside. No need to persuade the men, the body suit she was wearing did that job well. The sisters had printed colour posters that were fixed to the walls. They portrayed the dark suited figure in different poses and each was titled 'BB who is she?' in large text.

In an adjoining chamber, Philip and Heather sat in front of a video screen, scanning every new arrival.

"I don't see any young women with blue eyes and red lips," remarked Philip.

"She might be disguised. Contact lenses and change of lipstick is simply done. Look, here's Elizabeth!" exclaimed Heather.

A body suited figure had rushed into the hall.

"BB is waiting outside to sign autographs!" she yelled.

The hall cleared in a second and Philip and Heather rushed after them into the street. A small lorry had parked across the road with a video screen mounted on the rear. It displayed the words ' BB is here' with an animated sequence showing the figure back flipping across the screen. No driver in the cab.

Clarissa and Elizabeth joined them.

"Who was the driver?" asked Philip.

Elizabeth shrugged.

"I don't know. I was helping an old lady into her car when it arrived."

"How did you know BB was going to sign autographs? It doesn't say that on the screen."

"No."

"No what?"

"I didn't."

"Didn't what?"

"Didn't know."

Realisation struck like a giant gorilla landing on a mattress.

"Someone came in the hall and shouted," said Heather.

The sisters rushed inside like hyper charged gazelles with Philip and Heather behind. They entered the hall. Empty, apart from a third suited figure at the far end. She was sitting at the table and writing rapidly.

"Hello!" called Elizabeth and the woman looked up, a grin visible under the mask.

"You two look great! Clarissa and Elizabeth Hartwin, I believe."

"You know about us?"

"Who doesn't? I really appreciate this fan club idea and I've just signed lots of autographs for you."

Another smile and even Heather was captivated.

"What does BB stand for?" she asked.

"You didn't guess? That's disappointing. I'm Badger Babe."

"Wow! That's a great name. I love badgers. Why don't I ever think of things like that?" cried Elizabeth.

"Stupid of me. Should have recognised the typical head markings," added Clarissa.

"You look fantastic in that suit. I wish I had your figure," her sister continued.

Another brilliant smile.

"That's silly. It fits you perfectly."

"Really? I tried very hard to make it like yours but had to do it from memory."

"Got a camera?"

"Yes."

"Then take me quick before I go."

Elizabeth pulled out her phone and began to click rapidly. Then Badger Babe rose from the table and moved towards a door at the back of the hall. Heather glanced at Philip but he appeared to be transfixed by the vision.

"Wait! We're here to catch you," she called without conviction.

"You can try," grinned the woman and began a series of forward flips, ending with a leap directly over them. Within two seconds, she was gone.

Heather looked at her companions. Elizabeth displayed a strange expression, Clarissa smiled and Philip was still wide-eyed and silent.

"That went well then," she remarked.

"I'm in love, Clarissa," beamed Elizabeth.

"About time but I thought you preferred men."

"That's not important, it's the just the person. Wow! I hope those photos are good."

She began to check the media files on her phone and Philip finally showed signs of existence.

"A very remarkable woman," he murmured.

"She does have a somewhat magnetic persona," Heather responded but inside, she shared the general attitude of unbridled exhilaration.

"However, I suppose she does remain a criminal and we really should attempt to curtail her activities," Philip continued with lack of certainty.

"If I was her partner, I'm sure I could change her to work on the side of the law. A vigilante! We could go out together at night and clear crime off the streets!" announced Elizabeth.

Clarissa looked doubtful.

"I can't support that unless I match your DNAs. You'll have to find out her exact age."

"I don't care. I'm going to find her and marry her," insisted Elizabeth.

"But she may already be married," remarked Heather.

"I just know she isn't. Wow! Isn't it great being a woman?"

Philip regained some composure.

"I have reached a decision. We will allow Elizabeth one week for an attempt to convince Badger Babe to give up her criminal activities. If she fails, I will be forced to recommence the search and will most certainly succeed. Is that acceptable?"

Elizabeth nodded.

"Make it 72 hours. A week is much too long. I'll find her."

That evening, Heather was driving home with Philip when they became trapped in a traffic jam near the town centre. Horns were blaring but many had left their cars to join a crowd further on.

"We'd better see if my services are required," said Philip opening the car door.

They reached the edge of a milling throng who were gathered in a small square. A rope had been stretched between buildings and two figures were balancing on it, both wearing bodysuits.

"Badger Babe and Elizabeth," murmured Heather.

"Ad they appear to be arguing."

The pair seemed oblivious to their precarious footing, Elizabeth standing with one hand on her hip.

"...and if you don't stop thieving, I'll have to shoot you," she called loudly

"When someone doesn't agree with you then you always just go for your gun!" yelled BB.

"That's not true! I also use a laser rifle."

"Well, I'm enjoying the robbery thing too much to give up. Tomorrow, I'm going to steal the Golden Mask from the museum and no one's going to stop me!"

"You're wrong. I'll be there."

BB brushed a hand over her capped head before turning and marching back along the rope to disappear on the roof of a building. Now Elizabeth appeared to notice the onlookers for the first time.

"What are you looking at? Go away before I get annoyed."

She waved a pistol to emphasise and the crowd dissipated immediately. All except Philip and Heather.

"Don't worry, I wouldn't shoot you," called Elizabeth and then ran back along the rope in the opposite direction to Badger Babe. She was quickly lost to view in the murky roof.

""I'm afraid it doesn't seem to be going to well," remarked Heather.

"That's women for you," responded Philip unwisely to be met with a frosty pursed lips response..

A large crowd the next morning at the museum. Philip and Heather inside the main chamber where the Golden mask was on display. An invaluable Inca relic in a clear plastic case was in the centre with a uniformed security team around the walls. Next to a mask stood a grim faced Elizabeth, simply dressed in jeans and top with no sign of weapons.

"I suggest we leave," remarked Philip.

"You don't want to wait?"

"Follow me, dear."

He led her from the chamber and into the main hallway of the museum. Several doors leading off and he guided her through one of them.

"This is the 1960s room," she said.

"Exactly."

The room was smaller than the central chamber but a similar layout. The central display here was a toaster with a card that read ' this is polystyrene replica of a 1960s toaster as used in households of that era'.

A plastic showcase was apparently unnecessary for this article.

"If you recall BB's previous history of blunders, this is her most likely target," remarked Philip.

"Yes, I see. It's the most worthless exhibit in the place."

An untidy, slim figure in a baggy museum curator's uniform entered.

"Good morning, Badger Babe," Philip called loudly.

The figure straightened up and the white hair was removed to reveal a mask.

"How did you know?"

"Curators don't usually wear pink trainers. Conservative black shoes are more the style."

Now the girl stripped off the uniform to expose her trademark bodysuit. The startling blue eyes regarded them thoughtfully.

"You're not going to try and stop me, are you?"

"No but I will."

Elizabeth emerged from behind a genuine 1964 self-assembly wardrobe in imitation pine.

"You were in the other chamber. How did you get here?" exclaimed Heather.

"That wasn't me. I hired a double."

Now BB moved to the centrepiece toaster.

"Well, I'm taking it now. I have to do it. I mean, in normal life I'm continually pestered by men demanding dates and they never want to do anything interesting. It's so hard being a woman."

Elizabeth was at her side in a flash, eyes wide.

"That is so true. How many texts do you get?"

"Maybe 50 every day, all wanting to go out with me."

"Fliff! That's nothing. I get nearly that many in an hour. Just want me to go to parties and things. It would take me all day to get the lipstick on."

"I spent a year at college learning how to apply cosmetics. Think I've just about leant it now."

"Do you like experimenting with acids?"

"Never done that. Is it interesting?"

"What? Of course it is. You can try them all sorts of things to see what's resistant. I got through nearly all my clothes two nights ago."

"I'd like to try."

"We could do it this evening. A couple of hours catching muggers in town, then the acids and finish with a session on the firing range."

"Wow! That's the best offer I've ever had. Why don't any of the men I know want to do something like that?"

The pair wandered from the room, deep in conversation and Heather smiled and Philip.

"Isn't it great being a woman?" he asked rhetorically.

Almost no climbing 10 that night that the police cells were bulging with wrongdoers arriving every few minutes. They were nicely packaged with tightly tied ropes with evidence in the form of photos and signed confessions stapled to their clothing. Also attached was a business card. Just two words on it.

'The Babes'.

16 THE GARDEN SHED THAT ATE PEOPLE

Heather arrived at the office to find Clarissa writing in a massive diary.

"Arranging more brain surgery?" she asked.

"No, a double wedding."

"Really?"

"I've rescheduled my contractual affiliation with Burg and Elizabeth will marry Badger Babe at the same time."

"She only had her first date last night."

"I was the same with Burg. Our family doesn't waste time. Anyway, she told me about Babe and I've checked their DNA's. Perfect match. No wonder they were attracted to each other. So it's a double wedding in Hawaii."

"That means everyone will know Badger Babe's true identity."

"No. I found a legal loophole. Under a little-known Act passed in 1791 known as Identus Comicus Secretus, any person who hides their identity behind a mask is allowed to wear it and use an assumed name when they marry. I've also been nagging Elizabeth to make Badger Babe sign a contract."

"That's really not necessary. I didn't have one when I married Philip and we've been together a long time."

"Rocky and I did the kissy, cuddly thing last night. I didn't think I'd enjoy it but I did. Nearly as good as a brain replacement operation."

The fascinating conversation was rudely interrupted by the entrance of a large, florid man.

"Excuse me. Sorry you to interrupt and your pardon beg. Possible chance any the office of Mr Philip Caldrock, the renowned investigator this is?"

The man spoke with an unpleasant grin and Heather disliked him immediately.

"Yes. What do you want?" Clarissa responded sharply.

"I'm apologetic totally for like this intruding but enquire I would like to if it is at all feasible to actually see him for me?"

Now Clarissa rose from her desk.

"See him? You want to see him? Just walk in off the street and demand an audience with perhaps the greatest detective in the world? Think that everyone should jump about to your command, do you?"

The man gave a slimy look as he cowered visibly and began to ease towards the door. Heather reluctantly moved to stop him.

"If you can just wait a minute, I'll see if he's free."

She whispered to Clarissa as she passed.

"You've been reading that course about how to be a receptionist again, haven't you?"

"Yes, I think I've mastered it now."

"Well, here we prefer to be different from everyone else. From now on try to be nice and welcoming."

"Offer them tea?"

"No, that's too risky. Show our visitor into Philip's office."

Clarissa's face contorted into a savage smile.

"And your name, good sir?" she asked.

The smile appeared to scare him more than her previous rudeness.

"Pigworth Slugrat."

Philip was reading a newspaper when the trio entered.

"And who is this, Clarissa?"

"It's your wife, Heather."

"I meant the other person."

"Oh, him. Piggy Slugrat."

The red cheeks of the visitor glistened with sweat as he twisted his face into an obsequious smile.

"Nice that is. Call me Piggy most people."

Philip looked disdainfully at the man.

"Thank you Clarissa. Please take a seat, Mr Slugrat and recount your problem."

"My little difficulties are those that I hate to bother people with."

"I am here to resolve difficulties."

"So presumptuous it seems to ask you with someone else's worries to burden yourself."

"Mr Piggy, I mean Slugrat. Do not prevaricate further."

Heather looked at the visitor with distaste. He was distinctly fat with pink flabby cheeks, large stomach and just a scattering of hair on an otherwise bald head.

Sweat was now dripping from all visible skin and an unpleasant unwashed aroma began to fill the room.

"Please speak in your own words," she said in an attempt to speed up his departure.

"Thank you, thank you. Jumpy this business has really made me. It's the shed, Mr Caldrock. A killer it is."

"Shed? As in small garden building usually made of prefabricated wood or metal?"

"Wood. At the bottom of my garden it is. I do believe some form synthetic wood, of course not teak. Pre-coated it was with wood stain weather resistant. Light amber shade, pleasant rather."

His convoluted speech began to irritate Heather immensely but Philip appeared patient.

"You said it's a killer?"

"People it eats, yes."

"Are you a loony?"

"The truth it is. Already three people devoured."

"Then tell me the whole story and abbreviate it as much as possible," requested Philip, hand moving to his nose as the Slugrat body odour reached him.

"Four weeks ago the shed I got and swiftly erected using instruction manual well written. As clear and concise as could be. Diagrams even therein to component recognition facilitate. One week just it took to complete."

"Yes, yes."

"Saw this new addition did my neighbour Mr Fodder to the cultivated area at the rear of my house."

"Your garden."

"Exactly that's it. Expressed a desire, he did to commence a journey to my property and upon reaching he thereafter travelled to the rear of the land whereupon began he to examine and assess the positioned there structure. Described he to me subsequently an undeniable wish to ingress gain into the said erection, permitting interior examination thereby."

"He wanted to go in the shed?"

"Yes."

"Mr Slugrat. Perhaps you could accelerate your account somewhat by using more concise language," said Philip, checking the desk drawers for some form of aromatic room spray.

"Apologies my most sincere. He went in and was eaten by the shed."

"That part needs to be less concise."

"Into the shed Mr Fodder walked and door he closed. A few minutes after, concerned I became and attempted to enter. Door would not open. To the house to get a crowbar and force entry I went. Still closed on my return but opened immediately I pushed it. Empty was the shed."

"I see. And the next event?"

"My cousin, Gripeworm and his wife Nasta to stay with me came for weekend."

"Gripeworm and Nasta?"

"Them you know?"

"No."

"Shed very keen to look at was Gripeworm and out with him went I, morning after arrived they while Nasta house cleaning, cooking, washing. Inside went he and again it happened. Stuck door. To get crowbar went I. But amazed on return, open door found but disappeared he had."

"Perhaps he had come out again and returned to the house?" asked Heather.

"Unfeasible that must be, see him I was sure to. Nasta had lunch cooked. Roast beef lovely, tender with peas, potatoes and cabbage. Brought she had for after delicious ice cream log. Perhaps known to you, ice cream lump by chocolate covered that was decorated like a wooden log to look. A meal indeed, enjoyed greatly did I."

"Did you tell her that her husband had disappeared?"

"After meal, yes. Mentioned when finished my coffee."

"I will venture a guess that she went immediately to the shed," Philip declared, waving his hand in front of his nostrils.

"Indeed did she. Direct to shed and inside. Door closed and repeated circumstances. Returned I with crowbar and gone she had."

"Do you have any theories?"

"I'm sure is the truth that which I believe. On delivery vehicle, aliens substituted replica of shed. In fact is it living entity to sustain its existence on this planet must consume humans."

"Mr Wormrat."

"Slugrat."

"Yes, Slugrat. I perceive a common factor here. All three of these people disappeared whilst you were fetching an implement to open the door. They could simply have left the shed while you were absent."

"Are they where then? Seen since none of them."

"Yes, that is curious. Did you contact the police?"

"That did I but said they disappear every day millions of people. Wait for few years and turn up them again."

"Does this shed have any unusual features?"

"Noticed not that. A shed small and ordinary. Clever are aliens at object disguising."

"Then I propose to visit this structure later this morning."

Two hours later, Heather and Philip were regarding the shed. It was an almost perfect cube, just over two metres high and along each side. No windows and made of horizontal imitation wood pieces. A solid roof and the door was composed of vertical strips of wood. No gaps and impossible to see inside. Slugrat opened the door and Philip entered.

"Don't close it," said Heather instinctively.

Slugrat gave her a surly look but stood back as she looked inside. Completely empty. The flooring appeared to be made of two sheets of real wood, joined tightly in the centre. Then she saw it as she looked down. Faint markings.

"Did you notice this?" she asked Philip.

"Just natural blemishes in the timber," he responded.

Heather took a series of photographs for later study to confirm her suspicions.

"The only sensible thing to do is to put a chain around it to stop anyone going in," she suggested.

A negative grunt from Slugrat.

"Detective, find anything do you?" he asked.

Philip nodded.

"We now wish to consider our findings. Perhaps you will leave us for a time?" he replied, finding the open air didn't fully dissipate the Slugrat odour.

The man shrugged and marched back to the house.

Heather examined magnified pictures of the flooring on the display screen of her camera.

"Do you know what this is?" she asked, passing it to him.

"Still looks like normal lines in the wood to me."

"Philip, it's a summoning circle. Used by Satanists to call their master to appear on earth. There are two rings and a series of symbols between them. I read about the theory and practice of Satanic rituals a few years ago."

"The Devil? You think these people were transported to hell?"

"We need to keep an open mind."

"I'm presented with two possibilities. Either the shed is an alien artefact or it's a portal to hell. There is only one way to reveal the truth."

"If you're going to go inside, then I'm coming with you."

"No. I have a suspicion of the truth in this matter. I will enter the shed and close the door. You must wait five minutes and will then find it is apparently impossible to open. I want you to remain with Slugrat for exactly the period of time he normally took to find his crowbar."

"I don't like it. You could be dragged down to Hades by demons."

"Nevertheless, a man must accomplish those actions that might be required at any time where they become essential for one of the masculine gender to perform them. Let us call back the Slugrat."

A few minutes later, they were rejoined by the obese man.

"Just had doctor phone. Death certificates he has signed for the three who disappeared."

"What did he give us the cause of death?"

"Of course, eaten by shed."

Heather was nervous. A genuine fear for Phillip's safety bubbled through her but she determinedly suppressed it from view. Visions of demonic shapes, with clawed hands mauling his body, gripping his arms and pulling him downwards into a circular crimson pit in the centre of the shed. A sudden panic and she called him. Too late, he was already inside and the door closed.

"Do you have any devil worshippers around here?" she asked Slugrat.

"Here? No definitely, no. Satanic groups a couple of in the next street but not here definitely."

"What are these groups?"

"One run by Mrs Deman and called 'The How To Reach Satan From Your Own Garden Coven'. Other is 'The Dancing Around A Circle On A Wooden Floor In A Small Building Will Open A Gateway To Hell Society' run by Mark Overbeest."

Heather found it impossible herself to wait for the five minutes specified by Philip while Slugrat seemed a little less than optimistic.

"Him gone, that is. Never see again. Hope your insurance a good one was. Aliens cut him up probably for examination when they finish tests so suffering unspeakable pain only a week or two."

"Mr Slugrat?"

"Yes?"

"Be quiet."

Heather checked her watch and moved forward to try the door. It wouldn't open, resisting all her attempts.

"Go and fetch your crowbar. I will wait here," she instructed, as unemotionally as she could.

Slugrat disappeared into the house and returned a few minutes later.

"As soon as this I bring, door will open," he said.

Heather needed no persuasion and tried the door again. It opened easily.

"Just I said as," declared Slugrat.

The interior was empty and now Heather was worried.

"Philip!" she called but no reply.

Then she saw something. A message scribbled on the wall.

'Don't be alarmed. I will be back. Philip.'

"Maybe a pact with aliens he made," suggested Slugrat.

"Or Satan," added Heather with relief.

Philip had never let her down before and she was depending on him this time.

"Bother reporting to police, shall I?"

She nodded.

"Yes. Something tells me that Inspector Foxhole should be here."

30 minutes later, Foxhole had completed his summary inspection of the shed.

"Pretty obvious what happened," he remarked.

"How can it be obvious?" responded Heather.

"He went inside and then slipped out again while Mr Slugrat was in the house."

"I was here the whole time."

"Yes, yes. Everyone says that but I'm sure you looked away for a second. Checked your watch or glanced back towards the house."

"Inspector. Four people have now vanished in the shed. I have a theory that there is a gate to hell inside."

"A portal that manifested itself and the people were dragged down to Satan by a group of his evil servants? That sounds very plausible but I rather prefer Slugrat's theory of aliens. However, I believe that my looking away solution is the true one. The previous three could all have got out while Slugrat was in the house and Philip did the same when you were checking your watch."

"I kept my eyes on the shed."

"Yes, yes. Everyone says that but I'm sure you looked away for a second."

"You've already used those words."

"Yes, yes. Everyone says that."

"Then where is Philip?" she asked, breaking the circuit.

"Probably turn up in a couple of days in some remote village. Wandering around the streets and suffering from memory loss. Happens all the time."

Heather was about to get angry when her phone rang.

"Hello, dear. Please don't give any indication you are talking to me."

Her heart jumped but she masked her feelings. Making an excuse, she moved away to the other end of the garden.

"Philip, are you phoning from hell?" she asked in a whisper.

"Not exactly. Please encourage the Inspector to leave as quickly as possible and then I will reveal all."

The call ended and she returned to the others.

"Well, Inspector. I think you have wrapped up the case now. I'm sure you have other pressing matters to undertake."

Foxhole shook his head.

"No. I'm just exchanging views with Mr Slugrat here about the possibility of alien life forms in the outer galaxies."

"That phone call was from someone who thought they saw a spacecraft over the police station. It might still be there if you hurry."

"No rush. I'm sure it would have gone by the time I get there."

Now Heather attempted to physically shepherd him towards the house but he wouldn't move. Time for a final attempt.

"I heard a rumour that Badger Babe will appear in the town centre at any minute. Clarissa and Elizabeth could be with her, wearing their bodysuits."

Before the end of the sentence, he was dashing into the house.

"Duty calls," he shouted as he disappeared.

"Suppose as well you're going," mumbled Slugrat.

"No. I'm waiting."

"Want go into shed?"

"No thank you."

"You do, yes," he responded and grabbed her arms, pulling her forwards. Heather resisted, kicking him firmly on the ankles but he maintained his grip. She was trying to get away from the smell as much as his clutches.

"My master Satan wants you join him. Pointless is resistance."

"So you're a Satanist!" she shouted.

"That great honour have I to serve master from hell."

"And all that talk of aliens was just a diversion."

The slimy man giggled unpleasantly.

"Right that is. Some believed it, to think that!"

"As I thought, you created a gateway inside the shed."

"Actually I didn't, no. Thought it was just ordinary garden building when I ordered it. When neighbour disappeared, only then I realised must be gift from Satan to his most devoted follower. Purpose was send souls to him he wanted."

"So you encouraged your relations to go inside and then had the idea of getting Philip and myself for the next victims."

"Indeed yes. And more will there be. A tourist attraction will I make it and feed visitors from all over the world to shed."

"I need not ask if you are a loony," declared Philip.

Slugrat gasped , releasing his grip and Heather spun around.

"Philip! You're back safely. Thank goodness."

"I hadn't gone far."

"But you were sent to hell."

"To borrow Elizabeth's joint favourite word, no."

"Where then? Some other haven of Satan?"

"I was in the house next door."

"What?"

This time Heather and Slugrat spoke simultaneously and with equal disbelief.

"Having dismissed the ideas of aliens and Satanists, the case became very simple. There had to be a method of leaving the shed without using the door. The fastest way to discover it was to enter the shed myself."

"Slugrat tried to get me inside. He's a Satanist," declared Heather.

"I know and he is also extremely smelly. Those are two of many reasons why he is a deeply unpopular man. Others include his curious method of speech, eating habits, playing loud music during the night and general unpleasantness."

Slugrat leered vindictively.

"All right am I, who are wrong it's the other people. Satan will give me the leading the world power and then will I punish severely them for their rudeness to me," he shouted, waving his arms.

Philip wasn't disconcerted.

"Mr Fodder, his neighbour, found life becoming unbearable. When he saw the obnoxious Slugrat laboriously building the shed, he concocted a plan. Fodder already had an underground chamber beneath his kitchen, which he constructed in case of an invasion by Martians. He is a very practical person with knowledge of both construction and electronics and it was a simple matter to dig a full-size tunnel from the chamber to a point directly below the new shed. This only took a couple of hours and he had plenty of time to line it with concrete and install overhead lighting to facilitate safe transit."

"Under my shed, a tunnel?" gasped Slugrat.

"On the night after the shed was completed, Mr Fodder came up the tunnel, sawed through the wooden floor of the shed and then made significant modifications. He cut the floor across the centre and fitted an electric mechanism so that the two halves slid apart when he pressed a remote control switch. He also installed steel rods that rose up from below to insert themselves into holes he had drilled in the base of the door. This ensured it could not be opened. The rods were controlled by another button on the remote."

"Why?" asked Heather.

"Fodder was then in a position where he could sit in his house and observe the shed. At any time he wished, he could press the switches to fix the door closed or open the floor."

"But why?"

Philip ignored the question again.

"Then Fodder visited Slugrat, feigning interest in the shed. He had the remote control with him and when he was inside, it took just a few seconds to stop the door opening and then go through the floor, along the tunnel and back to his house."

"Philip! Will you tell me why?"

"A very simple reason. Repugnance. Like everyone else in the street, Fodder had been trying to get rid of his neighbour for a long time. His idea was that Slugrat would be accused of abduction, satanic sacrifice or simple murder. That should ensure incarceration by the authorities and his annoying presence removed."

"What about his cousins?"

"Fodder realised that his disappearance has not accomplished the objective. Then he saw Gripeworm and Nasta arrive. He was convinced that the police couldn't ignore three vanishing people and managed to speak to them whilst Slugrat was busy in the kitchen. They also despised their relation and readily agreed to the proposal. Consequently, both Gripeworm and Nasha went down the tunnel and have remained in Fodder's home ever since."

Slugrat ran to the garden fence to look at the neighbouring house. Three figures visible in the kitchen window, gesturing unpleasantly at him. He rushed back to the shed, screaming.

"All lies, it is! My master took them and replicas sent to earth. Human shells they are with demons inside! Lord Satan, give me a sign!" he yelled, opening the door.

A great red mist burst out from the shed, enveloping the screaming figure. It formed a solid, impenetrable wall for a minute and then began to disperse. Heather saw Slugrat was now lying on the ground, his pudgy face contorted.

"Is he alive?" she asked.

Philip strolled over to the body.

"Yes, I'm afraid so but I don't think he'll be quite the same now."

Heather moved to join him. Letters were painted in bright crimson deep across Slugrat's forehead. Just one word.

'Reject'.

17 THE MURDER MYSTERY MYSTERY MYSTERY

"A holiday," announced Philip as he read the newspaper on a sunny Sunday morning in the lounge of their house.

Heather was halfway through a massive tome entitled 'Minoan or Menoan. Which is it?'

"We had two weeks in Cornwall just last month."

"Yes but this is different," he responded, handing her the newspaper and pointing at a miniscule classified advert.

"It appears to be offering a murder mystery week at some hotel but I can't be sure without a magnifying glass."

"Constant detective work has made my sight as sharp as a cabbage."

"Cabbages aren't sharp."

"But they're good for your eyesight."

"I thought that was carrots. Or is it celery?"

"You're right, I could be thinking of lettuce. I'm sure it's not potatoes but it might be green beans. Or peas."

"What does the advert say, Philip?" Heather asked patiently.

"A week away from it all in a hotel on Sepulchre Island."

"Where's that?"

"Just off the east coast of England. It's not really an island, just a small patch of land about half a mile from the coast and joined to the mainland by a causeway barely wide enough for a car."

"And cut off at high tide?"

"The road normally stays just above the water when the tide is in."

"I'll check on the internet."

Some time later, all was revealed. Sepulchre Island was almost circular and barely large enough to contain the only structure, the Trettening Hotel. The building housed just 16 guest rooms and was bordered all round by extensive lawns. The hotel's webpage described the facilities in more detail and the primary attraction appeared to be lack of beach.

'No sand here to get in your eyes, sandwiches, drinks and swimsuit. We ensure that none of this unpleasant gritty yellow stuff is present on our island'.

Specialist holidays appeared to be the norm and a range of subjects was on offer. Heather checked a few examples.

'Finding Your Feet in Crocodile Collecting - for animal surgeons only'

'How to stop Painting – get portraits and landscapes out of your system and live longer'

'Mountain Climbing for Beginners – the first stage – ascending the stairs (bring strong boots)'

'Learn a Craft – retired captain teaches the rowing boat'

"Here it is. 'Join celebrity guests in our murder mystery weeks. Can you solve a baffling case?' I admit to being doubtful when you first mentioned it but I'm quite keen now," said Heather.

"And I have an idea to add a little pinch of fungus to our holiday."

"Fungus doesn't sound right."

"A pinch of cabbage, then."

"What is the idea?"

"We will go incognito."

"Under assumed names?"

"Exactly. Then, when I have triumphantly solved the mystery, I will reveal myself to all and receive their universal acclamation."

"I've just been reading about a prehistoric inscription in a recently discovered Minoan cave."

"What did it say?"

"The modest man is …"

"Is what?"

"The remainder had been eroded but I think everyone can guess the missing words."

"Eating celery?"

"What?"

"The modest man could be eating celery to improve his eyesight."

"Why would anyone write that on a cave wall?"

"Simple jealousy, perhaps. One of Mr Modest's more aggressive neighbours who was envious of his ability to discern a pterodactyl at 100 paces. I believe that I possess considerable and expansive knowledge in the field of modesty."

Heather sighed.

"I'll book the holiday. The next murder mystery begins on Friday."

Thursday evening. Heather drove carefully across to Sepulchre Island. The causeway was perfectly straight and supported by concrete blocks on the sea bed. A bright and warm evening with a cloud free blue sky, now a darker hue as the sun lowered to the horizon. An excellent example of the best English twilight.

"At least we'll have good weather, whatever the quality of this murder mystery," remarked Philip.

"Have we decided what name to use? I rather liked Mr and Mrs Brickhouse. It sounds so ordinary."

Heather wasn't going to admit that she found the idea of an assumed name exciting, a subtle declaration of celebrity status.

"Lord and Lady Dunderdale is definitely my preference," announced Philip.

The Trettening Hotel looked even smarter than in the photographs. A sprawling but roughly square white building of two stories. It had obviously been recently refurbished and everything was sparkling. Not a condition shared by the person behind the reception desk. A lean, unshaven middle aged man with wild dark grey hair. He wore just torn jeans and an originally cream shirt that had food stains all over it.

"You're the last pair. Booked in name of Lord Dunderdale, is it?"

Heather stepped in quickly.

"The Lord was unable to come. We are his close friends, Mr and Mrs Brickhouse."

"Okay with me as long as your money's good. I want 100 pounds deposit so flash the cash."

Philip took notes from his wallet and they were grabbed voraciously.

"Right. Room 13, first floor. Carry your own bags. I'm Grimedung."

"Yes you are," responded Philip.

The man gave a sly look.

"Have we met before? Maybe you knew my wife. She left me years ago for another man. Not Mrs Grimedung now."

"Some women have a curious habit of finding the most disgusting men attractive."

"Right on. Man she's with now is a real pig."

"Demonstrating that the habit can be repetitive. When is dinner?"

"Get down to the dining room at eight sharp or nothing for you."

Up the stairs. Again the decor was impeccable and everything spotlessly clean. They entered number 13. A spacious room with double bed and a balcony looking out to sea. Unpacking completed, Heather was taking a bath when there was a knock at the door. Philip opened it to reveal a revealing girl in a revealing short black dress with revealing lace front. Long dark hair, very red lips and revealing eyes.

"You are the Lord?" she asked revealingly.

"No. Brickhouse is the name. Lord Dunderdale couldn't come."

The girl looked disappointed.

"Pity. Are you a rich man?" she asked, scanning his clothing to confirm. Apparently satisfied with the value of his attire, she didn't wait for a reply and stumbled forward, gripping him tightly around the neck.

"So sorry. My heels slipped," she said breathily.

"My wife is in the bathroom," Philip mumbled uncomfortably but she didn't seem to hear and her grip didn't relax.

"My name is Manita and I am Brazilian. We are a country of passionate women and know when we like a man."

"My wife, who is in the bathroom, is not at all understanding and I am not a young person," he responded with clarity.

"I want more experience in a partner. I love to sit with man to watch sunset and TV."

Philip heard sounds from the bathroom and prised her hands from him.

"Thank you, Manita. We don't need anything at the moment," he said loudly as the bathroom door opened.

"Maybe see you later," whispered the girl and disappeared down the corridor.

"Who was that?" Heather asked.

"A maid, asking if we needed anything. Good service, I thought."

Heather nodded. She had seen the smudges of lipstick and rouge on his cheek but didn't mention them.

An awkward silence relieved as Philip's phone rang and he spoke for 2 minutes.

"A problem?" asked Heather as he finished the call.

"Merely a distraction. A newspaper has been stolen from a resident's letter box. That was Inspector Foxhole asking me for urgent help."

"Can't it wait?"

"I'm afraid not. I must return immediately but anticipate it will only take a few hours. I should return here tomorrow morning. Meanwhile, you must stay and note all the occurrences in order that I may triumphantly solve the case on my return."

"Very well, Philip," Heather responded with a sigh.

She watched him drive away and waited until eight before going to the dining room. Grimedung stood at one end, checking his watch with Manita beside him. A pair of people at four of the eight tables with a solitary man at one in the corner. Heather moved to a vacant table and sat expectantly. Another minute passed then suddenly, Grimedung looked up and struck a gong behind him.

"Eight o'clock so shovel down some food!" he yelled.

Manita sprang into action, rushing through a swinging door behind her and emerging with a tray full of steaming soup, fortunately in bowls. There appeared to be a time limit on the exercise as bowls were dumped on tables as fast as possible.

"Excuse me," said Heather as Grimedung wandered past.

"What's up with you?" he asked.

"I appear to be lacking in bread. A roll or slices of baguette perhaps?"

"Bread is it? You're asking for bread? And what is wrong with the soup, may I ask?"

All eyes turned to them.

"Nothing is wrong with the soup. I wish to partake of bread as an accompaniment."

A stunned silence.

"That's a great thought, they'd go so perfectly together. Some new idea from the luxury restaurants of Japan, no doubt."

He summoned Manita and bread rolls were dispersed to all tables at a lightning pace. Six minutes later the gong was struck again and soup bowls cleared to be replaced by plates of roast beef, beautifully cooked.

"I must compliment the chef," declared Heather as Grimedung passed again.

"Want more bread?" he asked.

"No. I wish to personally congratulate the chef on this excellent repast."

"Repast? Is that one of your Japanese words?" the scruffy man asked with added suspicion.

"A superb dinner," said Heather quickly.

"All righty. I cooked it."

After coffee was served at the end of the meal, a slim and attractive blonde woman rose from one of the tables.

"Hello everybody!" she shouted, displaying a heavily practised smile. The announcement was greeted by a polite murmur and she continued.

"I am your guide and hostess, Flitty Biteburg! Welcome everyone to our murder mystery!" she squealed.

Grimedung moved over whispered in her ear.

"Ah, I see. One of you is just a regular guest and not here for our special event. Mr Owen Dairy?"

The single man nodded with irritation.

"So you're not as welcome as the others although that doesn't mean you're not welcome but as you haven't paid to hear me say it, it doesn't matter anyway. Maybe it's best if you don't listen."

"Inform us of the fantastic mind conundrums which are to come before us in their unfamiliar guises of unfamiliarity," said a deep voice at the next table.

Heather was startled. The man looked exactly like Gluckweed Nightsock but he had been killed at Lord Gruntingdon's.

"Excuse me but are you Nightsock back from the dead?" she asked.

The large man stared at her. Same massive build, same long dark hair.

"Madam, I am Mainwaring Nightsock. Do I have the acquaintance of previous honour with your good self?"

"Mainwaring? You are related to Gluckweed?"

"My twin brother."

"I see. My condolences."

"In the tortuous yet ultimately fulfilling twisting yet stony path that is our allotment in life's rich, yet multicoloured circus, one does not ingratiate oneself with the creator of the aforementioned path by aimless discordance with one's fraternal relations."

Silence as Heather reviewed the initially impressive but tortuous statement for errors and then meaning.

"I referred not to the actuality of your existence as brothers but to Gluckweed's sad and tragic demise resulting from the impact of a pair of skis."

"Ah, yes. An unfortunate accident. I fear he will no longer be able to wear a baseball cap with propriety."

"He's alive?" exclaimed Heather.

"Indeed yes. Pronounced dead by Doctor Wilma Tryst but when the paramedics came, they were able to conduct paramedical repairs."

"Wilma said he was dead. She even kicked him twice."

"That was all she could do as only paramedics are qualified to kick three times. It is an essential part of the training course that permits the use of para in front of the standard medic. The third kick restored him to life and then it was a simple matter to glue his brain back together, using special paramedic adhesive. Gluckweed is now living in California where he hosts his own TV chat show."

"You are also a writer?"

"The sharp yet insidious fingers of modesty are wagging to forbid my verbal assertion of unsurpassed literary genius."

"Excuse me! Can everyone look in my direction please!" yelled Flitty, clearly unhappy with the side conversation.

When attention had been restored, she continued.

"Now I have bad news and very good news. The bad news is that the team of actors that we recruited at massive cost are all suffering from Ingapt"

"What is that?" asked one of the group.

"A disease of thespians. An acronym for 'I'm Not Going And Performing There'. But now the good news! The murder mystery will go ahead as planned with me playing most of the roles and others will be performed by Sam Throg, my assistant. Stand up Sam."

A dour looking youth rose sheepishly and sat down almost immediately.

"Now you must all leave your normal lives and come into the realms of imagination. All except you of course, Mr Dairy. Someone will be murdered tonight and you have to use your detective skills to find out the name of the murderer."

"One could speculate that the perpetrator of this homicidal act would almost certainly be yourself or young Mr Throg," remarked Nightsock.

"Maybe or maybe not but we are now no longer Flitty and Sam. We are a multitude of different people."

Grimedung grimaced.

"You're saying that you're using assumed names? I'll have the police after me," he said with concern.

"No, I'm really Flitty but I can also be someone else at any time."

"You can transform?"

Now Flitty got gritty.

"I am an actor playing different parts. You can understand that, can't you?"

A grunt in response.

"Now I want each of our guests to stand up and introduce themselves. Mr Nightsock first," she announced, checking a list.

The large man rose immediately.

"Mainwaring Nightsock. Like my brother, I am the author of a number of best selling novels. My works sit atop the mountains of literature, like eagles surveying the lowland of pulp writing with the disdainful look of a large bird that looks down, errr, disdainfully."

"Mr and Mrs Brickhouse."

"My husband is delayed but should be here tomorrow. He is confident that he will solve the mystery," declared Heather.

"Ms Ilena Baker."

A curvaceous blonde stood up and smiled brilliantly with added pouts. This didn't appear to impress Flitty.

"What do you do?" she asked.

"Why, I'm famous," responded the blonde in a mid-Atlantic accent.

"Mr Fleet Midwit."

An intense young man with carefully disarranged hair.

"Hi everyone. I think you've all heard of me," he announced.

Universally blank looks.

"Midwit Bird Call?" he added with growing disappointment.

More blank looks.

"My column in the Celebrity Pic Weekly where I write about the world of famous and infamous women?"

Sympathetic smiles and Flitty tried a rescue act.

"Great! A celeb writer!"

No response and she continued.

"Siko Pigswill."

A cherubic faced girl stood up and immediately began to sing.

"Love is like ping-pong, your turn then mine, when I do sing song, I'll serve you fine."

Polite applause.

"You should be on stage," said Flitty.

A sour look from the girl.

"I'm a singer. I've done concerts all over the world."

"Leach Rouse."

A slim, shifty eyed man with long, prematurely thinning, prematurely grey hair. In fact, premature appeared to sum him up totally.

"Painting is what I do. Only women though. I hope to get the chance to do a couple of you while I'm here."

"And finally, Potty Dirsnap."

A small bright eyed woman with grey hair.

"I expect you all thought I was Dotty Parsnip, the well-known amateur sleuth. I'm her twin sister but nothing like her at all. In fact, I haven't spoken to the silly old cow for 10 years. I am a science professor at a major university, so don't you forget it. If anyone calls me Dotty, I'll be very angry."

Flitty clapped her hands.

"That's super! So everyone knows everyone. We'll just have to wait until Mr Dairy leaves and then we can begin."

The man in the corner showed no signs of movement. He was drinking coffee and reading a newspaper, seemingly oblivious to all the eyes turned on him. An uncomfortable silence as the minutes passed. Eventually Grimedung sidled across.

"Want anything?"

Dairy looked up and nodded.

"Another coffee please."

"Have it in the lounge. Dining room is closed now. Private party. Manita, get him out."

The girl approached quickly. And revealingly.

"You rich man?" she asked.

"Yes I am."

Her eyes lit up and she tripped over something and fell into his lap.

"So sorry. You want me to uncrumple your clothes?"

"No thank you."

With substantial manual activity, she shepherded him from the room.

Flitty stepped forward again.

"Right. Now we'll begin. I am Lady Binki Watt who is bored with her husband. She has come here with Gordon Grant, the gardener at the hall where she lives. Sam will play Gordon."

The youth looked terrified as he pulled a script from his pocket. Flitty sat next to him and raised her voice two levels.

"Oh, darling. It's so wonderful to be together in this hotel under assumed names at last. I just couldn't keep going behind that hedge all the time."

Sam mumbled an inaudible response.

"What did he say?" asked Midwit, who was transcribing the conversation in a reporter's notebook.

"You weren't meant to hear his words. That's part of the plot," responded Flitty.

Nightsock waved a hand.

"Pray, dear lady. By what indication are we to distinguish between that speech which is intentionally suppressed and that which is purely of inadequate volume to obtain access to our hearing organs?"

"Good point, Nightsock," said Midwit.

"I know! You could carry a little red flag in your handbag and wave it when we're not meant to hear you," proposed Pigswill, bursting with pleasure that her brain was capable of generating the suggestion.

Now Potty clapped her hands.

"Listen you lot. Stop that yapping or we'll never have a murder. Just get on with it, Flatty."

"It's Flitty."

"I don't care. Go on."

The hostess gave her a look but continued.

"Oh darling, I've hungered for these precious moments, sharing trifle over a table together."

"Oh my god, Binki!" cried Sam, as manfully as he could.

Mystified looks from all, including Flitty. She reached over and turned Sam's script to the correct page. Red face but he managed to mumble the line nearly correctly.

"Yes, long have I acquired you from afar. Now I want to consummate."

Pigswill gave a gasp and there was a pause as Flitty nodded at Sam. He nodded back, appreciating the encouragement but then found her finger pointing at his script and finally spoke again.

"Now I want this consummate bliss to last forever."

Flitty was clearly unsettled.

"I thought never I would not hear those words. But my husband! He is a cruel and violent man who often uses a rifle."

She spoke to last part with clarity, looking round meaningfully.

"A rifle for shooting, dear?" asked Sam.

"I hate bloodsports. Poor little deer. What a horrid man," declared Pigswill.

"Shut up, Pignose or we'll be here all night," Potty admonished.

"You're very rude."

"I'd like to offer my full support to the lovely Siko, who I'd very much like to paint," Leach announced, leering in the girl's direction.

Flitty ignored everyone and continued.

"And I'm worried about my new maid."

"You mean Polly who was in the correction centre for homicidal maniacs and you gave her a second chance even though she killed lots of people using a wife?"

"A knife, yes."

"But you are also concerned about your husband's friend, Earl Slunk who has an insatiable desire for you but you have always refunded him."

"Refuted, yes."

"And the butler, John Smith, who has never liked you and has been arrested three times for straggling women but was acquitted."

"Strangling. Yes, Gordon, I'm worried about all of them."

"Oh my god, Binki!" cried Sam.

Flitty leant over again to turn back the page.

"Sorry. I meant to say I want you to come with me and even if you see ravenous loins, you don't need to worry."

A frightened cry from Siko.

"No, it's lions," Sam corrected.

Flitty glared but the distraction didn't help her concentration.

"You make me feel…"

A long pause as she turned the sheet and puzzled over the continuation. Finding the pages out of sequence, she began to scrabble through them furiously.

"Come on Flitty, we're all dying to know what you're feeling," said Potty brusquely.

Another glare.

"… so secure and wanted."

"Let us go to our room for a night of unbridled poison."

"Yes, passion."

"It says poison," responded Sam stubbornly.

"Well it shouldn't. The word is passion."

"If you say so."

"Yes, darling. Off we go," declared Flitty and taking Sam's arm, she guided him to the door.

Leach immediately rose and began to follow them.

"What are you doing?" asked Flitty.

"I'm coming to watch the bedroom scene," he responded.

"Well there isn't one. Go back to your seat."

"They were only going for a bit of poison anyway," said Potty unkindly.

The pair left the room but Flitty re-entered immediately.

"Now I'm Polly, the maid of Lady Watt," she announced and paused before continuing.

"This must be the place where those two are staying. I've always hated that Lady Watt, ever since she employed me as a maid. I had to tell myself to keep my homicidal urges under control. I know her room number now and I'll take photos of the two of them to show to the Lord."

Exit Flitty and enter Sam, clutching his script tightly.

"I am Lord Watt. I followed my wife's car. Can they be here together?"

Enter Flitty.

"Good evening, Lord Watt. I am the hotel manager. How may I help?"

"I'm looking for a wife."

"Your wife did you say?" she corrected

"No, it says a wife," responded Sam with determination.

"Give the boy a chance, Flitty. Let him have one if he wants," called Ilena.

"But he doesn't. He's got one and is looking for her."

"Maybe he wants to change. I'm free at the moment and the boy's rather cute," retorted the inflated blonde.

Now Sam's face glowed like a red beacon. Flitty pursed her lips before continuing.

"We have no one here registered under the name of your wife."

"I just had a feeling," mumbled Sam, still gazing at Ilena who seemed to revel in the attention.

Flitty urged him from the room and then she returned again.

"Now a new scene. Sam is playing Earl Slunk and I am John Smith, the butler."

"Where is that maid, Polly? I followed her here," she declared in a deeper voice.

Her companion entered.

"My goodness! You are John Smith, the butler of Lord Watt, aren't you? I am Earl Slunk," he declared.

"Yes I am John Smith."

"I found out something about your past, John Smith. Come, Smith. Let us go to my room to discuss a proposition."

"Ah, so you want to propose something to me?"

"You will be forced to agree, John Smith because you are here at last, Inspector. The body is in the next room," said Sam with certainty.

Puzzled looks and another correction of page sequence.

"You will be forced to agree because I know about your paste," he corrected.

"My past? Oh no!"

"Hold on. What was the butler's name again?" asked Midwit

"John Smith. They said it 20 times," retorted Potty.

"Is that John with an H?"

"Yes," responded Flitty.

"And Smith with a Y?"

"What?"

"No, Watt is the Lord. I mean this butler, Jim Smythe."

Flitty didn't respond and squeezing her lips together, she pulled Sam outside again.

Then they both re-entered.

"Now we are Lady Watt and Gordon again," she said.

The script problems seemed to be unnerving Sam.

237

"Well Binki, we've been to our room but we both felt like a little drunk before returning," he mumbled.

"A little drink, you say. Yes, I need one."

"To calm your nurse?" said Sam, eyes now constantly flashing towards Ilena.

"Nerves? Yes."

"Binki, there's something I need to get off your chest."

"You want to tell me something? Go ahead while I drink."

"I'm going to come clean. I'm already married."

"You can't be! Who is your wife, Gordon?"

"I don't know. A year after our marriage in a little village church in Cornwall, I lost my memory and can't recall anything. I was found wandering the streets and have no idea who my wife could be."

Nightsock stirred himself.

"May one enquire as to the judgemental gymnastics by which this gardening person was able, in one respect to remember the church in which the marital knot was bound whereas his cranial content summarily dispensed with other information, including the physical appearance and characteristics, not to mention the name of his spouse," he asked in tortuous fashion.

Flitty looked downcast for a second and then grinned cheerily.

"All such factors must be considered in your deductions, Mr Nightsock."

"My condolent apologies for it would seem that my mental faculties are as rapid as the raging torrents that course their way down the Andes to the plains of the Maya, thereupon to irrigate and bring forth fresh life to the soil and the crops thereon that the honest, hard-working populace have so earnestly tended to ummm…"

He tapered to a halt, lost in a self-made verbal rain forest.

"It could be a man," remarked Potty.

"Tending the crops in the Andes?" asked Pigswill.

"No, you silly girl. This Gordon could have been married to a man."

"You've got inside knowledge?" Midwit enquired sharply.

"Of course I haven't, I just mention the possibility."

"We can ask him if he's gay," suggested Ilena.

Potty sighed.

"There's no point. He's lost his memory."

"That's stupid. Losing memory doesn't affect his orientation."

"Don't call me stupid, you blonde airhead. I'm a highly qualified university professor."

"So you say. For all we know, you're probably some unemployed shop assistant."

Flitty clapped her hands.

"Now everyone, we're all here to have a good time."

"Was that scene part of the mystery?" asked Fleet.

"No, Mr Midwit."

"Okay but it's a bit confusing. I mean, how can we be sure?"

"I know! You could wave a little flag when it's part of the mystery," squealed Pigswill.

"You really are dumb, Pigsty. How realistic would that be if people waved little flags all the time," Potty observed.

"I like the idea. Siko is an intelligent and very attractive woman," remarked Leach ingratiatingly.

Now Potty turned on him.

"You'd say anything to slime your way into a woman's underwear. Leave the girl alone," she vipered.

"I certainly have no desire to paint you although you're supposedly female," he retorted.

Flitty return to the script in desperation.

"Oh my goodness! So you're married, Gordon and you don't know who your wife is due to memory loss."

Sam nodded solemnly and she continued.

"But darling, what will become of us? I was hoping to arrange a divorce and marry you but that seems impossible now. If you don't remember your wife, it could be any woman at all, even Polly the maid."

"It might have been me," interjected Ilena, smoothing her blonde hair with a smile.

Throg's discomfort became painfully obvious as he stumbled back to the script.

"Errr, I just want to have your baby."

A sharp look from Flitty and he backtracked.

"Sorry. I mean 'yes it could'."

"I just want to have your baby. You're the only one for me now," said Flitty with all the passion of a cabbage leaf.

"Let's forget everything tonight and just abandon ourselves to our emotions."

They started to move towards the door and Leach rose from his seat again but an iceberg look from Flitty stopped him.

"Oh, my. I feel a little unwell," she said, clutching her throat.

She fell into Sam's arms but the Throg muscular constitution proved inadequate for the task and she slipped down to the floor.

"Owww! My elbow!" she cried.

"Elbow, interesting," remarked Midwit, writing it down.

Nightsock waved a finger.

"It is my considered opinion that the reference to the hinge mechanism that is part of the upper human limb was not a component of the performance although as I myself have emphasised in one of my best selling novels, it is a perpetual conundrum for the human race to distinguish between that which is in veracity realism and that which is, by the verdict of some, a transient part of unreality although many will propound that this unreality in itself could be as true as the very granite bedrock of this planet that sits beneath our feet like the muscular arms of mighty Atlas."

Siko looked dubious.

"I don't think that's right, Mr Nightsock. An atlas is a book of maps and it doesn't have elbows that hurt," she observed accurately.

"I'm okay, it's only a bruise," cried Flitty, bouncing to her feet and glaring at Sam. She closed her eyes and bent slightly towards him.

"Oh my god, Binki!" he said.

"I've been poisoned!" cried Flitty, placing a forearm across her brow.

"Sure it's not passioned?" remarked Potty cruelly.

Flitty ignored that and carefully placed herself on the floor. Sam moved dutifully to stand over her.

"She's dead!" he said in a monotone.

"Oh no!" squealed Pigswill with a sob.

This unsettled Sam again.

"Don't worry Binki. I'll find out who did this and they will pray for it."

An uncomfortable pause until Flitty got to her feet.

"It's okay Gordon! She's alive!" yelled Pigswill joyfully.

Flitty patiently held up a hand.

"No. Lady Watt is dead. That's the end of the scene. Now you have to find her murderer. There are more scenes tomorrow and later you'll get a chance to interview everybody. What we do now is to put you in pairs and the winning couple will receive the trophy."

"I'll pair off with Ilena," announced Leach.

"No, Mr Leach. We pick the pairs at random. I've put all your names in a bag and we'll draw them now."

"But there are only seven of us as Mr Brickhouse hasn't arrived yet."

"It's not a problem. You others pair off and I'll be with my husband when he comes," responded Heather.

No one seemed particularly happy with the result. Midwit with Pigswill, Nightsock with Ilena and Leach with Potty.

Flitty spoke again.

"There's a lot more to come so you can't reach any conclusions yet. Get ready for the continuation of the mystery tomorrow! I suggest you get acquainted with your new detective partner tonight. "

"I'm not too keen on that," remarked Leach, looking across at Potty.

"And you're not exactly my first choice," she retorted.

Nightsock stood up and faced the group, his countenance benign.

"Now, now all you good people. Are we not here but for a fleeting moment of life's great voyage and should we not imbibe in full the succulent mead that is placed before us in bowls of pewter and gold? I launch myself into the maelstrom of mystery with eyes open and lightning brain at full throttle, like the racing car of deductive faculty that speeds along the twisting track, o'er mounts and screes in the rich pageant of exotic ummm, pageantry."

"Well said, Nightsock," responded Midwit unexpectedly.

Pigswill clapped her hands.

"This is going to be great! I'm looking forward to getting together with you, Mr Midwit."

"Call me Fleet."

"Let's start now. We can go to my room if you like."

Leach sighed as they departed.

"We'll Potty, I doubt if I can stand you for more than a minute but I suppose we can try," he offered gallantly.

"It's unlikely but just possible that you are not the most repulsive man I've ever encountered. We'll go in the corner by the window," she responded

As they walked away, Nightsock and Ilena were engaged in deep conversation, or more accurately deep diatribe from the Nightsock branch of the partnership. The blonde moved to occupy a sofa against the far wall.

"Please come and join me, Mainwaring," she enticed.

He did the joining and immediately found her leg pushed against his.

"I can read men like a book," she began.

"One can only trust that my prologue is of sufficient incentive to demand further exploration."

"You've heard about me?"

"Only that your photograph is displayed with unerring regularity within the celebrity columns of certain newspapers and magazines with which I am not familiar."

"My real name is Brenda Overbach-Ward but I changed it to Ilena Baker when I was 18. I don't sing, act or anything like that. I just started to turn up at celebrity parties. All I did was to say I was the girlfriend of the host and they let me in. I got friendly with all the reporters and cameramen and that's it!"

"It may be that the populace would speculate on the method by which you are able to acquire sufficient finances for such an existence."

"It's easy. I just tell these well-known people little stories to deceive them and they give me money."

"In what fashion?"

"Most celebrities are really dumb and depend on a bunch of advisers for any contact with the real world. Pigswill's a perfect example. I just go up to one and say my car's been stolen and they give me thousands of pounds for a new one. Obviously I have to act it up a bit and do some body pressing but it's pretty simple. In case you're wondering, I've never slept with any of them. I'm actually a very puritan woman, despite my appearance."

"And what pray, is your considered opinion of our fellow detectives?"

"I know Fleet. He's often at the parties. He's young, earnest and not very bright. Leach is a schoolboy, despite his age and Potty shows a hard surface but she's soft inside. Pigswill is everything people think I am and more. I'm not sure about Mrs Brickhouse."

Midwit was in a chair in Pigswill's room while the innocent faced girl sat on the bed.

"Isn't this super! Who do you think did it?"

"We haven't got all the facts yet."

"That Sam is quite cute and Nightsock is so intelligent. I love men with brains. Leach is obviously someone with experience. Older men are so attractive, don't you think?"

"I really wouldn't know," responded the youthful Midwit in disappointed fashion.

"Well I'm not getting married yet. I need to try every man I meet until I find the right one."

"You've known many?" he responded, brightening up.

"572 as at today. I keep a record of each of them and give them a score out of 10. The highest so far is three."

"Maybe you have high standards?"

"Me? All I want is someone honest and faithful."

"Right."

"And a great lover."

"Okay."

"And rich."

"Right."

"And not possessive, so I can have other men friends."

"Okay."

"And he's got to be famous and take me to all the celebrity parties."

"Right."

"And really good-looking."

"Okay."

"And well built."

"Right."

"Want to try for it?"

A pause.

"Well…"

"Come back here later tonight."

"Right. Your name is rather unique isn't it?" asked Midwit, changing the subject while his luck was in.

"I knew you'd like it. Clever, don't you think? I sat for a whole hour with my agent to come up with it. It's so feminine, makes you think of sunny blue skies and fluffy clouds."

"Does it?"

"Pigs will fly, you see!"

"Ah yes. Clever."

"Then my first name is very romantic. O kiss me, backwards. Except we had to miss the first three letters because Emssiko would sound horrible."

"What's your real name?"

"Celeste Amour. Terrible, isn't it? And so common."

"Siko Pigswill is definitely very unusual."

"I think I might get painted by Leach. He seems keen on the idea."

"Speaking as a man, I suggest he has rather more in mind than just painting."

"A sculpture then? That would be great. I could be on display outside an important building, like a nightclub."

At breakfast the next morning, Flitty and Leach were having a slight altercation.

"… but I was investigating the mystery," he protested.

"I'm saying you can't search my bedroom early in the morning or at any other time," Flitty responded.

"I had an idea that Polly, the maid had concealed an important clue under the bed."

"Well she didn't. Where's Potty? You two should be working together."

"She's not very sociable. I offered to paint her but she refused."

Flitty turned to face him, hand on hip.

"Mr Rouse. May I suggest that your approach to the female gender is somewhat one track. Perhaps you should consider a less unwelcome technique."

"Absolutely. I will most certainly take your advice. Perhaps you could explain it fully whilst I'm concentrating. I can do that best by painting you."

Flitty beamed.

"There you go. That's so much better. I'd be very happy for you to get me on canvas."

With this amicable agreement, they parted and Leach joined Potty at the table. Flitty posed, waving her hand.

"Morning everyone. I hope you had a really good rest and your faculties are as sharp as razors. Except you of course, Mr Dairy."

The solitary man granted her a baleful look and returned to his newspaper.

"Our mystery continues in one hour. The next scene is outside!"

Now Midwit rose to his feet, waving a sheet of paper.

"I transcribed all my notes last night and prepared a spreadsheet with all we have so far. I'm selling copies," he announced.

"I'll have one. You can bring it to my room with you when you come tonight," cried Pigswill, smiling sweetly at him.

The remainder of the meal passed quietly, apart from a ferocious whispered argument between Flitty and Sam that appear to relate to his refusal to wear female clothes.

An hour later, the group gathered outside on the grassy lawn at the rear of the hotel. The sea beyond was calm and azured and Nightsock appeared stimulated by the landscape.

"Ah, sweet nature. For the golden disc ascends like a king to his midday throne, casting clarity upon the lands and waters whilst bringing a joyous light to we insignificant bipeds that trawl our furrows of existence like the sparrows in a field of corn that flutter solemnly to seek the worms of existence from this fertile earth."

"Wow! Can you write some lyrics for me? Maybe we could get together later in my room?" proposed Pigswill.

"He won't have time for that because we'll be studying clues," Ilena said sharply.

Flitty had changed into a short yellow dress and looked particularly disappointed that Sam was still in the same jeans and T-shirt as the previous day.

"Right everyone, this is the next scene. You all remember Polly, the maid who was an apparently reformed, homicidal maniac?"

Fleet checked his spreadsheet and scrabbled through his notepad.

"Was she the one who strangled women?" he asked.

"No, that was the butler, John Smith. Polly is the maid who was given a second chance by Lady Watt. She killed people with a knife."

"Hold it everyone! That's right. The spreadsheet got it wrong. I'll correct it and issue a new copy," declared Midwit.

Pigswill brightened.

"You can bring that tonight as well," she said.

Flitty forced a smile.

"Right, so we all know who Polly is. Today she's going to be played by Sam."

Her companion looked distinctly uninspired as he stepped forward and spoke in the deepest voice he could manage.

"Here I am outside the hotel where Lady Watt is staying with Gordon Grant, her lover. I don't approve of it at all but if she runs away with him, I'll have the chance to marry Lord Watt and live a life of luxury. Hello, there's a small house over there. I'll see if anyone lives in it."

"Now you have to imagine Polly is walking towards a little house near the hotel," said Flitty.

"Is it whitewashed?" asked Leach.

"If you like."

"Then it's reminiscent of my most famous painting, 'Little House By The Sea' that I finished two years ago. You can purchase full-colour prints from my website."

Leach produced a leaflet from his pocket and held it up. It was indeed a small house and sea was definitely present. That was the background, largely masked by a cavorting young woman who dominated the picture.

Flitty looked at him with disapproval.

"Now we will proceed. Polly goes up to the house and the door opens."

"My goodness," Sam said dourly.

Flitty looked at her script.

"Yes, it's me, Polly. Molly, your identical twin sister."

"Polly Molly? A weird name," remarked Potty.

Flitty drew a deep breath and rearranged.

"Yes Polly, it's me. Your identical twin sister, Molly."

"Twins! Right, now we're getting somewhere," said Fleet scribbling in his notepad.

"What on earth are you doing here?" continued Sam.

"We haven't seen each other in five years but I found out you were working for Lady Watt and followed you to this place."

"Are you still working as a chemist?"

"Yes I am."

"Amazing…"

Sam stopped as a sudden gust of wind caught Flitty's short dress.

"Amazing indeed," concurred Leach.

"The errant breeze of Mother Earth that curls about our flesh like the loving arms of, ummm, Mother Earth to pull us close to the eternal bosom of…" Nightsock hesitated.

"Mother Earth?" suggested Potty with sarcasm.

He nodded sheepishly. Flitty was now battling to hold her script whilst controlling the dress with her other hand. She refused Leach's offer to assist with the latter.

"Yes, Polly you were saying there is an amazing resemblance between us. In fact, anyone could mistake me for you."

The dress event had unsettled Sam.

"Don't you get so thigh and mighty, Molly. You don't fool me, I can see it all."

"I think everyone did," remarked Potty.

Another gust of wind and Flitty's struggles received help from an unexpected source.

"Madam, I believe this will be of assistance," said Nightsock, removing his belt and fastening it around the disobedient dress. It looped around her three times but seemed to do the job.

"Thank you, Mr Nightsock. Very gentlemanly."

"It is but nothing, Madam," he declared loftily as his trousers fell down.

It was some time before the performance continued. Nightsock's belt was back in place and Flitty now had rope knotted around her thighs. She had tied it with grim modesty to hold the dress tightly but the downside was that it made leg movement almost impossible.

"Right, where were we?" she asked, thumbing through her script.

"Polly told Molly she had seen it all," said Ilena helpfully.

"Well I don't care what you say. It's my life and I'll do what I want!"

"Charming. I was just trying to help," miffed the blonde.

"No, that was Polly. I mean Molly."

"Oh, right."

"Off you go, Sam," instructed Flitty.

He looked puzzled for a moment and then began to walk back to the hotel.

"Is he still Polly?" asked Fleet, note taking.

"No, no. Come back here!" shouted Flitty.

Sam returned for another whispered conversation. Then he stepped forward.

"Sorry about that. If you do, I promise you one thing. You will not live long."

"If that's how you feel, Polly, there's nothing more to be said," Flitty declared before turning with difficulty to the audience.

"Molly slams the door and Polly walks away in an angry mood. Now we go inside the little house and I'm still Molly."

"I'm getting my Pollys and Mollys a bit mixed here," said Midwit.

"Why? It's very clear to me," remarked Potty.

"Don't be so nasty to Fleet. Why not try being nice to people?" suggested Pigswill.

"I don't expect to be told what to do by an amoral girl like you."

Pigswill beamed with delight.

"Amoral, amore. You're saying I'm full of love and it's so true. And I don't mind telling you things. I guess I just naturally love everyone."

"I need some," said Leach.

"The gift of love overcomes all obstacles in our torrid existence that draws us like lemmings to the very edge of those cliffs of anger and hatred that immerse our very souls in their dank and insidious liquid which flows fresh from the cuts and wounds that righteousness, ummm, makes on the putrid flesh of evil, ummm, things," mused Nightsock.

"Come on Molly," Heather encouraged with a sigh.

Flitty raised her script again.

"Well she's not going to stop me. Ah, a knock at the door. It sounds like the person I have duped into helping me to become the next Lady Watt. He believes I am my twin sister and I'll get rid of him as soon as I achieve my objective. Of course, he doesn't realise that."

She performed a door opening mime.

"Earl Slunk, my darling. It's so good you see. I mean good to see you."

"Yes, my dear. I capitulated to your seduction and am now at your command. Have you heard the tragic news that Lady Watt is dead?"

"Really? How sad for you as I know you always had an unrequited desire for her."

"I did, Polly but I always liked you when I saw you during my visits to the Lord. Now I realise that I don't want any other woman."

"I'll make some coffee while we talk."

Polite applause as the scene ended.

"Now we go to another part of the island, where a lone man is looking out to sea," announced Flitty.

Sam strode away from the gathering and convincingly portrayed a lone man whilst accomplishing the looking out to sea function admirably. So well, in fact that he didn't check his script. An embarrassed silence as Flitty attempted to walk over to him but the tight rope round her thighs made movement impossible.

"Read the script, Sam," she yelled.

He waved a hand of apology and began to read. From his gestures it must have been a speech to savour but unfortunately he was some way from the others with his back turned.

"What did he say?" asked Fleet, pen poised over pad.

"The wise deer rests in Gulf Mysol," responded Siko, who was nearest to Sam.

"Gulf Mysol? That's where I holidayed last year. It's in southern Spain," gasped Ilena.

"But why would an animal go there? Great clue!" declared Fleet with enthusiasm.

"Maybe the deer is the killer!" exclaimed Siko.

"Unlikely. Poison isn't their usual method of attack."

"Well done, Flitty. You've really got us thinking," remarked Potty.

"Nice line, Sam!" Ilena yelled and he turned and waved happily.

Flitty was now red-faced and struggling to reach Sam but was prevented by the rope. Eventually, she pulled it off and strode over to the still waving youth. Gripping his arm, she marched him back to the gathering. By this time, deer talk was prevalent.

"I've heard that some African deer have amazing eyesight. They can spot a predator 50 miles away," said Fleet.

"You mean lions or should I say loins?" asked Ilena sweetly.

"But why wise? That's the important word for me," he responded.

Potty nodded agreement.

249

"You're right. The question here, folks is what a wise deer knows that a dumb one doesn't."

Flitty interrupted brusquely.

"Please stop, everyone. Let's roll it back and pretend the deer thing never happened."

"Are you Polly or Molly now?" enquired Leach.

"This isn't part of the performance. Now Sam will do the line again. As I said, we have a lone man looking out to sea."

Her companion began to walk off again but she grabbed him firmly by the arm and pointed at his script.

"The demise of my dearest is engulfing my soul," he declared.

"Hello Lord Watt. It's me Polly, your maid," responded Flitty.

She moved away and then walked up to him. Another gust of wind threw her dress exposingly upwards but she didn't appear to care now.

"What on earth are you doing here?"

"I've come to you in your hour of need and you can depend on me to be beside you always if you need something."

"Why Polly, I didn't realise. You know that I've always found you…"

He broke off as the mischievous wind really got down to work on the dress.

"Get on with it, Sam," shouted Potty.

"Yes, ummm, you know I've always found you in bed thinking about how attractive you are."

A sqeaky gasp from Pigswill.

Flitty moved in for another whispered conversation before he apologised.

"Sorry, missed a line. You know I've always found you intriguing and many times have I lain in bed thinking about how attractive you are."

Suddenly a piercing scream. Followed by several more. Manita was running towards them from the hotel.

"He's dead! Dead! Dead!" she yelled, her face a mask of horror, dread, fear and lipstick. And Pink Sunrise number 37A rouge.

Potty didn't hesitate. She gripped the girl and slapped her. Then she did the same to Siko who had joined in the screaming for no apparent reason.

"Who is dead?" asked Fleet, writing down every word.

"Mr Dairy. Murdered!" bawled Manita from a distance of two paces.

"Then how is he gazing out of his window?" asked Heather.

They all looked up to see Dairy staring solemnly down at them.

"It's a ghost! He's come back to haunt us!" screamed Manita.

Now Potty resumed the slapping but with extra enthusiasm in the blows.

"Tell us exactly what happened," said Heather.

"I went to his room with morning tea and he was lying in bed with his eyes closed. It was terrible?"

"Perhaps he was asleep?"

A long silence and then Manita began to walk back to the hotel, mumbling apologies.

"Well done, Flitty. You really had us going there for a moment. I didn't realise Manita was in your play," remarked Leach.

A puzzled look from Sam but Flitty grasped the life raft.

"As I said earlier, anything may happen now you are in the world of imagination."

That attracted Nightsock like a moth to a bedside lamp.

"Ah, the realms of the imagination that are reminiscent of a…"

Potty interrupted quickly.

"Reminiscent of rabbit ears maybe. Let's get on, shall we?" she said sharply.

Nightsock looked deeply offended although Pigswill was oblivious to the tension.

"Sorry, I don't get it. You mean because rabbit ears listen in pairs? How is that like imagination?"

"It was not my simile," remarked Nightsock smugly.

Fleet waved a hand.

"I think I know. They are large aural extensions in the same way that imagination is an extension of reality except that it's both aural and visual."

"Maybe the rabbit is friendly with the deer?" observed Ilena dourly.

"Will you all shut up and let's get on with the performance," shouted Potty.

Flitty jumped in quickly before arguments started.

"Right, we've just seen Polly and Earl Slunk saying that they're attracted to each other. Their conversation continues. Go on Sam."

"It's not my line," he responded.

"Yes, here it is," she said, pointing at his script.

"You haven't said that yet."

"It doesn't matter."

"I'm getting confused."

"Oh very well. As do I!"

She noticed the blank looks and enlarged.

"As do I think about you in bed at night."

"Polly, I would have you tomorrow for a wife but it cannot be while Lord and Lady Watt still live. Apart from me, they are the only ones who know you were in a correction centre for homicidal maniacs after killing lots of people with a knife."

"That's not true! Gordon knows as well," Pigswill cried.

"I think that's part of the plot," advised Heather.

"Well, I like Gordon. He's romantic and so good-looking. Not like that's horrid Earl Skunk."

"Sam is playing both of them, you stupid girl," Potty declared.

A baleful look from Pigswill and Flitty continued although looking as if she wished to be somewhere else.

"But haven't you heard? Lady Watt has been murdered."

"That's great news. So if something were to happen to Lord Watt, we could go away together and live in my villa in the Caribbean."

Flitty waved a hand.

"That's the end of the scene. Now we'll go inside and you'll have the chance for your first interview with any of the characters you choose."

Back in the lounge soon afterwards and Fleet was studying his spreadsheet.

"First we have Lady Watt but she's dead," he declared.

"Let's have a seance!" suggested Pigswill but was ignored.

"Then there's Lord Watt, his friend Earl Slunk, Polly the maid and Molly, her twin sister. Finally we have Smythe, the butler."

"You forgot gardener Gordon," remarked Potty.

"I put a tick against him in the already dead column. He is still alive then?"

"Yes, unless he fell on his shears."

"Okay. I've got another column to mark who each of them is sleeping with. Molly and Earl Slunk, Gordon and Lady Watt."

"Lady Watt is dead and Earl Slunk wants to sleep with Polly but it's unclear if that's happened yet," said Ilena.

Nightsock intervened.

"Yes, madam but as Polly and Molly are identical, it can not be ascertained whether it is the former or the latter who may have or may not have been sharing a duvet with the notorious Earl."

"What about the deer, Mr Midwit? Is that on your bed sheet?" asked Pigswill.

"Ignore them and let's have Lord Watt on the stand," Potty declared.

Flitty sighed with relief.

"As Sam is just filling in, I'll sit with him and help out with the answers. Now here you are official private detectives who have been called in to solve the case," she responded and sat at the table alongside the youth.

Potty began.

"Did you know that your wife had a lover?"

Now Flitty had written the words 'yes' and 'no' on a piece of paper and pointed at the negative.

"No," replied Sam.

"How did you know your wife was here?"

Flitty scribbled a note and handed it to Sam.

"I saw her dive off and cased Arthur."

"I used to have a boyfriend called Arthur," announced Pigswill.

"Me too," remarked Ilena.

"Well it wouldn't be the same one. My Arthur is now a big star."

"So's mine."

"He's the drummer with the Ripping Velcros."

"And my Arthur is."

A pause before Pigswill continued.

"I knew him longer than you."

"How long?"

"Oh, ages," responded Pigswill cautiously.

"I've known him on and off for years."

"On and off what?"

Flitty stepped in at this point.

"Sorry ladies, there is no Arthur. What Sam meant to say was 'I saw her drive off and chased after her'."

"He looks like Arthur," and Pigswill remarked sullenly.

"So what you're saying is that we need to delete this Arthur character from our records?" Fleet enquired, ferociously amending his notes.

Potty continued at increased volume.

"And my next question. What is your relationship with Molly?"

"He doesn't know her," Flitty responded.

"Let the man speak for himself," protested Fleet with support from Pigswill.

Flitty sighed and wrote on the paper.

"I don't know her," read Sam.

"You're lying! She's your maid!" declared Potty triumphantly.

A silence as Fleet cross checked his spreadsheet.

"Hold on, Potty. I think you're thinking of Polly."

"Yes, Polly. That's what I said, wasn't it?" she blustered.

"Ah, what a dilettante is the human tongue. It curls itself with gay abandon around our M's when we so fervently desire it to moistly form around our P's," mused Nightsock.

"That sounds disgusting," squealed Pigswill but didn't look disgusted.

Flitty scribbled another note for Sam to read.

"Yes, I know Polly well although her mental condition remains a concern."

"I want to ask something. How do you feel now you're not married and therefore available?" enquired Pigswill.

"My wife's death has deeply upset me."

"And do you like younger women?"

"I don't think I want another wife," read Sam but he gazed adoringly at the questioner.

Now Fleet had written more notes.

"I'd like to quiz the butler," he said.

"I'll play him," answered Flitty to save writing fatigue.

"Good. You are Jim Smythe, the butler?"

"Yes, I am John Smith."

"And you strangle women?"

"That's a lie! I was acquitted. I'll get my lawyers on you!"

This unsettled Midwit.

"Really? No, I meant to say it is alleged that you strangle women."

Flitty was into it now.

"But you didn't. This will cost you a lot, Mr Midwit."

"Look, I'll offer an unreserved apology. Even put it in a newspaper."

"Not good enough. I want compensation and I want it now."

Midwit's forehead glistened with sweat.

"I can offer you 100 pounds, cash."

"100? Ridiculous. I'm looking for 10,000 and I won't accept a penny less."

"I'll have to sell my car and maybe remortgage the house," he whimpered

"That's your problem. You should have thought about that before making such slanderous allegations in front of witnesses."

"I heard him say it, Mr Smith! I'll come and testify and I'll make sure I wear a grey suit," shouted Pigswill.

Midwit turned to her in desperation.

"I thought we were friends. I mean, last night."

"For goodness sake, this is just a performance. We can say what we want," Potty declared dismissively.

"It wouldn't matter to you because you haven't got a reputation to protect but I'm a famous singer," Pigswill said tartly.

"Well, I've never heard of you and all I've seen here is a stupid girl."

"Right. I'm calling a lawyer. Can we share one, Mr Smith?"

Flitty had calmed down a little.

"No, Ms Pigswill. Potty is correct. This is just part of the act."

Ilena had been checking her make-up in a hand mirror but now looked up.

"At this rate, we'll be lucky to finish this mystery before Christmas," she said dispassionately.

"You're right. Let's keep talk to a minimum and let these two get on with it," Potty agreed.

Assenting murmurs although Pigswill remained somewhat prickly.

"Any more questions, Mr Midwit?" asked Flitty.

He shook his head.

"Is there anyone else you'd like to ask questions of?"

"If you see Gordon the gardener then tell him to come to my room later. I'd like to console him over Lady Binki," said Pigswill.

Sam blushed and his eyes opened a little but he didn't have the courage to respond.

Pre-dinner and Heather was back in her room when the phone rang.

"Hello dear."

"Philip. I thought you were coming here today."

"A slight delay. The newspaper said it was just the tip of an iceberg. It now appears a magazine was also stolen."

"Magazine?"

"Yes, taken from the same letter box. Significantly, it was Canary Monthly, a periodical that could have some impact in this case."

"Why would a bird be of importance?"

"Not just a bird. A yellow bird. That is the significant factor. I still expected to resolve matters swiftly and hope to join you tomorrow."

"I'll keep making notes. Bye Philip."

"Good-bye, dear."

The next morning dawned bright and sunny, the heavens were purest blue and a hot day was forecast. Everyone wore smiles of joy and optimism, a new vigour in their step. That was in Trinidad.

Sepulchre Island was also under a clear sky but a depressing cloud of utter desolation and despair hung over the hotel, reflected in the persona of those within.

The atmosphere had the opposite effect on Flitty. As breakfast was completed, she bounced to her feet.

"I hope everyone had a really deductive night!" she shouted cheerily.

A general mumble appeared to indicate that it hadn't been.

"Well the good news is that there could be another murder today!"

This didn't seem to spread a lot of happiness but it did at least encourage Midwit to start writing in his notebook.

"One wonders at the coruscating ambience of post-repose somnolence that wallows as a hippopotamus in the mud bath of our subconscious," observed Nightsock wittily.

"That made no sense at all," remarked Potty.

"My dear Madam, those words are famed throughout the literary world as the initial sentence in my acclaimed novel, 'A Fantasy During Slumber Within The Darkness Of The Midpoint Of The Hottest Season'. One of the few books ever to receive a five star rating in the annual awards of NOPE."

"Never heard of the book, never heard of NOPE."

"The Nightsock Organisation Prize for Erudition? A much sought after recognition among authors."

"An organisation you own?"

"Purely in terms of ownership, dear lady. The awards are bestowed by a totally independent committee of which I have the honour to be chair."

Potty's expression turned fearsome and Flitty rapidly continued.

"Now we're going outside again. The weather is lovely."

Heather noted she was wearing trousers this time. They gathered on the grass where a semi circle of chairs had been placed. Then Flitty continued.

"This scene introduces two new characters into our plot. You'll have to think of Sam as a woman."

"I can't do that! He's a man!" cried Pigswill.

More embarrassment for Sam but he came through this time.

"Look, actors are doing it all the time so you'll have to use your imagination," he declared.

"It takes one with true masculinity to play a woman," remarked Ilena, obviously impressed.

Pigswill reacted swiftly to the competition as if she had experience of this sort of thing.

"I'm glad you agree. As I said, Sam is a real man in every sense of the word."

The youth glowed with the attention, little realising that he was purely that little thing with feathers being flogged to each side of the net in the badminton match of death that is a battle of esteem between women.

"So off we go," declared Flitty, bringing Sam back to reality by jabbing at his script.

"Oh right. Well we're here now on this sad occasion," he said.

"Yes, we are the sisters of Lady Watt who have rushed here after her dreadful murder. There were three of us sisters but now only you Dolly and me, Holly remain."

"Yes, Holly as we live together, we spent some time making our plans. We will find the murderer and they will pay for it!" Sam announced dramatically while studiously avoiding the admiring gaze of Pigswill.

"You seem very positive Dolly but I know that you've never liked our sister. You said you hated the way she married a Lord to improve her status."

"Well, it's interesting to hear you say that. You tried to kill her once by dropping a brick on the head."

"I was only demonstrating the laws of gravity, Dolly."

"And where were you, Holly on the day she was killed? You went out in the morning and didn't get back until late."

"I was just shopping for a new black dress."

"I didn't see you bring one back."

"They didn't have my size," said Flitty, greatly encouraged at the lack of interruptions.

It didn't last.

"I know a good dress shop and they'd certainly have one to fit you," remarked Ilena.

"But I know a better one," cried Pigswill, still competing.

" I haven't even told you the name of my shop."

"Mine's sure to be better. I have to get outfits to wear on stage in front of thousands of people but you just need skimpy little things for parties."

"She's got a point, Ilena," supported Potty.

"What would you know about dresses, Dirsnap? I've only ever seen you in shirt and trousers."

"That's because I'm intelligent and a university professor. I don't need to flaunt myself around to earn money."

"Hold on! I think I've found an important link here," shouted Midwit.

All eyes turned to him expectantly as he double checked his spreadsheet and notes. Then he looked up triumphantly.

"The maid and her sister plus these two sisters of the deceased all have a first name with the letter Y at the end," he declared.

"So what?" asked Potty, balloon poppingly.

"Well, there could be a relationship between them. I'm thinking that the letter Y is an important factor in this case."

Siko screamed with delight.

"He's right! Polly, Dolly, Holly and Molly. They're all in on it. It's a massive conspiracy. A gang of murdering women. We'll need the police to round them up."

Her enthusiasm wasn't shared by the others.

"Better warn them that Polly is a knife killer," added Ilena incitingly.

"Was that the end of the scene?" asked Leach, ignoring the revelation.

"Yes. Now we're starting another one. It's in a room at the hotel. Go on Sam."

"Hello Polly, you've come to my room as I asked," he said.

"Yes I have, Earl Slunk."

"Then let me kiss you."

"No. Not until you do something for me."

"What?"

"I want you to kill Lord Watt. Then I'll be free to run away with you."

"It is an agonising choice for me. Should I murder another human to gain access to your favours or should I deny myself these pleasures in the name of integrity?"

"Favours? Like wedding favours?" asked Pigswill.

"In your case he'd need to murder someone not to get them," Ilena knifed.

"You know you can't resist me. Wait! Someone's entering!" Flitty continued.

Sam walked to the other side of her before reading the next line.

"I made a mistake and came in the wrong room. Hold on! You are Earl Slunk and you are Dolly the maid!"

"Shouldn't that be Polly?" asked Midwit and Flitty nodded before speaking.

"Oooh! It's Gordon the gardener. The man who seduced my mistress with his silken tongue and muscular body."

"Wow! He's back! I just love Gordon," cried Pigswill.

"Yes it's me. Now I find you two in intimate circumstances."

"It wasn't that intimate," remarked Leach.

This filled the time while Sam moved back to his original position.

"What do you mean, sir? I will not have my reputation besmirched by a common servant such as yourself."

"Oh, Earl Slunk. You didn't seem concerned about my reputation. Perhaps you are not so obsessed with me as I thought you were," observed Flitty/Polly.

Sam changed positions again, checked his script and continued.

"Don't think that, my dear. I just forgot to mention you."

Now he moved to position B.

"Ha! So the two lovebirds are already arguing. A thought has occurred to me. Both of you had good reason to murder my love, Lady Binki Watt."

"A malicious slander!" declared Flitty

A whispered conversation ensued.

"That was my line," said Sam.

"It doesn't matter."

"It matters to me. I've got fans out there."

"What? You're just filling in."

"They like me."

"I'm with you, Sam!" cried Pigswill.

Nightsock rose ponderously to his feet.

"Madam, I believe it to be the considered and unanimous opinion of we, the onlookers, that the lad should be accepted in a fair and equitable manner to be a significant character amidst the gripping and tangled tale that you place before us as a cuisine chef presents his most treasured and carefully prepared repast to a select and in some cases distinguished number of aficionados of culinary excellence."

"Don't you dare make any assumptions about my opinion," said Potty with some venom.

"I fail to perceive the justification for your aggressive manner."

"You said unanimous. That means you are presuming your pompous statement has my support."

"Pompous! Pompous? Madam, in all my many years of scribing words of excellence and giving innumerable speeches and lectures, I have never been referred to by that description."

"That can't be true," remarked Ilena.

"What? Another female anaconda burying her fangs into my universal reputation as perhaps the most modest and unassuming figure amongst the dazzling lights of the greatest literary talents in recent history?"

"My dog's got more talent than you," responded Potty, warming up.

"You compare me to mere canine? If I were in the animal kingdom, I would dominate all others as a veritable Colossus of Rhodes amongst the inferior fauna that mingle in mindless mundanity within the forests and plains of those domains in which the lesser creatures reside."

"What's its name?" asked Pigswill.

A pause as everyone searched for an appropriate piece for the jigsaw question. Finally Potty replied.

"His real name is Grotto of Tranquillity. He makes me feel so relaxed and his eyes are like pools of shining water."

"Yes?" enquired Ilena.

"Yes what?"

"You said that's his real name so what do you call him?"

"I'm not telling you."

"I'll have a guess," offered Leach.

"Don't you dare."

"Is he a sheepdog?" Pigswill continued.

"No, a Bonsai Alsatian. A new Japanese breed, like a tiny version of a real Alsatian."

"And you call him Gertie," suggested Midwit.

"No, I do not."

"Okay, okay. I'm just getting the names right on my spreadsheet."

"This is not part of the performance."

"Hold on. Your name finishes in Y as well. Listen everyone, I think we've cracked the case wide open."

A terrified squeal from Pigswill.

"Potty, how could you murder that woman?" she screamed.

"Shut up you stupid girl."

"I know! You wanted Gordon for yourself. I mean, a dog is nice but you obviously needed a man as well."

"Well Potty, it looks like your life of crime is finally coming to an end," remarked Ilena sourly.

261

"Do they still use the electric chair?" added Leach, stirring with some pleasure.

Flitty plucked a schoolteacher character from her repertoire.

"Now come along everyone. We all know that Potty isn't part of the mystery so Sam and I will just finish off our scene. You remember that Gordon had surprised Earl Slunk and Polly the maid in the hotel room."

"A malicious slander!" cried Sam quickly with a smug expression.

"Don't you dare accuse us of murder, Gordon," added Flitty.

Sam in position B.

"Yes Polly, a woman who was in a correction centre for homicidal maniacs would say that. And I also know about Molly."

Back to position A.

"Who is Molly?"

Position B.

"Ha, ha, wouldn't you like to know. I'm going now."

"He's gone and slammed the door after him," said Flitty in confirmation.

"Does he sit on your lap?" asked Pigswill.

A mystified silence.

"Sam? Certainly not," Flitty responded vehemently.

Midwit checked his spreadsheet.

"No mention of lap here. Is this lap in the sense of a circuit of a running track?"

Nightsock stirred again.

"One would speculate that the location described by Ms Pigswill refers to the central portion of the human body whilst it is in a seated position. Thus the question posed must relate to an object or objects that may be positioned thereon. Here we find an important clue within the statement. The word sit indicates an animate entity and my intellect, that has the ability to transform the incomprehensible into the trivial, provides an immediate response. A canine quadruped of the genus Japanus Bonzai Alsatianus."

Ilena glanced at him.

"Sorry Nightsock, what did you say? I dozed off for a minute there. It's pretty obvious Pigswill is talking about Potty's dog. The one she calls Grotty."

"Don't you dare say that name. He's Grotto of Tranquillity to you," responded Potty.

"And the next scene!" Flitty yelled above the tumult of invective.

Surprisingly, silence fell.

"Right, now we are outside a room at the hotel. I am the manager again."

She began to mime the unlocking and opening of a door but the portrayal didn't seem to get through.

"Are those code signals?" asked Fleet.

"Yes! She's turning her hand. Like giving something," responded Siko.

"Giving us information. Right, you call it out and I'll mark it on the spreadsheet."

"Now she's holding something round. A ball!"

"Maybe it's tennis?" enquired Ilena.

"And now she's pushing with her other hand. Like in the sales at the clothes shops. It's as if she's trying to reach something."

"Hold on! I've got it. The ball is a grenade and she's pushing through a crowd to throw it at someone," Midwit burbled.

Pigswill was almost overcome with excitement.

"I went to Grenade for a holiday last year. It was lovely. I remember sunbathing nude on the terrace of the villa."

A pause as everyone waited for Leach to speak.

"You're thinking of Grenada," he said unexpectedly.

"Oh, yes. What's grenade then?"

"It's like a small bomb."

Now Nightsock started.

"My hyperactive senses indicate a connection. One is presented with a bomb and a person at the sales. The salient words here are bomb sales."

"A weapons dealer! Yes, you've cracked it, Nightsock!" cried Midwit.

"But who is it?" asked Potty.

Midwit checked the sheet.

"Got it! Only one person with the wealth and influence. It's gotta be Lord Watt."

"I think he was a deer smuggler as well," announced Pigswill.

Now Flitty was showing the strain.

"Don't be so stupid. I was miming the unlocking and opening of the door to a hotel room."

"Yes, yes. You would say that," Midwit responded with a knowing smile.

A sigh from Flitty but she continued.

"Oh my goodness. A body!"

Now Sam joined her.

"Hello manager, you remember me. I am Lord Watt. Hold on. That's John Smith, my butler! The one who strangled women!"

"Careful, Sam. He could take you to court," advised Midwit.

"The trick here is always to use the word alleged and then you can say what you like," added Ilena.

This unsettled Sam.

"But I'm only reading the script."

"That's no excuse in law," said Leach firmly.

"Come on Flitty, get your lawyers on him. He's a nasty deer smuggler and should be locked up," demanded Pigswill.

No immediate response from the fair-haired woman. Her chin firmed up.

"We will not continue until your inane comments cease."

Nightsock immediately offered support.

"In this respect, you have my complete and utter agreement, madam. As a wordsmith of international repute, it pains me indeed that my aural orifices are so continually assaulted by such uninformed chatter that passes through the air as silken winged eagles, steering their unseen path through the gathering clouds of nirvana."

"Shut up," responded Flitty.

"Yes madam."

"Right. Now we will carry on and I don't expect further interruptions."

Even Sam waited for her to nod before continuing.

"Yes, your Lordship. He's dead, poisoned by the look of it."

"Wait! Was that a scream I heard?"

Siko started to speak but bit her lip as Flitty stared severely at her before continuing.

"Now imagine the manager and the Lord walking into another room where a maid is standing next to the open door."

"What is it?" asked Sam in his lordly voice.

"Two more bodies. Why, it's Dolly and Holly, the two sisters of Lady Binki Watt."

"I knew them well. Are they also dead?"

"Yes and both have also been poisoned."

An uneasy silence as the audience stared appealingly but with mouths firmly clamped. Midwit almost whimpered with the effort of restraint.

Flitty milked the moment, revelling in her power. Then she gave a faint smile, like an over promoted official.

"Very well. Are there any questions?"

The dam burst and a torrent of speech cascaded from all directions, welling up like a giant tidal wave and threatening to submerge the two actors in its amplitude. Finally Potty's voice held command although Nightsock continued an unfathomable whimsy that involve pastures, mountains and primarily, a solitary pink flower.

"I'm talking now," Potty announced.

Nightsock halted somewhere between stamen and pistils.

"Thank you. So you've given us three more murders. When do we start to solve them?"

Another supercilious smile from Flitty.

"From this moment. You now have to find the killer or killers."

"The spreadsheet needs some work. So Polly and Dolly are dead then," said Midwit.

"Holly, not Polly," responded Flitty.

"I haven't got a Holly here."

"Was her second name Day?" asked Ilena innocently.

"Holly and Dolly, the two sisters. You must have them," declared Potty.

"What? The spreadsheet got it wrong again. I've got Hilly and Dolly."

"No woman is called Hilly," declared Pigswill.

"One of my friends is called Gilly. That's only a letter away," offered Ilena helpfully.

Now Sam stepped forward manfully.

"Now listen everyone. It's pretty simple. Lady Binki Watt was poisoned and also her two sisters, Holly and Dolly. The butler John Smith has now been murdered the same way."

"You're so masterful. Please come to my room tonight and explain it all to me," breathed Pigswill receptively.

"I thought I was coming?" complained Midwit.

"I've already scored you at two so time to move on."

A glum silence from Midwit but Nightsock seemed encouraged.

"In this world of alligator eat alligator there must always be those who triumph, triumphantly and those that fail miserably."

"You only got a one and you know exactly why," Pigswill added venomously.

Nightsock blushed, stammered and blummered as Potty took charge again.

"Right. We've got four dead. The suspects are Lord Watt, Polly the maid and her twin sister Molly, Earl Slunk and Gordon the gardener."

"Yes, that's exactly right Ms Dirsnap," agreed Flitty with relief that someone had been taking notice.

"So now you want us to pair off and start solving the puzzle."

"That's the idea. Each pair is free to interview any of the characters. That could give you important clues."

"Siko doesn't want to pair with me now," whimpered Midwit.

"Don't be silly, of course she does," responded Flitty.

"No I don't. I want to be paired with Gordon," Siko said emphatically.

"Well you can't because he's fictional."

"I'm okay with Nightsock. One is more than enough for any woman," observed Ilena.

"Thank you, madam," the big man responded, testosterone suitably assuaged.

"And I'm getting to like my Potty," announced Leach.

All eyes turned to the little woman in expectation of a vehement response. It didn't arrive.

"Very well, Mr Rouse. We will unquestionably be successful in winning the prize for detection."

Nightsock raised a hand.

"There I must contradict you, madam. My own capacious deductive abilities are already leading me to a conclusion and I am sure I will achieve this climactic moment with Ms Baker."

Ilena beamed.

"No doubt we will, Mainwaring. Who shall we interview?"

Potty got in first.

"We will begin immediately by quizzing Molly in private," she announced.

"And I want Gordon privately," demanded Pigswill.

"Only if you do it with Midwit," Flitty stated firmly.

"Yes, that's okay with me," came the quick response.

Flitty turn to Sam.

"I think you can handle it but call me if necessary," she instructed.

"Great! We'll do it in my room," enthused Pigswill.

"No, you will not. All interviews will be held in this lounge."

"Let's go in the corner. Come on Sam," said Midwit and the trio settled on a sofa with Sam in the centre.

Flitty paused.

"Unfortunately there's just Sam and myself so you other three will have to listen in with one of the groups."

"Nightsock and I will go to Sam," offered Ilena quickly, noticing the youths face was now a rich red as Pigswill endeavoured for the closest proximity on the sofa.

Potty and Leach moved to the opposite corner and Heather followed as Flitty took a chair to face them. The questioning began and all appeared to be organised. Not for long.

A minute passed before Sam gave a cry and Flitty bounded over like mother antelope.

"What's happening here?" she demanded, noting that Ilena had usurped Midwit's position next to the youth.

"It's just that they're whispering things," mumbled Sam.

"Siko and Ilena?"

"Yes."

"Right."

Now mother antelope turned feral and hands moved to hips.

"You two ladies will come with me now."

Pigswill and Baker trailed her to another corner where one of those discussions between women commenced. The words couldn't be heard but the visual indications were more than sufficient. Not really a discussion, more a full-scale verbal assault by Flitty.

Nightsock unwisely lumbered across to them, drawn by some irresistible male masochistic urge. Leach and Midwit followed with Sam, the same undeniable instinct guiding their limbs.

Finally, Potty marched over in a take charge manner but it was too late. A full-scale skirmish of invective that was now degenerating into a women versus men battle.

Heather waited alone as the volume increased. She was the only one to notice Manita rush in, screaming. Disappointed by the lack of attention, the maid left the room until the hubbub had subsided and then re-entered, revising the screams upwards.

"He's dead! Dead! Dead!"

"Who? asked Leach

"Mr Dairy"

"Asleep again?"

"No, he's really dead this time. We called a doctor."

Now Heather stepped forward.

"I must now reveal myself. I am Heather Caldrock, assistant to Philip Caldrock, the well known investigator. I propose to take charge here."

Gasps from the others although Heather caught them asking each other if they'd ever heard the name. She waved a hand for silence.

"Now Manita. Tell me exactly what has happened."

"I went to Mr Dairy's room this morning."

"Bringing his breakfast?"

"No."

"Then why were you there?"

"Do I have to tell you?"

Heather sighed.

"And what did you see?"

"The door was locked from the inside so I went back to my room and got dressed. Then I called Mr Grimedung. He opened it with his master key and there was Mr Dairy on the floor. It was terrible."

"The cause of death?"

"I don't know. The doctor has just arrived so you can ask her."

"Why did you say it was murder?"

"He had a look of terror on his face, as though he had seen some horrifying monster."

"It could have been the deer," offered Siko.

Heather ignored that.

"Now this is important, Manita. Were any of the windows open when you entered the room?"

"No. Just one window there and it was closed and locked. I opened it immediately."

"Why?"

"A strange aroma in the room. It was like something but I just can't think what."

"Like a man's bedroom?" asked Potty.

"Yes, that's it."

Heather began to turn away.

"I'm going to see the doctor. You can return to the hotel but you must not leave the island," she announced.

Potty's chin firmed up.

"Don't you start telling me what to do, Mrs Coldsuck or whatever your name is. You have no rights whatsoever and do as I please. In fact, as a matter of principle, I propose to leave immediately."

Nightsock moved alongside her, like a huge tugboat beside a coracle.

"Whilst I invariably desist from the use of such strenuous language, I wish to announce that I share the feelings of Ms Wordsnap."

"Dirsnap," she corrected.

"Indeed madam. A name of veracity if ever I heard it."

The curious couple turned towards the hotel just as a single dark cloud scurried to a positioned directly above and commenced precipitation.

"Only a shower," remarked Midwit, looking upwards.

As if this was a challenge, the cloud's relations stormed to support their lone offspring. The wind intensified and rain poured down. A wild scramble to the hotel and all were sopping wet as they entered.

Grimedung awaited them.

"You're dripping on the floor. Stop it now!" he shouted.

"It's pouring with rain. Didn't you notice?" Potty responded.

"Don't care. Look, you dripped again. Get out, all of you. You can't come in here with wet clothes."

Potty flushed and stepped forward. Then stopped as he produced a shotgun.

"I mean it!" he bawled.

A scramble outside. Torrents of rain descending now. No hesitation from Pigswill. She stripped off her drenched outer garments and threw them in the porch, leaving just the underwear.

"If any of you gentlemen want to bring my clothes to my room later, I'd be very grateful," she announced, disappearing through the entrance.

No one else seemed particularly keen to follow her example and Sam was distinctly affected by the event, eyes wide and mouth open. No hesitation from Leach who pounced on the discarded clothing and attempted to wring it out although the rain quickly reversed the procedure.

Heather began to walk along the wall of the building.

"I'm going to get in. You can follow or not, as you see fit," she declared, somewhat vexed by the previous response to her assumed command.

They followed as she turned down the side of the hotel and opened a fire door that had been left unsecured. This led directly to a flight of stairs and all quickly returned to their rooms.

Heather was soon descending, dried and freshly attired. A sole woman in the lounge as she entered.

"You are the doctor?"

"Doctor Rigor," responded the woman, a cold faced, square personage with short cropped brown hair.

"I am Heather Caldrock, assistant to Philip, the investigator and I propose to supervise the investigation pending the arrival of the police."

An unexpected response from Rigor.

"My goodness. You are really Philip Caldrock's wife? I'm a great admirer of his."

"Ah, right. That's very kind, Doctor. Now what facts can you provide on this strange death."

"Not a lot really. Mr Dairy died between 11.38 and 11.39 last night. The cause of death was a rhinoceros."

"What! In this hotel?" exclaimed Heather.

"A metal representation on a table in this room. It impacted on his cranium with fatal results. My medical oath prevents me from disclosing how the ornament could have accomplished this."

Heather moved close to the woman and whispered in her ear.

"Doctor Rigor, you will appreciate that during our investigations, I have been privy to many medical secrets. You are referring of course, to the fact that human or animal representations possess one good jump during their existence."

The chunky doctor beamed.

"Yes indeed I am, Mrs Caldrock. I should have recognised that you would have known about it."

"I understand that Mr Dairy was found on the floor?"

"Yes. I suspect he had been sitting in a chair when the rhino clobbered him. To use medical terms, the impact caused his body to fall forwards and to one side, eventuating in his final position on the floor."

"We must also consider another possibility. A person could have picked up the ornament and struck him with it."

"Then how would you explain the locked door?"

"The murderer could have locked it when they left."

"Good point."

Siko and Leach entered the lounge in mid argument.

"But you said bring your clothes to your room," he protested.

"I said later. That means later when I'm free. I don't want men banging on my door when I'm busy."

"Yes, what was Midwit doing there? I'm keeping the clothes until I have an invite," Leach responded, clutching the garments.

"Very well. I'll tell you if I'm ever available."

The doctor observed the newcomers with distaste and packed up her bag.

"I must be going now. The corpse has been wrapped in a carpet and Manita has placed it in the cellar, ready for the police."

Leach saw a new opportunity.

"Hello. You're the sort of woman I'd love to paint."

"Go away, you disgusting old man. I'm leaving."

"No you're not. Have you seen outside?"

A quick glance through the window underlined his words. Torrents of water gushing from the roof and the sea was invisible in the deluge. Siko produced a mobile phone and then screamed in horror.

"No signal! No signal!"

Grimedung entered, nearly smiling.

"Looks like we're cut off. I've tried the main telephone but it's not working. The line must have been broken in the storm. Or maybe it's been cut deliberately."

Another scream from Siko just as Potty arrived with Nightsock and Fleet close behind.

"What's going on?" she asked.

"We're trapped here! No telephone!" squealed Siko.

Now Flitty and Sam joined the throng.

"Shall we carry on with the play or would that be a bit impolite to Mr Dairy?"

"He's not going to care," observed Potty.

Heather stepped forward.

"To confirm my previous announcement, I am taking charge of this investigation, particularly as it's obvious that the police will not reach us for some time. I have the support of Doctor Rigor," she added, wary of Potty's response.

"The talons of deduction must be inserted into the rancid flesh of this whole calamity, to extract the gleaming orb of truth!" declared Nightsock.

"What do you want us to do?" asked Midwit.

"I wish to ask you all a few simple questions. Where is Ilena?"

A screaming figure burst into the room. Manita.

"She's dead! Dead! Dead!" she screamed, screamingly.

Doctor Rigor grabbed her by the shoulders.

"Speak clearly girl. What has happened?"

"She's dead! Dead! Dead!"

This time at a lower volume.

"Who?"

"Ms Baker. In her room. Murdered."

"Take me there immediately."

The two women disappeared and Siko began a fresh outbreak of screaming, eventually physically silenced by Potty. Silenced and unconscious. Potty glanced down at her.

"That's better. So what's your verdict, Caldrock?"

"I am gathering facts. Where were you between 11.30 and 11.45 last night, Mr Midwit?"

"I was in bed. Siko will confirm that."

"I see. Mr Nightsock?"

"The delicate digits of slumber had not yet gripped me but I was in a reclining posture. The veracity of this statement can be confirmed by simple interrogatory communication with Mr Midwit or Ms Pigswill."

"And you, Mr Leach?"

The lean man looked less than gruntled.

"I was working on a painting."

"By yourself?"

"Yes. Then I went down to the kitchen to get a sandwich."

"What time?"

"About 10.30."

"Did you see anyone?"

"No. After that I wandered round for a while."

"Did you go past Mr Dairy's room?"

"Yes, at least once. After half an hour or so, I went back to my room and stepped fitfully for about 30 minutes. Then I went to the kitchen again."

"Another sandwich?"

"No, a glass of milk. I did another wander around the hotel and finally went to bed."

"Thank you," Heather said with finality but Leach continued.

"I woke again 20 minutes later and went downstairs."

"To the kitchen?"

"No. To get a book I'd left in the lounge."

"And then you wandered round once more."

"No. This time I did a thorough circuit of the hotel. I visited every corridor in the building before returning to bed and to sleep."

"Right."

"I woke again 15 minutes later but this time I didn't go downstairs."

"Good."

"I just wandered around my own level. Round and round. By that time I was so tired I went back to my room and I fell asleep immediately."

"Until this morning?"

"Yes."

"Thank you, Mr Leach."

"Yes, it was three in the morning. So I got up and came downstairs for a cup of tea."

"Perhaps we can abbreviate your account, Mr Leach. How many times in all did you leave your room between entering it last night and leaving it for breakfast this morning?"

"38."

"Excellent. Thank you, Mr Leach. It seems that Ms Pigswill has now recovered."

The girl scrambled to her feet.

"Where am I?" She asked dizzily.

"We're being interrogated," said Potty.

"Oh right."

"I only wish to know of your activities last night," enquired Heather unwisely.

"Really? What everything?"

"Just the essentials. Mr Midwit claims that you can confirm he was in bed."

"Did he?"

"And as Mr Nightsock declares that he was with Mr Midwit, it's possible that you may also verify his account."

"Yes."

"Yes meaning you confirm they were with you?"

"It's possible that I could."

"And do you?"

"Maybe, maybe not."

"Another good smack could get her to answer," remarked Potty.

Siko screamed.

"No! I'll talk! I'll tell you everything!"

"Yes?" Heather encouraged.

"Yes, everything."

"Well?"

"I'm suffering from memory loss as a result of being hit by Potty."

"It's okay. You can tell them," offered Fleet.

"Who are you?"

"I'm Fleet Midwit and this gentleman is Mr Nightsock. You remember."

"No. The memory of you two men coming to my room last night is a complete blank."

At this unsatisfactory state of the questioning, Doctor Rigor returned.

"Ilena's dead all right. On the floor of the room with a cracked cranium. Just two possibilities. One is that someone could have banged her on the head with the wooden mallet that lay beside her body."

"And the other?" asked Heather.

"An accident. She could have fallen out of the window."

"But she was in her room."

"She could have fallen out onto her head and rebounded from the ground back up through her window to finish on the floor."

"Rebounded?"

"The cerebral cortex is very bouncy, like a giant spring."

"The time of death?"

"Just before breakfast."

"I was wandering about the hotel then," offered Leach.

"I was in my room and I've got two witnesses," declared Siko tritely.

"I thought you'd lost your memory," remarked Heather.

"Yes I have."

"Then how can you remember the fact you had two witnesses?"

A pause.

"I wrote it down on a piece of paper," Siko said desperately.

"Where is this paper?"

"I can't remember."

"I was with Siko," announced Midwit.

"And Mr Midwit will verify that I was with him," declared Nightsock.

"Sam and I were together, rehearsing our lines," said Flitty.

All eyes turned to Potty.

"No need to look at me. I've got a perfect alibi. I was watching morning TV in my room."

"Anyone could say that," remarked Midwit.

"But I can tell you all about the program. They had three guests. An actress who had appeared naked in a film and was promoting it, a male singer who had bedded a load of celebrities and was plugging his new song and a woman novelist who had just posed nude for a men's magazine. She was hyping her new book."

"Okay, that sounds conclusive," admitted Midwit.

"Where is Manita?" asked Heather.

Rigor responded.

"I instructed her to carry the carcass to the cellar. Strange, she should be back by now."

"Could be a story in this. I'll find her," said Midwit and left the room with the doctor.

Nightsock stepped forward.

"In order to occupy the chronological period that will elapse before Mr Midwit returns, I will recount an amusing anecdote. I use the word amusing in a modest fashion as those who have heard this trifle claim it to be, without reservation, a paramount of hilarity, an unquestioned pinnacle in the field of that human emotion we know as humour."

He ignored a groan from Potty before continuing.

"To use a dramatic artifice, the story commences in an ancient and distant land, a fragmented nation, every part of which is divided into territories that one could call sectors and each of these is controlled autonomously by noble Lords who defend the perimeters of their region with the utmost aggression. In order that the populace are completely aware of the sector on which they stand, a distinctive visual aid lies at the borderline of these territories and it is guarded and patrolled continuously by armed men in the employ of the Lord."

"Why not women?" asked Potty.

"Ah, madam. We are in a time of unenlightenment when the male gender accomplished domination by their innate strength and overbearing manner."

"Women have also got that. Were these Lords all men as well?"

"I presume that to be the case."

"It's nothing short of appalling."

"I agree with Potty," said Leach, surprisingly.

Nightsock squirmed.

"Ah, now I do recall further details. Indeed you are correct. Some of the Lords were of the female gender as were a proportion of the vicious warriors who guarded their land."

Now Siko started.

"Women are not vicious," she protested.

"Ms Pigswill, this is a land purely of the imagination. It is hypothetical, illusory and existing entirely in the realms of fantasy."

"So it's not real?"

"No."

"Get on with it Nightsock," insisted Potty.

"Yes, well. I recall that I was describing the boundary markings of the territories. They were delineated by a relatively narrow strip of white cloth, a broad ribbon if you will."

"How big were these territories?" interjected Leach.

"Oh, some miles across, perhaps."

"Wow! That's a huge amount of material. I performed once in a dress that was made only of pink ribbon!" exclaimed Siko.

"Rather lacking in coverage then, I would think," Leach remarked wistfully.

"It was wound around me hundreds of times. It looked great but when I was moving around on the stage, it started to slip down. They called an interval and had to staple it together quickly. I remember I needed two men in my dressing room afterwards to get it off. They had scratches all over them afterwards."

Nightsock interrupted loudly.

"A young maiden, daughter of one of the Lords, had fallen in love with a prince who resided in the adjacent territory. He was also the offspring of the Lord of that domain."

Potty shook her head.

"That's not right. A Lord's son can't be a prince. His parents must have been a King and Queen. You haven't told us that there was a monarchy. I'm totally against that sort of inherited power," she declared frostily.

Now Pigswill lifted her eyes to the ceiling.

"Unless he was the illegitimate son, born to a woman who lived alone in the forest. A handsome King arrived one night on a winged horse and they grabbed the opportunity for one night of passion together. He flew off the next morning, promising to return but on his journey, he was attacked by a dragon and killed. The woman never knew this and every day she…"

"I'll proceed then," Nightsock said firmly.

"It's just that I can't resist princes."

"I studied my family tree and I might be one," said Leach quickly.

"To return to my most amusing anecdote. The maiden and young man who claimed to be a prince, were avidly obsessed with each other but the line of the tape precluded any physical contact betwixt them. Upon every morn, the maiden waited on her side of the boundary, gazing into the glistening pools of his eyes, desperate for the caress of his hand, the embrace of his arm and most of all, the sweet touch of his lips. But it was denied to her. The constant presence of the guards, both male and female, made any contact of a tactile nature impossible."

"Poor prince, he must have been desperate," sympathised Siko.

"Did I mention that I'm almost certainly one of them?" persisted Leach.

"And then, one night, an idea occurred to the maiden. She would tie a rope to the top of the tree to bend the upper foliage in such a manner that it overhung her side of the malefic ribbon that separated them."

"What tree?" asked Potty.

"That on which the branches of which he always sat," Nightsock replied brusquely.

"You didn't mention it before."

"Not that it is in my nature to disagree, in particular with a woman, but I clearly stated that the prince always sat amidst the branches of a tree when meeting the one with whom he was enamoured with."

"I'm afraid she's right, you didn't say that," supported Leach.

"One of my albums was called 'Making It Under Trees'. Shall I sing something from it?" offered Siko.

"I suggest that Mr Nightsock finishes the story," Heather said.

"Thank you madam. We are now reaching a crescendo of this remarkable tale. So, during the night, the maiden had tied the tree in such a fashion that it was leaning over her side of the divisive ribbon. Thereupon, when the next morn did come, the pair again went to their regular places. the man in the tree, as I distinctly mentioned before and the girl on her usual stool."

"You didn't mention the stool either," remarked Potty but was ignored.

"Perceiving an opportunity to finally reach his amour, the young man climbed carefully along the branches to attain her side of the border line. But alas! In the excessive excitement that consumed him at this long sought-after moment, he slipped and fell upon the ground."

"Did he rebound?" asked Potty. Ignored again.

"His body lay almost in its entirety on his own side of the ribbon but just the part of one hand had passed through the invisible barrier and lay on her side of the tape."

"Was he dead?" asked Siko expectantly.

"He was not, although temporarily immobile from concussion. The aggressive guards within the maiden's territory witnessed the occurrence and rushed to the body. Perceiving an invasion of the land by the man's extremities, they cut off all the fingers that had encroached."

"Urggh, that's horrible," exclaimed Siko.

"The maiden rushed to recover the severed digits and called to her erstwhile lover. 'My darling, what shall we do now?'. To which he responded, 'You can always give me a ring'."

Nightsock guffawed violently but no positive signs from the others.

"Chopped fingers dripping with blood. I think I'm going to vomit," announced Siko.

"Your last statement implies the existence of telephones in this oppressive feudal country. That doesn't sound right at all," declared Potty.

"Yes Siko, I'm definitely a prince. If you like, we can talk about it later in your room," offered Leach, indicating that his mind had clearly been elsewhere.

Doctor Rigor returned alone.

"Sorry it took a bit longer than expected," she said with a grin.

"Did you find Manita?" asked Heather.

"Yes. Only fainted. Right as rain now."

"Where is she?"

"Oh, carrying the corpse down to the cellar."

"Corpse?"

"Didn't I mention it? Grimedung was lying dead in Manita's room. She saw him and fainted but she'll be absolutely fine, so no need to worry."

"How did Grimedung die?"

"Hard to say. I mean, I couldn't ask him, could I?" chortled Rigor.

"You must have some idea."

"Yes. Death consequated from a blow to the head from the heavy candlestick lying beside him. The angle of the injury tells me that it was used by a human."

"Right or left handed?"

"The probability is that they had both. The proportion of people who have lost one or a pair of hands is very small."

A screaming entered the room in the form of Manita. She was quickly joined by Siko for no apparent reason. Potty leapt into action again, swinging fists in all directions.

Some time before order was restored and Manita could speak.

"He's dead! Dead! Dead!" she cried.

"I know and you've carried Mr Grimedung's corpse down to the cellar," responded Rigor.

"No! No! Mr Midwit! Dead!"

"Show me immediately."

The pair departed swiftly.

Flitty and Sam returned from the dining room and Siko quickly updated them with the latest casualty report.

"Never mind. The weather looks awful and the sea has risen well above the shore of the island. We just got a narrow strip of land between us and the approaching waters. Within a couple of hours we could all drown. If we're not murdered first," Flitty said optimistically.

"I think I'll go off by myself for a while without telling you exactly where I'll be. It's good to be alone when there's an unknown murderer about," remarked Sam.

Flitty nodded.

"Excellent idea, Sam but I've got to stay here and keep everyone's spirits up," she said as her companion departed.

"I have another amusing anecdote," offered Nightsock but Flitty shook her head.

"What we need is a bit of get away from it all fun. Forget the murders and our imminent drowning, let's show that we're going to enjoy ourselves. Look, there goes Sam!"

Through the window, they could see the youth marching towards the incoming sea. Blinding rain hammered down as he entered the waters and was quickly lost to view.

"He looked as if he was hypnotised," remarked Leach.

"That's terrible. I once appeared at a theatre alongside a hypnotist. He put me under and as soon as someone spoke the keyword, I had to do everything they told me. I still do it," declared Siko.

"What was the word?" asked Leach with some urgency.

Doctor Rigor returned before she could reply.

"Right, that's Midwit done. Manita is carrying him to the cellar now."

"We just saw Sam walk into the sea," remark Potty.

"That's okay. Just a standard drowning. I could do with a nice cup of tea now."

"Allow me to accomplish the preparation of this required beverage," said Nightsock nobly and left for the kitchen.

Leach moved closer to Siko.

"You were just going to tell me the word that makes you do anything I want," he said appealingly.

"That's bunk."

"It's just not fair," Leach responded, leaving the room slamming the door.

Potty laughed.

"Stupid man. You told him the word was bunk."

"Yes mistress, I will do everything you ask," declared Siko with a dull smile.

"Right. Do not obey anyone who says the word bunk. Now wake up."

Siko blinked her eyes.

"I feel great. Like a big weight has been lifted from me."

Manita rushed in screaming again.

"Mr Leach and Mr Nightsock are both dead!"

"Where is my tea?" demanded Doctor Rigor.

Manita looked contrite.

"Sorry, I'll go and fetch it."

"I don't suppose we'll see her alive again," remarked Flitty but the girl was back within seconds, holding a steaming mug.

"It could be poisoned," offered Potty helpfully.

Rigor hesitated.

"You're right. I need to complete a rapid medical test before it gets cold. Take a sip of tea, Siko."

"Why me?"

"It's obvious. I'm a doctor, so I could possibly save you if it's poisoned. But if I take it, there's nobody else here qualified in doctorship."

The logic of the argument struck home.

"Oh, okay then."

Siko took a gulp, then another and another. The mug was soon empty.

"That was my tea," complained the doctor.

"Yes, lovely. Thank you," the young singer responded.

"Manita, would you fetch me another mug?" asked Rigor.

As the girl rushed out, she shouted an afterthought.

"With tea in it!"

"Just six of us left now," Siko remarked cheerfully.

"And one must be the killer," added Flitty.

Heather moved forward.

"Not necessarily. It's very conceivable that one of the supposedly dead people is still alive. We were all in this room when Leach and Nightsock died, for example."

"Except Manita. It must be her," Potty observed.

"Perhaps but there's another possibility. An escaped lunatic, a murderer could have got to the island."

Siko clapped her hands together.

"Wow! My brother is a lunatic and he's killed lots of people. He could have escaped!"

"I also have a homicidal, blood crazed brother," remarked Flitty.

"Me too," added Potty.

Doctor Rigor looked aghast.

"You look aghast," said Heather.

"No, it's askance," responded the medic with aplomb.

"It's pretty obvious that Manita isn't coming back, so it's down to us now. We've all been in this room together so it must be one of the alternatives I mentioned," Heather insisted.

There was a sudden banging at the front door, clearly audible over the raging storm. Siko screamed but followed the others as they ran to the hallway.

"I'll do it," declared Potty.

She opened the door to receive a dousing of rain. An oilskin clad figure outside. He pushed his way in and slammed the door.

"It's a man!" screamed Siko and received a mighty cheek slap from Potty.

The visitor pulled back his hood. A young, commanding figure.

"Hello. I'm a police officer. Just passing by when I got caught in the storm. Any tea?"

Siko clicked into normality.

"Police? That's great. Come to my room and I'll get you all nice and dry."

"I'll be fine. My name is Inspector Jim Ewing," he responded, stripping off his oil skin to reveal a blue suit.

The medical person stepped forward.

"I'm Doctor Rigor. We've had a little trouble here. Quite a few people murdered."

"Excellent. I specialise in murder investigations."

"Come with me and we'll have tea while I bring you up to date."

The couple disappeared towards the kitchen and the others returned to the lounge.

"Where's Flitty?" asked Siko.

Heather looked around.

"I thought she was with us. She probably went to the kitchen."

"That police officer didn't look genuine to me," remarked Potty.

Heather nodded.

"I agree. No one could have reached here since the rain started so he must have been around the hotel all the time. That makes him a prime candidate to be the killer."

"Unless he is one of the supposedly murdered people who is not really dead and is now wearing a disguise!" declared Siko with satisfaction.

"He's tall and slim. No one looked like that," Potty responded dismissively.

"Yes they could. The smaller ones could have elevated shoes and if it was Nightsock, he could have worn a sort of corset to make him look thinner."

"Plus a rubber mask over his head?"

"Absolutely. We can soon check. I'll make some excuse to make bodily contact with him."

"I don't like it. It could be dangerous," advised Heather.

"Not really. I've done it lots of times with lots of different men."

"I mean if he is really the murderer, you could be killed."

"Oh, I see. Right. While I'm grappling with him on the floor, Potty can stand over us with something heavy. If he tries to murder me, she can biff him on the head."

"I'm up for that," Potty said with enthusiasm.

"Grappling on the floor?" asked Heather dubiously.

"Of course, every girl knows how to do that," Siko responded primly.

Inspector Ewing returned.

"Doctor Rigor is having a second mug of tea. I thought I should proceed with my investigation."

He wasn't at all prepared for the Siko onslaught. She leapt up to hug and kiss him, her propulsion carrying him on to his back.

"What!" he shouted as the girl's hands trawled all over his body. Meanwhile, Potty had grabbed a metal vase from the shelf and stood over them.

"Make my day!" she yelled.

"He seems like a normal man but I'm still checking" burbled Siko.

Another four minutes before she was reasonably satisfied with her explorations.

"He's all real," she yelled but still clung on with excessive intimacy.

He dragged her off and got to his feet.

"Attacking a policeman is a serious matter but I'm prepared for to ignore it for the moment."

"You can come to my room later and question me thoroughly," offered Siko.

"Perhaps I will. Anyway, now Rigor has told me the whole story, I think I can solve this case. While I was outside, I checked everywhere and there's definitely no one else on the island," said Ewing.

"My new options are that either one of the dead isn't dead or you are the murderer," announced Heather.

"Just one of the missing people wasn't pronounced dead. The same one who wasn't present in this room during the murders. Manita."

"Of course. I knew it was her," Potty concurred.

Doctor Rigor returned with a fresh mug of tea.

"Just found Manita. Dead in the kitchen cupboard. No more screaming, thank goodness."

"We've also lost Flitty," added Siko.

Potty rushed to the door.

"I'm not going to wait here to be picked off like fleas on a camel's back. I'm going out there to face this killer, whoever or whatever it is. Stupid to sit and wait like caged jaguars as if we were tethered goats waiting for the lion, octopuses waiting for the shark, slices of ham in a hyena's dining room, pieces of cheese on a hamster's table, lumps of plastic at a laser gun party, helpless planets approaching a black hole, packets of chocolate biscuits at…"

"Yes, thank you," interjected Ewing.

"I wanted to know about the chocolate biscuits," complained Siko but he ignored her.

"I agree with Potty. Let's go and search this place. There are five of us, so we'll be all right together."

Heather shook her head.

"You four go but I'll stay here. I know who the murderer is but I just need to check my notes to be sure," she announced.

"Who is it?" yelled Siko.

"I won't tell you until I'm certain. Off you go now."

They left her alone on the sofa and she pulled out a notebook. Heather didn't know the murderer but was using the traditional tethered chocolate biscuit ploy, a proven favourite in books and films. She began to write out the list of characters, ticking those who were now declared dead. Then she did know. An awesome certainty flowed through her.

A faint noise outside and the door opened.

Siko Pigswill.

"I think I left my lipstick behind so I came back to get it."

She was still searching when Potty marched in.

"I came back to get Siko," she declared.

A few seconds later, Inspector Ewing and Doctor Rigor appeared, claiming they had returned to find the other two.

"Actually, I really came back to see if you were dead," Siko admitted.

Heather looked beyond her. A smiling Flitty had just entered. Then she fell on her face to display a big knife sticking out of her back.

"Is she Polly or Molly now?" enquired Siko.

Rigor rushed to the body and pulled out the knife.

"She's going to be all right for just a few seconds before she dies. Listen, she's saying something."

They could hear Flitty mumbling indistinctly and then Rigor turned her face up.

"I'd just like to tell you the name of the murderer. Yes, I know who it is and I'll give you their name now without further ado or delay in any way as I'm going fast and I'm determined to say the name before I finally expire so I'll speak now because if I don't then I'm sure to go just at the moment before I fully reveal the name of the one that did it…"

"I'm betting she's never going to tell us," remarked Potty as the diatribe continued.

"… and now I will finally name the name that is actually two names, being the first and second names of the one I will name…"

"I'm sure I left my lipstick on the table," remarked Siko.

"It on the floor by the chair," Heather responded helpfully.

"… so here it is, without saying another word about how I'm going to say a word about it, I'm going to gasp out an identity that will be the person who has committed these foul and malicious acts. These terrible crimes that are repugnant to all of us and even…"

"I think the storm is clearing," remarked Ewing, looking out of the window.

Pigswill rushed to join him.

"Yes! Let me try my phone. Wow! It's working now and I've got loads of texts. Fantastic! One of my friends has had her hair cut shorter!"

"… so this is the moment when I speak the name and you'll notice that I've given no indication of whether it is a man or woman in order to preserve the dramatic impact of the disclosure because if I said he or she, it would immediately narrow the suspects down and I don't want to do that as some of you could have a particular person in mind and…"

"Anyone want tea?" asked Potty.

"Look, the sun is coming out and the sea is going down. There's a car coming across the causeway," announced Siko.

Heather moved to the window and smiled.

"It's my husband."

"… I'm sure you're expecting it to be the one you least expect because there's no surprise if it was someone one very obvious and you'll all feel very let down but I want to be very clear here in saying that this does not mean you can dismiss the patently unpleasant people as it could be a double bluff in the sense that…"

Heather saw the car pull up outside and rushed to open the front door.

"Hello dear. Delayed by the little shower I'm afraid," he said.

"We need to talk," said Heather, guiding him to the kitchen.

"Did you solve your case?" she asked, bringing two mugs of tea to the table.

"I did. You recall that newspapers and a canary magazine were stolen from the letterbox of a house?"

"Yes."

"The adjacent building had been converted to flats and I found that one of them was occupied by the Vicki Chest, the notorious canary trainer."

"Not a name I know."

"She had coached her canaries to pluck the newspapers from the neighbour's letterbox and bring them to her."

"A little canary couldn't carry a newspaper."

"Not alone but Vicki had trained them to work as a team and 27 were required to transport the newspaper."

"For what reason?"

"To provide a fresh lining each day for their cage, a new carpet for them if you will. Unfortunately, one morning the winged throng espied the canary magazine in the letterbox and they were irresistibly attracted to a rather gorgeous specimen that disported in all her yellow feathered finery on the front cover. Consequently, they filched the magazine, no doubt harbouring some plan to crop out the picture with their beaks and hang it over the perches where they slept."

"So you worked out that the thieves were a number of canaries, based on this magazine being stolen?"

"I wish I could say yes. Unfortunately, the real clues were a number of fallen feathers near the door and a series of photographs taken during one of the thefts by a passer by."

Heather smiled.

"Now I need to tell you what's happened here."

She spent some time describing all the events in detail.

"Do you know who did it?" asked Philip, brain bulging with Dollys, Mollys and Pollys.

"Yes but I was waiting for you to arrive so you could announce it. I know that's important to you."

"Not as important as you are, dear," he said, kissing her cheek.

"Philip?"

"I will speak a few words and then you will announce the solution."

She led him into the lounge.

"… therefore as Plato once said 'speak openly and you will be heard' or perhaps it was someone else and anyway the principle is still correct in that the naming of this name will…"

The others were now gathered at the table, drinking tea and chatting.

"This is my husband, Philip Caldrock," declared Heather.

Inspector Ewing looked a little miffed and rose to his feet.

"Amateurs. We don't want in business police this is meddling," he declared.

Doctor Rigor punched him in the stomach and he dropped back into his chair.

"That should cure it. He was suffering from what we call word mislocation," she said doctoringly.

Siko was excited.

"Wow! The famous Mr Caldrock! Would you like to come to my room later to reveal the solution?"

Philip nodded.

"No, I wouldn't. Can someone stop that woman talking please."

Rigor walked over to Flitty who showed no sign of completing her incessant speech.

"Actually, I was wrong. I think she'll recover," the doctor remarked.

Flitty lifted her head.

"What! That's not fair. I wanted to raise suspense to unbearable levels before I finally slumped back just at the very instant I was going to announce the name and then, in my final moment, I was going to move my finger in the dust on the floor to leave some unfinished word or symbol that seemed to make no sense but in fact would…"

Rigor struck her on the jaw and silence reigned at last.

"A little general anaesthetic to help the recovery," she murmured.

Philip nodded.

"Thank you. I have to announce that I am not going to solve this mystery," he declared.

Cries of disappointment before he continued.

"I must tell you all that my wife is essential part of our investigations. She is not only my assistant but my partner in every sense of the word. Heather will now tell you how she alone has resolved this case."

He took a seat and looked towards Heather who has now lost for words.

"Did I offer to paint you?" enquired Leach.

"No, Mr Rouse and I'm grateful for that. Where should I begin? First, we are told there are a number of dead bodies in the cellar."

"Maybe they'll come back to life as vampires. One of my songs is about them. It's called 'A Bite with Me'," Siko squealed.

Heather ignored her.

"I believe there are more events to come but the murders so far were not random killings. I am certain that the victims were selected. The guests here were not aware of each other's identities until they arrived and so they could not have planned the murders. Similarly, the people involved in the hotel could not have prepared a strategy in anticipation as the event was not entirely under their control."

"Could have just been a killing spree by some crazy person," remarked Inspector Ewing.

"I think not. That sort would not have been so careful to conceal their identity. A full-scale attack would have been more likely."

"So you think the murder mystery people are the killers. Not Flitty by the look of her and Sam was drowned."

"Maybe Flitty stabbed herself in the back to divert suspicion," offered Siko.

Doctor Rigor snapped her fingers.

"Good thought. I didn't check the wound. Could have been a retracting blade knife with fake blood."

"So who is the murderer, Mrs Investigator Caldrock? Flitty or Sam?" asked Potty with some sarcasm.

Heather gave her a look.

"The average person sees only what is presented to them visually and aurally," she said and immediately regretted sounding like a Philip clone.

"Wow! That is so deep," gasped Siko.

"I'm waiting for an answer," Potty insisted.

"I've got no more evidence than you. Think about Flitty's response much earlier when told by Nightsock that the criminal in her little mystery had to be Sam or herself."

Siko thought hard.

"Umm, she said something like maybe yes, maybe no."

"That's right. I can't see any reason why she didn't just say yes unless there was actually another person involved in the performance. Someone that I will call man number three."

"He can't be just a number! He must be a real person!" protested Potty.

"Yes he is."

"It has to be Nightsock. He was full of long words like an actor," concluded Siko.

Heather nodded.

"No. Man number three is Mr Owen Dairy."

Gasps of astonishment.

"But I saw his body. He wasn't breathing," said Doctor Rigor.

"I studied acting in depth three years ago. All drama colleges teach their students the way to pretend death during their first year. It's an essential skill when playing Shakespeare."

"But what is the motive, Heather?" asked Ewing.

"A little inspired guesswork here. It's clear that the murder mystery performance included a surprise conclusion where Dairy would suddenly reveal himself as some escaped lunatic or whatever. By this late appearance, he was reduced to a secondary role, even below Sam Throg. He therefore planned to kill Flitty and Sam in retribution for this demotion."

"But why murder the hotel people?"

"They further demeaned his stature by hustling him from the dining room when the play was beginning. That sealed their fate."

"But killing the guests makes no sense," Potty remarked disbelievingly.

"Fleet saw Dairy murder Grimedung so he had to be silenced. Ilena saw him killing Fleet and Nightsock saw him killing Ilena."

Siko clapped her hands in delight.

"That's great! I'm safe because I didn't see anyone being murdered."

"Stupid girl. She just told us who did it so we're all at risk," advised Potty.

Siko paused.

"I wasn't listening. I don't know what Heather said," she yelled loudly.

Inspector Ewing rose to his feet.

"Keep calm everyone. We just need to stay together. It's not as if anyone's going to come through the door with a submachine gun."

Dairy burst into the room, carrying a submachine gun.

"Think you're clever, do you?" he snarled.

"Well I am but I'm not sure about the others," declared Potty.

Heather attempted a desperate ploy.

"We can't possibly expect Elizabeth to rush in here and disarm him, can we?" she asked as loudly as possible.

Everyone looked at the door but no newcomers.

"Who's Elizabeth anyway?" asked Dairy.

"It's not important," Heather said with resignation.

"I want to know," insisted Potty.

"It doesn't matter."

Come on you can tell me, I'm a doctor," Rigor demanded.

A babble of encouragement filled the room before Dairy shot a burst of bullets into the ceiling.

"If you don't talk, I'll kill you. Then we'll know."

"That's stupid," muttered Siko.

"Who said that?"

"It was this silly girl," betrayed Potty.

"Well, it was stupid. If you kill her she can't speak."

"She could write it down," Dairy responded.

"Only if you kill her a bit so she could still use her hands."

"Too difficult. I'll just shoot you all now."

Siko squealed.

"No! Someone has to make a sacrifice. Kill the men and let the women go!"

Dairy puzzled for a moment.

"How will I know for sure?"

"What?"

"You could be a man. A cross dresser."

"Doctor Rigor could examine us all. I'm definitely a woman."

"You would say that. You could all be men and Doctor Rigor would lie about your gender."

"He's got a point," said Potty.

Pigswill gave her a sour look.

"Well, let the youngest go and kill the old ones then."

"Why?" asked Dairy.

"Because I have all my life in front of me and people like Potty have most of it behind them."

The grey haired woman looked a trifle annoyed.

"Stupid girl. It should be the other way round. What's the point in killing people who are nearer to death? That's more like rescheduling rather than murder."

As she spoke, Ewing leant forward and whispered in Pigswill's ear.

"I saw that. What did he say?" asked Dairy.

"I couldn't hear properly because that old woman was talking and he was whispering something about me jumping on you while he's subtracting."

"I clearly said I will jump while you're distracting him," Ewing declared with irritation.

"No point in telling Pigswill anything. She's got no brains at all," Potty remarked.

Now Flitty had regained consciousness.

"I'm going to tell you the identity and I won't be stopped. You'll all know the murderer the moment I give you this name information and you'll…"

"You can shoot her whenever you like," advised Rigor.

"Yes, I've decided she will die, just like the others."

"The ones you didn't murder?" enquired Heather.

"Yes I did. Killed them all."

A pause as Heather moved to face the gathering.

"No you didn't and I think it's finished now."

Mystified looks as she continued.

"You could say we have three murderers here. First I'll deal with the mystery performed by Flitty and Sam. The murderer is Gordon, the gardener. A complex plan to inherit all the assets of Lord Watt."

"Why should a gardener inherit?" enquired Potty.

"Because he was actually the brother of Lord Watt who had left the family home when a child. He carefully modified his appearance to be unrecognisable and obtained the job as gardener. All he had to do was kill her and her husband

and he would then inherit everything. The first stage was to seduce Lady Watt and later entice her to a weekend at this hotel, leaving a clear trail for her husband to follow. He would kill her first and then murder Lord Watt. Unfortunately, others also followed the trail and Gordon's simple plan to murder the couple became more complex. He was seen by Smith, the butler putting poison in Lady Watt's drink so he had to die. Dolly and Holly saw him murder Smith so they were next."

"Not Gordon! It can't be! He was coming to my room tonight," moaned Pigswill.

Flitty perked up at this statement.

"That's disgraceful! Young Sam? Are you insatiable?"

"No, I'm English and I don't care who knows it."

"Poor kid. Drowned himself just when Siko was ready for him," remarked Rigor.

Heather smiled.

"My congratulations on your efforts to mislead me."

"What are you talking about?" asked Ewing.

"Now the second set of murders. They were designed in such a way to indicate Dairy, man number three, as the culprit. We can call him the second murderer."

"You said he didn't do it," remarked Ewing.

"That is correct. It was what I was meant to believe. In fact, the principal murderer is Sam. He is not the callow youth he portrays but a much older actor with an unusually young appearance."

"He was with us when most of the people were killed," said Flitty.

"I said he was the principal murderer. He was assisted by his wife."

"What! Married?" moaned Pigswill.

"Yes. His wife is Manita. She accomplished the first killings and he took over after his feigned drowning."

"But Manita was also murdered."

"Sam killed her when her job was done."

"But his motive, Heather? His motive?" demanded Ewing.

"Initially, it was to take control of the acting troupe that performed here but Manita was killed for another reason."

"Why?"

"Because he became obsessed by the attractions of Siko Pigswill and saw an opportunity to pursue a lucrative career as her spouse and agent."

Siko bounced to her feet.

"Wow! He killed people for me? That's so romantic."

"You didn't tell me this before," exclaimed Ewing.

"Of course not. It's all part of the murder mystery performance that includes you, Gordon, Lady Watt, Mr Dairy and all the deaths here. Almost everyone in this hotel has been acting, including Grimedung. Just one exception, apart from Philip and myself. Siko Pigswill."

"I've won! I've won!" cried the girl joyously.

Rigor shook her head.

"This can't be true. I confess that I'm an actress but I thought I was the only one."

Heather smiled.

"Yes, that was the clever part of the plan. Sam and Manita were hired as a pair but all the other actors were recruited individually. Each of you thought you were the only performer in the hotel. An ingenious strategy that ensured added realism in the performance."

Flitty rose to her feet and opened the door. All the other supposedly dead characters entered the room.

"Wow! That was brilliant, Flitty," congratulated Siko.

Heather shook her head.

"No, no. Flitty is only one of the actors. The author and producer of this complex tale is of course, Potty Dirsnap. Or should I say, Dotty Parsnip."

The little grey woman looked at her glumly.

"Thought I'd fooled you this time," she muttered.

Philip joined Heather, placing an arm around her waist.

"I have never been able to deceive my wife and consequently your chances were less than zero," he declared emphatically.

www.ingramcontent.com/pod-product-compliance
Ingram Content Group UK Ltd.
Pitfield, Milton Keynes, MK11 3LW, UK
UKHW041258180426
11947UKWH00008B/547